Tactical Civics™
For Church Leaders

TACTICAL  CIVICS™

For Church Leaders

A Handbook to Teach, Guide, and Support
the Repentant Remnant to Restore our Land

David M. Zuniga

Founder, Tactical Civics™

Books by David M. Zuniga

This Bloodless Liberty

Fear The People (Fourth Edition)

Our First Right

(Book One) Tactical Civics™

(Book Two) Mission to America (Second Edition)

A Republic to Save: Essays in Tactical Civics™

Grand Jury Awake: Tactical Civics™ Field Handbook, Vol. 2

Tactical Civics™ Ready Constitution

A Tax Honesty Primer

Tactical Civics™ for Church Leaders

Tactical Civics™ High School Edition (31-unit homeschool tutorial)

The Great We-Set™

No king but King Jesus

Time to Start Over, America

Coming Titles

*Taking America Back: The Tactical Civics™ Vision
for the Patriotic American Business*

(Book Three) Engine of Change

(Book Four) The Banished Bureaucrat

(Book Five) The Greatest Awakening

Changing the American Mind

*The Statesman's Manual: A Citizen-Statesman's Guide to Writing and Enacting
Legislation Conforming to the Constitution and Supporting the Rule of Law*

Dedication

For every 'remnant pastor' in this Republic who will faithfully preach the Word and teach the saints their duties before the LORD and over our servant government, presently in cynical, arrogant violation of the U.S. Constitution, thus having become our domestic enemy.

May this book, and our organization standing behind it, inform and enlighten, edify and encourage, equip and support these men of God as they support our home mission, urging their flocks to take up every American's duty to superintend and enforce our Constitution.

May our repentance together in this perilous time bring a fitting end to the peril, as the LORD lifts His hand of judgment for our sins and abdication, that the world might join us in glorifying the High King, Jesus Christ, and that future generations may keep the faith.

The Most Important Page

Below is our most important Tactical Civics™ infographic. It depicts the hierarchy of American government.

We The People (collectively, not individually) must live 'above the line', superintending and enforcing the Constitution by serving in Grand Jury and Militia in our counties (our Romans 13 authority and duty).

On the other hand, We The People make every public servant (city, county, state or federal) take an oath to obey the Constitution. As such, when on duty they must live 'below the line', or face God's ordained magistrate – We The People in Grand Jury and Militia.

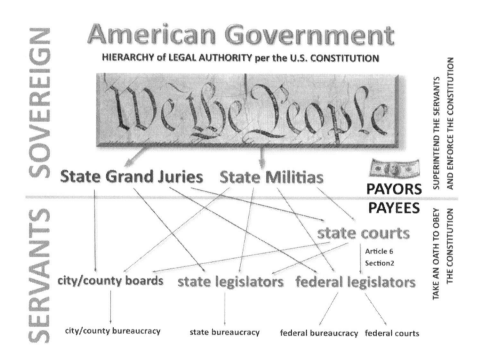

CONTENTS

(Appendices on next page)

APPENDICES

FOREWORD

These testimonials from several pastors associated with Tactical Civics™ demonstrate that this is easily attainable for any pastor who desires it.

Martin C. Bonner
Pastor, Abundant Life Christian Fellowship, Everett, WA

I have wrestled with defining my pastoral duty under Jesus Christ to the Republic in which he has placed me. To love God is to love my neighbor. Thus, I have always taught the churches where I pastored that Christians have a spiritual and civic duty to shoulder within this Republic. For years, I have encouraged believers not to shrink back from voting and speaking out on public issues just because it looked to them like it would never change.

However, I had done too much study of history to promote the Republican Party or Democratic Party, but believed that they worked together as a perfect ratchet system that was taking us over a cliff socially and morally. That said, voters always have to choose who they are going to vote for, so I encouraged prayerfully deciding. A large number of Christians across this land do not vote, but part of me understood and sympathized with their position. Still, I felt we had a duty before God not to give up on America to our dying day.

Pretty much every 'save America' group that I connected with, very quickly proved to be just another group sucking money out of concerned citizens, while the problem continued to get worse. What to do? Pray for America to repent and keep voting!

When I was presented with the mission of Tactical Civics™, I realized quickly that this organization was different. Its teaching on repentance wasn't new; that's been taught since before our Republic. Its recognition of all that is wrong with America wasn't new, except for one thing. There was something that the average American could do that was more than voting, being vocal in their social circles and running for office. The historical tools for holding our political servants accountable had never been on my radar as options in our civic duty.

1

I am not seeking a Christian theocracy over America, but neither am I looking to abdicate my place to those who would take us down a 'progressive' road to ever-greater serfdom. I have much more hope for America today because I believe that God in His mercy has shown us the door of repentance at just the right time. I like Tactical Civics™ because it isn't pointing to a presidential or congressional candidate as the answer (and of course, your dollars). Rather, it is the time-honored, and God-honored, message of growing up and disciplining yourself, for your sake and for the sake of the people in your life.

I'm still learning, but I'm no longer ignorant of that long-forgotten duty of every American to participate in law enforcement and to protect the rights of the generation that is coming up behind us.

Ed Gonzalez

Pastor, The Faith Center (also Academic Dean, Faith Bible School) Ft Myers, FL

As governments grow increasingly corrupt, we hear the question, *"But doesn't the Bible teach us to submit to our ruling authorities?"* There was time I would have said yes, and continued what I considered to be spiritual pursuits while I allowed corrupt (criminal) activity in the government to run rampant.

Today, pastors everywhere have been intimidated by the Supreme Court and the IRS using the misapplied doctrine of "Separation of Church and State." This was not always the case. During our Founding Era pastors were often part of the Black Regiment, or Black Robed Regiment, from the black robes they wore while preaching. They preached about everything that pertained to life, whether spiritual or temporal. They preached the Gospel *and* about taxes, government, education, and the military.

Historian B.F. Morris said, *"The ministers of the Revolution were, like their Puritan predecessors, bold and fearless in the cause of their country. No class of men contributed more to carry forward the Revolution and to achieve our independence than did the ministers... By their prayers, patriotic sermons, and services* [they] *rendered the highest assistance to the civil government, the army, and the country."*

But I did not know any of this. I only knew that something was very wrong with our Republic and that if there was anything I could do, I must. Not just for myself but for the church and for my children and grandchildren. Then the Lord led me to Tactical Civics™ and began to open my eyes.

The most impactful thing I learned was the exegesis of Romans 13. (Chapter 1). Romans was written when the highest authority in government were the Caesars. Paul says to submit to the higher authority; but we are not under Caesars. In these United States, there is one human sovereign (a collective term, not individual): We The People. And as you read it, you immediately see that *We The People ordained* the highest human law in the land, the U.S. Constitution.

So then, if we (especially those in public employment and elective offices) are to submit to the higher authority, that means submit to the Constitution that we established and ordained! That means that enforcing the Constitution is the purest application of Romans 13 that we could ever achieve.

As a pastor, I fully endorse Tactical Civics™. I have found it to be the only peaceful, lawful, true solution to restore our beloved Republic. I encourage you, pastor, to look at Scripture in this light and determine that you will not be one who gives tacit approval to crime and corruption. At the very least, identify leaders in your congregation who are civic-minded, encourage and empower them to do this vitally important, urgent task of restoring our Republic.

Paul Michael Raymond
Pastor, Reformed Bible Church (also Founder, New Geneva Christian Leadership Academy) Appomattox, VA

What we know, that too many others (especially pastors) do not, is that the culture is the report card of the church. As it stands now, the church has failed as a result of pastoral failure to engage the culture for the crown rights of King Jesus. As a result of faulty hermeneutics, reading of Christian type fantasy novels and Biblically unfounded speculations from such men as John Nelson Darby, Charles Ryrie, Hal Lindsey, Tim LaHaye, and David Jeremiah, the Church has relinquished the world to the secularists, Marxists, anti-constitutionalists and anarchists.

Why bother, they say, to polish brass on a sinking ship? So, like rats fleeing a sinking vessel, the institutional church retreats from her duty to change the world. This retreatism denies, negates, and repudiates the clear teaching of the Great Commission of both the Old and the New

Testament (cf Deut 1:28-29, Matt 28:18-20) which calls the Christian Church to take dominion by subduing the earth with Truth by the authority of the Christ. Through the victorious, conquering work of the Lord Jesus Christ, the Church is given all power on earth to defeat that which is in rebellion against God and His Christ. (Luke 10:19) Thy kingdom come *on Earth*....as it is ['modeled'] in heaven.

Most churches hold to dualism which teaches that the world belongs to the devil and all Christians need to do is hide out and be holy until the Lord returns, or that Christians should have nothing to do with politics, the culture, law, and public policy; just preach the gospel. Not only does this fly in the face of Holy Scripture; it argues against the history of the Church, especially during the days of the Reformation.

There is a pandemic in the church; a far greater threat than COVID-19; that is the plague of *historical amnesia*. Too many pastors are content with preaching therapeutic messages to their congregation for fear that if they challenge them with real action, they may lose members. They instruct their people in lessons of morality without calling them to challenge the powers of anti-Christian ideologies, practices and those who should be called to account. While lamenting over what *is*, and what *ought* to be, they whine over the wicked affairs of the republic.

I have been preaching for 30 years that the Kingdom of Our Lord is now and His victory is efficacious. Whether that harmonizes with your eschatological understanding or not, everyone functions according to their eschatological presuppositions. If you believe the restoration of our republic to its original constitutional Christian glory is hopeless, you will refuse to fight. But, if you believe that through the power of God's victorious Spirit, the victory is ours, then you will not only fight but you will teach future generations to do so as well. This mindset is what I call Tactical Recon (tactical reconstruction) and it can be realized through the efforts of Tactical Civics™.

Tactical Civics™ is essential to restore our Republic to its original moorings. Reconstruction, I call it. Without realizing it, in concert with my congregation I've established a local (proto-)Militia unit, and have networked with other county proto-Militia units, pastors, attorneys, and county officials to convince church leaders to carefully consider their commission to revitalize our Republic through Tactical Civics™, for I believe this is how pastors can again become the 'tip of the spear' as God restores our Republic.

PREFACE

In America, you really are who you *think* you are.

Before you begin learning about one of the best kept secrets in our blessed Republic, I need to frame this study of Christian citizenship in our American context, with several bedrock concepts to prove why our civilization is so special. To many Americans it appears that we're about to lose it forever.

First shocker: the Marxist takeover of this republic is over 160 years old already; not some new attack on our rule of law.

Second shocker: our domestic enemies are merely one tool in the hand of our Creator as He judges us for six generations of refusing to glorify Him, instead glorifying man and chasing after self, stuff, and sin.

Third shocker: *the worst may be yet to come.* Scripture teaches that God chastises those whom He loves.

The Buck Stops at Your Pulpit

But the Word also teaches that God is faithful to restore us when we repent. As you well know and often preach, that formula appears often from Genesis to Revelation. And since I Peter 4:17 teaches that this judgment must come to pastors first, this is a 'repentance manual' for you to first learn, and then to teach if you see fit, in sermons if you can. Or at least delegate to a leader in your flock, the goal of planting the Tactical Civics™ chapter in your county.

That person – and you, in sermons over time – can begin to teach the shocking but powerful and liberating truths about American history and civics in this book, *They must be told, so the People know what to repent of!*

We do not ask or expect pastors to lead a county chapter. We ask only that you inform your flock and let natural leaders rise to the challenge, then give the Tactical Civics™ chapter a welcoming place to meet. Our 7-week *Mission to America* crash course book is designed for Sunday schools and small group church studies.

The hour is late, and the enemy determined. We need the responsible remnant among America's pastors to know that our home missions organization exists! Then, your church becomes the body of Christ reforming in tangible, lawful, peaceful *action* in the community.

Universities and Seminaries Don't Teach This

I assure you, these things aren't taught in schools, colleges, universities, seminaries, or law schools; our team had to dig them up for ourselves. Because these united States are not China, we had the *freedom* to do so. Because We The People entrusted only ourselves to enforce our highest law (as this book will demonstrate), we have the *duty* to do so. Because Jesus Christ is High King of all creation, including this republic of States, the American pastor has the duty to point out to the saints where they have abdicated this most vital duty.

It's ludicrous to preach against all the sins of corrupt government, when We The People *alone* have the authority *and solemn duty* to arrest it! The entire world is in the grip of demonic forces. Corporations as powerful as national governments; billionaires with absurd delusions of grandeur; tyrannical governments seeking to kill, steal, and destroy with an eye to greater domination than they already possess!

The body of Christ in America owes it to our brethren worldwide to not merely sit by and watch these shamelessly bold criminals tearing our civilization apart, but repent our abdication of duty in a new way of life.

AmericaAgain! Trust and its action mission Tactical Civics™ are simply a collection of normal Americans whom God is inspiring to stand up, crawl out of the shadows of faithless gloom, wash ourselves in His Word, and repent our abdication by doing the chores. I always reiterate, "repentance is an action word". And I always speak about doing the chores because I grew up on a ranch on the Texas/Mexico border where we raised poultry, hogs, goats, and beef cattle.

Fourth shocker: all of us have chores by virtue of being born in this Republic, including duty for regular service in Grand Jury and Militia in your county. Don't worry; in this book I will demystify both of those thousand-year-old institutions of Anglo-American law enforcement. They are the 'pointy end' of doing the chores.

Fifth shocker: at this point, *no other people on earth have this authority or duty.* Our system of law is unique on earth, and predicated on those two ancient institutions *of the People* for *enforcing law.* When the People refuse

6

to do these chores, mankind's sin nature takes the controls. Rule of law disintegrates. As you know, *we're there right now.*

By the grace of God through the regular counsel of the Holy Spirit, 44 Christians on our team have invested more than 67,900 hours in due diligence and R&D as of this writing, to produce a coast to coast chapter network and a small library of eye-opening books including *Grand Jury Awake* and *American Militia 2.0,* practical handbooks for serving in both institutions at the county level.

Our mission is to have the repentant remnant find and join us, applying Romans 13 and II Chronicles 7:14 to our terrible plight today. We repent our abdication of duty and serve in any way we can (including auxiliary support) in the two ancient institutions, as intimidating as such service may be to the ignorant.

Sixth shocker: when serving on Grand Jury, *your Panel is the highest authority in the court system.*

What you will learn in this book, almost no Americans know, including well-meaning Christian judges, district attorneys, and state and federal legislators. They are ignorant of basic American civics because their teachers were ignorant of them…because *their* teachers were, too.

The Story in Your Head

Alasdair MacIntyre wrote, *I can only answer the question 'What am I to do?' if I can answer the prior question "Of what story do I find myself a part?* [1] A narrative is just a story. As you know, in Greek, μετα- (meta) means after, beyond, or behind; something comprehensive or transcending. So a *metanarrative* is an all-encompassing, grand story within which all other stories exist. Like a framework; not as big a framework as *worldview,* but a grand story. Unbelievers have a belief system in which naturalism and evolution are the metanarrative. The Bible presents the metanarrative that you and I believe, as did our Founding Fathers. Our culture was built on that metanarrative, and *it alone will save and restore our culture.*

What we tell ourselves about ourselves, even if all the facts aren't real (perhaps only ideals or wishes), we all conduct our lives based on our personal metanarrative. As I write this, the latest fad in metanarratives

---

[1] Alasdair MacIntyre, *After Virtue: A Study in Moral Theory*, 2nd ed. (Notre Dame, IN: University of Notre Dame Press, 1984), 216.

is a 50-year-old retread from drug-addled Hippies, called 'Critical Theory' or 'Social Justice', that Marxists teach their 'useful idiots' who consider themselves losers. So these young people lash out at 'winners'; the diligent, godly, successful, and contented. *Worse is coming.*

America's Four Unique Bulwarks

Besides Scripture, Americans have three more unique bulwarks that have built our systems of law, economics, government, and culture.

Some people choose the metanarrative of naturalism (everything is the result of random natural processes that began with ambitious slime), or of Hinduism (everything is an illusion created by an impersonal reality), or other religious frameworks. Others trust the Bible's metanarrative that everything is created by and for Jesus Christ. Your metanarrative will radically affect how you conduct and understand your life.

Look around the world; beliefs lead to profoundly different results. For instance, if you live in China, no matter how capitalism grows around you, you can't escape the fact that there are 1.4 billion other individuals, swarming to and from their huge apartment buildings and scurrying around on mass transit like insects, all of whom have been brought up in a 5,000-year-old culture of autocracy and conformity. As a Chinese citizen, you simply cannot believe or operate like an American, having actual power to pursue evildoers and take an active part in your legal system through Grand Jury and Militia. But that's not only unthinkable in China; it's unthinkable in England, Canada, Norway, and *everywhere else on earth.* America is blessedly unique via four bulwarks built over centuries: 1) The gospel of Jesus Christ; 2) The U.S. Constitution; 3) Grand Jury; and 4) Militia; that's just We The People when we 'execute the Laws of the Union, suppress Insurrections, and repel Invasions'.[2]

No other people on earth will ever have these four unique bulwarks.

Dishonor Where it's Due

Before I brief you on your authority and duty when serving on Grand Jury: be careful what words you use, and the honor that you bestow with your punctuation and terms. That honor is *not* warranted today.

The former dean of Stanford Law School, Larry Kramer, in his 2004 book, *The People Themselves: Popular Constitutionalism and Judicial Review,*

---

[2] U.S. Constitution, Article I, Section 8, Clause 15.

posits that We The People got in this mess by forgetting that *we*, not the supreme Court, are the last word on the U.S. Constitution's meaning.

Oh, and *never* trust anything written by a lawyer or spoken by a politician (including sheriffs and judges) until you take the measure of the person *by actions*, not words. These people are trained to deliver pretty words. Notice the pit we're in, despite all their passionate speeches? Sane people don't think highly of speechifying 'professionals'; we'll sooner trust a farmer, mechanic, grandmother, or truck driver.

In retraining Americans to perform the duties and exercise the authority that we've had for over 230 years *over* our Constitution and its creatures, Tactical Civics™ employs a new writing convention in all of our publications. We The People, the (collective) sovereign in this Republic, must learn to capitalize 'People' and never capitalize the label or office of our servants: mayor, commissioner, sheriff, senator, congressman, president, justice, governor...

And *especially* we don't capitalize *judge*. If any species of servant has shown utter contempt for the Constitution, it's the egotistical petty emperors in black frocks. Likewise, we refrain from starting a sentence with the words *federal* or *government*, because we refuse to capitalize them.

Oh, we're fully aware of the 'rules' of address and punctuation in which we were programmed in school, college, university, in those writers' grammar manuals, and by every level of our servants, media, and corporate America. But just because my arrogant jailers want me to keep pulling my own cell door shut, does not mean I'll do it. Showing honor to people who look down their noses to steal from you, lie to you, and despise you, *their employer*, deserves nothing but *dis*honor.

Up until now, too many cynically believe it's enough to crack politician jokes like, "How do you know when a politician is lying? When his lips are moving." But with our rule of law on the cliff's edge or perhaps already in free-fall over the cliff, this is no time for jokes or cynical resignation. It's time to return to our chores.

If Americans understood the extent of their power to arrest corruption when they serve on Grand Jury, the roster of Grand Jury volunteers would include half the population of each county. As you will see in a few pages, we have inherited an ancient and now totally unique system in which the People themselves are the final authority to stop the 'bad guys'. In this Republic, by the grace of God, We The People made ourselves the top of the pecking order; the only human power *above* the Constitution.

This little book will teach you what no law school will, because they are a major part of the problem all around us. But the wonderful thing is, truth can still be known, and…

Some days, the world just changes.

CHAPTER 1

Applying Romans 13

Many quotations are attributed to Thomas Jefferson but are not actually his. One of these was by John Barnhill in 1914, *"Where the people fear the government you have tyranny; where the government fears the people, you have liberty."*

Thomas Jefferson didn't say it, but the saying is true; and it applies to other human relationships, such as parents who spoil their children until they eventually fear them.

Faced with corrupt and tyrannical government, too many Christians let criminals off the hook by using Romans 13, *"Let every soul be in subjection to the higher authorities, for there is no authority except from God, and those who exist are ordained by God…For the authority is not a terror to those who do good, but to those who do evil. Do you want to have no fear of the authority? Do that which is good, and you will have praise from the same…But if you do that which is evil, be afraid, for he does not bear the sword in vain. He is a minister of God, an avenger for wrath to him who does evil."*

How Christians Pervert This Scripture

Consider this in the context of our American republic, outlined in the Preface; we are not ancient Rome under Caesars so who are 'the higher authorities' in our system? See the first three words of our Constitution: *We the People* collectively are *over* the Constitution.

The first Chief Justice of the U.S. supreme Court, John Jay, wrote, *'The People are Sovereign… (A)t the Revolution, the sovereignty devolved on the People and they are truly the sovereigns of the country… the Citizens of America are equal as fellow Citizens and as joint Tenants in the sovereignty.'*

It is our power and duty to see that the law is enforced when servants 'do that which is evil'. Instead, our arrogant, sociopath servants have been training us to fear *them*.

We the People, the parents who gave birth to our government, must instill proper fear in criminal hearts. In Chapter 9 you will learn how

America's sovereigns will have our state criminal courts 'bear the sword' against any member of Congress or our state legislature who violates our highest law.

Good Guys Have Nothing to Fear

"Do you want to have no fear of the authority? Do that which is good, and you will have praise from the same."

A future action step, the Tactical Civics™ Good Guys campaign, will support those who run for Congress standing for our 19 reform laws and against D.C. lawlessness. But for those freshmen who decide to follow their bent elders in powerful committee chairs, we don't need to do this the easy way. We can make them fear the authority instead.

Explained in Chapter 9, our Indictment Engine™ is unprecedented, but the process will become easier with each felon that we indict, try, convict, and incarcerate via State Criminal Court, with the perpetrator's family assets seized.

Now, let's review the civics because schools have not taught this for generations: We the People, in the U.S. Constitution, create, define, and severely limit our federal servant in three branches for 17 enumerated services, and for *absolutely no others*. And what are the only duties that We the People stipulate in the Constitution that we ourselves must perform? Grand Jury and Militia duty.

Because we have been ignorant of our Constitution and never taken the law seriously, our servants violate it just as impudently as Mexican narcoterrorists violate Mexico's laws. Isn't it silly to see millions of frustrated patriots with not an inkling of civics, wondering when oh when the Department of Justice and FBI will start rounding up…their criminal *bosses* in Congress?

State-Sponsored Terrorism

With generations of Christians providing render-unto-Caesar cover, D.C. organized crime employs *fear* to defraud its sovereigns. *Terrorism* is defined as violent acts or threat of violent acts, intended to create or instill fear in victims.

Sociopath is an apt label for many in Congress, but beyond Congress' own violations of law is its *criminogenic* nature, teaching state, county, and city agencies in its bent path.

No organization is so feared by so many as Congress' IRS. Millions of Americans work their whole lives but never manage to get ahead. Congress' IRS operation skims every payroll account, allowing criminals in D.C. to live as royalty at your expense while productive Americans do without.

In the TACTICAL CIVICS™ Training Center, in the Books & Resources area, we offer a free PDF edition of my paperback book, *A Tax Honesty Primer* to demonstrate why I and tens of millions of other Americans no longer fear the Wizard of Oz. Almost 25 years ago, Joe Banister, a former IRS CID Special Agent turned Tax Honesty spokesman, gave me his book exposing the agency's criminal operations.

I took it to my pastor and elders at my 'reformed' church…and received nothing but veiled threats. No one wanted to even consider what this *reformed* IRS enforcer was trying to tell America!

For over 28 years, I have been a law-abiding Nontaxpayer; free of congress' financial crime. IRS agents tried to coax or threaten me back "into the fair share line" 14 times in the first decade as a Nontaxpayer. All 14 times, I sent them home empty-handed, and they never touched a hair on my head or a dollar in my accounts. That's what happens when the gaslighting wears off, you tell the truth and obey the law, and you force congress' gaslighters to do the same!

Your servants control your life, property, and future. Making illegal 'laws' for us, Congress exempts itself. They have been counterfeiting our money for 150 years. They invite millions of illegals over our border and force taxpayers to pay welfare, healthcare, incarceration, and 'free' government schooling costs so they can gain these illegals' votes and their industry puppeteers can gain the cheap labor.

Meanwhile for their sovereigns, they track, record, and store our conversations, emails, travel and purchase records; fine us for using our own land; regulate everything from lightbulbs to toilet flushes, and legitimize perversion as 'marriage' while muzzling our pulpits.

Our own abdication created the Caesar that threatens history's most blessed Christian civilization. Repentance demands that we never again apply Romans 13 to our constitutional republic as if we are ancient Rome. Repentance is an *action* word!

Pastors Need Repentance, Too

As their sovereigns, our servants' staggering expenditures, frauds, and abuse of office should fill us with righteous anger, to assure that the higher authorities arrest their crimes as we will outline in this book. Criminals had a powerful public relations and propaganda machine for five generations. Now the worm turns. "If you do that which is evil, be afraid". Now it's *our* turn, Congress.

Paul's Romans 13 directive to 'the higher authority' – We the People and the U.S. Constitution that we ordained – applies to every American pastor, elder, deacon, teacher and evangelist. You see, your calling is not only to preach the Word but to call the People to repentance and to good works that demonstrate to the world that our repentance is genuine.

This is not China. Here, church leaders have the same God-given liberty to speak out on issues as does every American. But as a leader in a local church you also have a *duty* to speak out on moral, ethical, and constitutional issues. Even if you touch on a political party, campaign, or candidate. Of course, you should not campaign for any candidate; but free speech is the God-given and constitutional right of *every* American.

The Cell You Built

The American church that has incorporated itself under IRS Section 501 classification to attract donations, is conditioning its members to seek financial gain (tax write-off) in Pharaoh's fiefdom rather than doing good works for God's Kingdom. By submitting under secular authority of corrupt servants of your corrupt servant Congress, you turn civics on its head. I recommend Peter Kershaw's HushMoney.org; it teaches you to reorganize as a Free Church, leaving 501c3 imprisonment.

But even if you do not, nothing in IRS rules prohibits any church from engaging in Tactical Civics™ – the People's duty and power of popular constitutionalism.

Even 501c3 churches are encouraged by your state's election division to conduct 'voter' registration efforts as long as you don't do so on behalf of any candidate or party; that's reasonable. Frankly, so are IRS guidelines:

501c3 Churches May:

- Conduct nonpartisan voter registration drives
- Distribute nonpartisan voter education materials
- Host candidate/issue forums (all viable candidates)
- Allow candidates/elected servants to speak at services
- Educate members about pending legislation
- Lobby for legislation (spending only a small amount of their budget on lobbying)

501c3 Churches May Not:

- Endorse candidates from the pulpit on behalf of the church
- Contribute funds, services, mailing lists, or equipment to candidates or PACs
- Distribute materials that favor one candidate or party
- Pay fees for partisan political events from church funds
- Allow candidates to solicit funds while speaking in church
- Set up a PAC that would contribute funds to candidates

501c3 Pastors May:

- Endorse candidates in their capacity as private citizens
- Lobby for legislation in their private capacity
- Participate fully in political committees independent of the church

501c3 pastors may **not** endorse candidates from the pulpit on behalf of the church, but they can do so on their own behalf.

Resources for 501c3 Churches

A pamphlet summarizing the legal aspects of pastor and church involvement in the culture war is *Pastors, Pulpits, and Politics* published by Western Center for Law and Policy. You can read it and order the booklet from them here.

There is similar material at the Liberty Council, the American Center for Law and Justice, James Madison Center for Free Speech, and many others. In other words, pastor, even if you are stuck in the 501c3 cell, you're covered every which way from Sunday.

So. Nothing keeps your church from joining the repentant remnant for Christ and the Constitution. This book is our tool for American pastors to teach what they will not learn anywhere else: true repentance means the American People finally performing our duties in the highest office in American government, by enforcing the Constitution and glorifying Jesus Christ, as was once our way before a watching world.

CHAPTER 2

American Idol

Brace yourself for this chapter. It will shock you and may make you angry. But as Christ taught, the truth will make us free. Just like Russians or Chinese, *we were lied to in school.* Hard truths of our history must be faced and hooted off the stage in our homes, churches, schools and colleges if we are to avoid the godless collapse evident in all other communist countries, especially across Europe.

One of the most destructive frauds promulgated by government and private schools is that Lincoln was a great president. In truth, he was the most ruthless, destructive president in our history. Americans are ignorant of the affinity that Lincoln had for Marx and his Communist system. Even as liberals banished the Confederate flag and hundreds of statues, those who think Lincoln was a hero are more ignorant of our history than a Russian is, of his.

If you think I exaggerate, the first resource I recommend is available at no cost. _Reading Karl Marx with Abraham Lincoln: Utopian Socialists, German Communists, and Other Republicans_ is a 2011 article in The International Socialist Review, the communist news source of record, describing the mutual admiration between Marx and Lincoln.

The first book is _Forced Into Glory: Abraham Lincoln's White Dream_ by Black scholar and author Lerone Bennett Jr. Impeccably documented with many original source quotes, Bennett paints Lincoln as the consummate White Supremacist and mendacious snake-in-the-grass.

The second book is _Lincoln's Marxists_ by Al Benson & Walter Kennedy. It delves into the ties between Marxism, Lincoln's unconstitutional new national army, and the neo-nascent GOP that rose from the ashes of the Whig party. It is a second shocking exposé of our most execrable president and his U.S. Army generals, _proud followers of Karl Marx._

The third book exposing Lincoln's true character and the lasting destruction he wrought is _Lincoln Unmasked: What You're Not Supposed to Know About Dishonest Abe_, by Professor Thomas DiLorenzo. After igniting a fierce debate about Lincoln's legacy with his book _The Real Lincoln_, DiLorenzo now presents stunning new evidence to explode the popular myths about Lincoln. A shocking portrait of a political tyrant, manipulator and opportunist; the antithesis of American schools' idol.

The fourth book to banish idolatry of America's hijacker is _America's Caesar_ by Greg Durand (two volumes). With a huge number of original source documents, Durand paints a picture of a nineteenth-century agnostic attorney representing riverboat operators and railroad barons; whose only use for Jesus Christ was to charm the masses. This portrait of the most destructive man in American history makes Bill Clinton appear as a saint in comparison.

The fifth book is _The Unpopular Mr. Lincoln,_ by Larry Tagg, a compilation and analysis of public statements and articles during Lincoln's rule. According to his closest associates, Lincoln was the most despised president in our history.

The sixth book is _A Century of War_ by John Denson. It provides copious original source documentation of Lincoln's Northern mercantilist handlers making him defy his cabinet to sucker the South into firing the first shots at Fort Sumter, where no one was killed or even wounded.

You need not take my word for the fact that our former idol was a monster. Read any of these resources and you will take the red pill and know that *we have work to do.*

Modern Conservatism is Destructive Denial

If you are not ready to dethrone the god of American government school legend, consider your condition. Our present descent into tyranny while the People do nothing suggests that Americans may have mass insanity. The simple precursor is *cognitive dissonance.* When truth is presented it flies in the face of everything the victim thinks he knows, so he rejects it.

The programming of once-godly, productive, tough-minded folk began in the generation of Marx, Darwin, and Lincoln. Since that generation, we increasingly turned from God to accept every imaginable sin and a few unimaginable ones. The wages of such rebellion is God's judgment.

So we wander in the desert, oblivious to where we have been and what happened there. Like dumbfounded hijack victims, we (pastors included) stare out the windows. *Our only path to sanity is repentance.*

A second aspect of our national insanity is actual insanity as defined. In the psychological phenomenon called *Stockholm syndrome,* or *capture–bonding,* hostages begin to bond with their captors and eventually even to love and defend them. The victim begins to consider any brief cessation of abuse to be an act of kindness by his captor.

Another defense mechanism known as *Normalcy Bias* may come into play, as we saw in the two oldest generations of former Soviet subjects after collapse of the USSR. In the victims' minds, nothing could alter the conditions to which the victims had become accustomed.

This insanity affects not only Hillary's and Bernie Sanders' socialist snowflake Millennial Generation (born 1980-95) but also millions in Generation X (1965-79), the Baby Boom Generation (1946-64) and the yes, even the Silent Generation (1925-45).

Fallen Stalin

A European blogger describes a display of communist statues that had been removed from public squares in Lithuania:

'Families with young children roam the park and it is no exception to see young children posing with Lenin or Stalin while their dad is taking a picture. It is also a

strange experience to visit…souvenir shops where you can buy mugs or small glasses with a portrait of Stalin on it. Why would anyone buy a mug with the portrait on it of he who ordered the death of millions? … Bizarre but true.'

A park filled with former tyrants' statues is less bizarre than the Lincoln Memorial's shocking idolatry; testament to the power of American school propaganda in place of history. Our schools, like those in China and Russia, have been teaching propaganda. And the worst part is, *they still do.*

As you trace history, you discover that our new Washington D.C. master began destroying America's two vital law enforcement institutions, Grand Jury and Militia, during the *War to Enslave the States* (its most accurate name) and in 12 years of armed 'Reconstruction' that followed that overthrow. A powerful new mega-bureaucracy hijacked our Constitution, transforming formerly sovereign People and States into serfs, and itself into our master.

You see, American Communism did not begin with Obama. Read any of the books linked in this chapter; you will see that it began with Lincoln and the 37th and 38th congresses (both GOP-heavy). Isn't that amazing…and depressing?

If you perform due diligence but still prefer to honor Abe Lincoln, then don't just hate the Confederate flag. Hate the U.S. Constitution too, as Dishonest Abe did.

And if you do decide to stay comfortably in propaganda-land, please don't blame me for bringing you this hard truth. Blame your teachers, whose comfortable traditions – whose *lies* – you prefer to liberty.

CHAPTER 3

Granite Dome Syndrome

This lesson is the transcript of the most popular 'TED Talk' I have delivered so far on our Sunday night national conference calls. It's the best way I know to prepare you for this new way of life; by showing you how the hired help has twisted American civics, and our lives, all backwards and upside-down.

I'll discuss Granite Dome Syndrome, Moral Hazard, and our abdication of our sovereign prerogative that has resulted in full-blown Washington D.C. Communism and Fascism. I mean *literal* communism and fascism as Marx and Mussolini defined them.

Let me first define sovereign prerogative. *Sovereign* just means one who exercises the supreme, permanent authority. That's established in the opening three words of the supreme Law of our Land. In its first decision in 1793, *Chisolm v. Georgia,* the U.S. Supreme Court held that the *People* are the collective sovereigns in our form of government.

Prerogative means the exclusive right and power to command, decide, rule, or judge. So this will be a key Tactical Civics lecture because it will give you civics knowledge that you won't hear *anywhere* else but that's vital for overcoming the psychological conditioning that you've suffered all your life.

So. First, *this* idea.

The power to *think* – to initiate and conduct those electrobiological processes called human thought – is the most profound gift that God gave mankind alone, among all species of His creatures on earth.

Because rational thought is our most valuable possession from God, it's especially discouraging and dangerous to see how few Americans spend much time actually *thinking* about *important* things. With each passing year, our days and weeks and years seem to be more packed full of noise. Of *busy*-ness and amusements that you only realize at the *end* of life were a total waste; worthless. Yet we spend the vast majority of our lives on these frivolous things.

Tonight, I want to challenge you to start doing things differently. And further, I want to challenge you to winsomely and in a friendly and helpful tone, also start influencing those around you to do the same: to just start *thinking* about things that matter in life, and to start immediately tuning out worthless nonsense when you see or hear it.

In the whirl and din of our Internet-and social media-mediated lives today, it's harder than you think, to just tune out every message that's just distraction on Facebook and YouTube and the like. The average American 15 and 20-year-old, as much as 60- and 70-year-old, is like a child at an arcade, wasting hours every day that they will never recover; that they *could* spend thinking about and doing things that might change their family's entire history.

So that's the challenge; my first point tonight. If you want your life to count when you leave this earth, stop wasting precious hours on *nonsense*. You can't get those hours back.

Now tonight's main subject. I want to break down criminogenic American government into several psychological artifacts of mass-conditioning so you start to perceive how the system creates and maintains its oxen: 'taxpayer', 'consumer', 'voter'. Not responsible members of a collective sovereign; on the contrary, just *oxen*.

I've spoken before on these calls about public architecture – what I call *Granite Dome Syndrome*. I've explained to you what happens right in the first week after a legislator or even their staffers get an office space under a granite dome. You've seen the incredible scale and opulence of the state capitols and of Capitol Hill. Not only the sheer scale and celestial beauty of the frescoed rotundas and massive colonnades, but the dining rooms with gold-trimmed china and silverware. The overstuffed leather chairs. The tapestries, portraits, and Persian rugs.

I've explained how this does for those public servants exactly what it would do to *you* if you suddenly were given a palatial mansion. You'd wake up every day and see all around you the fact that you're now *very* special in society. This deference *to our servants* is trained into American schoolchildren from a very early age.

Okay, so we know what Granite Dome Syndrome does for the servants, but what does it do to the sovereign…to us? Well, it does the same thing as if you lived in a 70-year-old blighted tenement house, and you walk into a marble-floored 20,000-square-foot, 14-bedroom mansion. You definitely are *not* able to conceive of yourself as the boss of the person in that mansion, right? So Granite Dome Syndrome is a no-brainer, and we need to do something about it.

Until we take them out of those palaces – by the way, I propose that you start calling your statehouse the *capitol palace* from now on. So at least when the snot-nosed legislative aide looks down his or her nose at you, you'll keep in mind that the young fool is the servant of your *servant*, and you're the *boss* of their boss!

Okay, now a *second* element: Moral Hazard.

In economic theory, the principle called *Moral Hazard* holds that the larger a taxpayer population grows, the less each taxpayer will care about a given expense because it impacts each one so little. Notice how central governments tend to be more corrupt and opulent as a function of population. The larger the victim pool, the less each victim feels the hit. That's Moral Hazard.

The label *Moral Hazard* derives from the phenomenon that when times are good and taxpayers aren't hurting much, the corrupt activities, agencies, bureaus and debt load that would normally make you furious, don't bother you. Because the hit is spread over a lot of people, each one doesn't feel like it's worth the trouble to confront it. Even if they're presented with a practical arrest mechanism for the crimes, *they just won't bother*. That's what makes it so dangerous.

Now, a *third* element of criminogenic tactics: *distance*.

Our feral government puts legislators far away from their communities. The sovereign can't see who they meet with for breakfast, brunch, lunch, cocktails, or dinner. This distance makes it very unlikely that you'll take the time or spend the money to check up on them. If you don't see their day-to-day shenanigans with attorneys and consultants for corporations and special-interest groups, it's as though it's not even happening. Do you see how these factors add up?

A *fourth* element is *unaccountability*. What difference will it make when we pass the Bring Congress Home Act (see Chapter 7) and not only bring them home and cut their salaries and limit their terms, but also demand annual audits of our servants' expenditures, posted on a public website? Isn't it *ridiculous* that we've never demanded this before? And why on earth do we, their employer, not get to determine their salaries but allow *them* to do so themselves? Pure irresponsibility.

Now the *fifth* element; I will call it 'mass civics deception'. Fraudulent labeling of the lawless form of government we've allowed to grow right inside the shell of our supposedly constitutionally-limited one.

D.C. Communism is never called by its accurate name, yet the D.C. government today meets all ten of Karl Marx's stated goals in *A Communist Manifesto*. Why don't we call it what it is? *Propaganda.*

The same goes for Washington D.C. Fascism.

Mussolini defined *fascism* as the alliance of central government with the corporations, to control the people in the service of the State. Ending D.C. Fascism is simple; after we strip them of their Granite Dome palace, we begin filling those legislators' seats ourselves, and we stipulate in law that legislation *must actually be written by legislators* and specifically *not* by industry. A dirt-simple shunt to organized crime.

When we break down U.S. House districts into small, local ones and take congress out of Washington D.C., then we can enforce Article I, Section 8, Clause 17 – that's where We The People grant congress exclusive legislative jurisdiction over the District of Columbia. Think how nice that will be when congress isn't there anymore but all the D.C. *tentacles* remain there. The responsible remnant can end D.C. Communism and Fascism *without firing a shot.*

You see how the American mind is conditioned, and why young people seek careers in politics. Political careerists *never* lose their granite dome, perks, and pay; better pay than private-sector jobs. And what about us? Well, if we oxen fail to pay property tax on our *paid-for* farm, home, or shop – we lose everything to the arrogant hired help when *the sheriff* sells it on the courthouse steps.

So the *sixth* element of corrupt government is closer to home. The *ad valorem* property tax scam in America stokes the fires that make us fear our servants. You fail to pay for whatever your legislature wants this week, and you'll face your county tax collection lawyers and your friendly, neighborhood sheriff!

That's the *predator* aspect of the crime spree; what about the *parasite* army? Well, that's the *seventh* element of criminogenic American government. *Criminogenic* means it teaches criminality by example…and that's precisely what government in D.C. and your state palace has done. It has taught your county, city, and school district bureaucrats and boards to be as criminal in their presumptions as congress is, with its $22 trillion+ debt burden palmed off on *our* backs.

So. The parasite army is a huge catalyst, a multi-generational welfare horde including 30 million illegal aliens, riding the coattails of our corrupt servants and 20 million public employees in agencies, bureaus and departments at all levels. That's *50 million people* extorting and bleeding productive America!

Our First Right and the Bring Congress Home Act are our last serious line of defense against rogue states that declare themselves *sanctuaries*. From under those granite domes, the state governments of California, Colorado, Illinois, Massachusetts, New Mexico, Oregon and Vermont have declared their states *outlaw territories*, against law and against the interests of productive citizens. Close behind are many cities and counties in Iowa, Pennsylvania and Washington State.

With state governments proclaiming rule of law dead, do you see how Obama's administration including 'Resident' Biden, Hillary's open corruption, Bernie Sanders' candidacy and George Soros' astroturf hordes forged a coordinated attack by American Communism against rule of law?

This public, shameless rebellion against Productive America is straight out of Saul Alinski's book. It's the Cloward-Piven Strategy in full metastasizing cancer mode. We will explain how these tactics took notes from the long history of success in the infanticide and sexual perversion communities.

TACTICAL CIVICS™ is the answer – but sincere repentance is Step One. As we've explained, Americans have been taught to self-label as *taxpayer* and *voter* like farmers use the terms *ox* and *mule*.

The war, banking, and oil industries piled on because no conditioning tool works as well on mules and oxen as the shock of war: Lincoln's war, Wilson's, FDR's, LBJ's, and the open-ended Bush-Clinton-Bush-Obama-Trump war were a one-way ratchet; a growing burden on productive America.

But things are finally changing, and TACTICAL CIVICS™ is the point of the spear, even though we're only a mustard seed today. You see, the ox is beginning to despise the growing blue whale on its back, but there are still millions of complaining, fearful, angry, cynical Americans on social media every day who (even the angriest among them) suffer from Granite Dome Syndrome without even knowing it.

So. Now you know more about your mental and emotional condition and its origins, than you did a few minutes ago. This book is designed to prepare you to break free, and help forge a far better life for your flock and your own grandchildren than your grandparents handed down to your parents.

Let's review TACTICAL CIVICS™ again, and how it will work. We all know the problems: every day, Americans are more fearful, angry, frustrated and cynical about America's direction. Abortion, perversion and transgenderism even in grade schools, Congress opening our border to hundreds of thousands more illegal aliens to add to the tens of millions already here. Cheap labor for industrialists and free votes for evil politicians. Muslims are winning elections to city, county, state governments and to the U.S. Congress.

Antifa rioters and random shooters pop up as regularly as clockwork. These planned distractions keep us from noticing D.C. mega-crimes. They give state and federal tyrants more reasons to disarm the law-abiding citizenry, and frighten and destabilize Americans, at least the more limp-wristed ones, to reject the idea of constitutional Militia more than ever.

Some governors are so wicked now that they're *openly* destroying our civilization. Some state legislatures are actually pushing the murder of not only pre-born infants, but those who have already been born. As Christians warned a decade ago, the homosexual army expanded the gaping hole in our morals to now allow pedophiles and transgendered perverts to follow. Marxists are pushing so-called Critical Race Theory to further tear our civilization apart. Where will this end, and what can *you* do to help?

To reiterate, AmericaAgain! Trust is a charitable trust and member organization whose mission is to recruit, train, support and organize the American remnant in a new way of life called TACTICAL CIVICS™, the result of over 66,000 hours of research and development by 45 volunteers. It is unprecedented; the only full-spectrum action solution in our republic. TACTICAL CIVICS™ has discrete milestones, detailed processes and personnel plans for execution, and metrics for reaching each milestone before proceeding to the next one.

The unique, powerful facts of American civics are that We The People, as the *creators* of all three servant branches in Washington D.C., are the *only* human authority *above* the US Constitution. Collectively, we occupy the highest office in our government. No other population in history has had that lawful authority.

TACTICAL CIVICS™ includes five unprecedented objectives...

First: We restore our original law enforcement institutions: the county Grand Jury and the constitutional county Militia, and most importantly, we *jointly deploy* them. Eventually, every county Grand Jury can have the lawful firepower of its corresponding constitutional Militia to serve and arrest potential criminals in public office at the school district, city, county and state levels, as well as members of Congress when we finally have them living and working full-time in their own communities.

TACTICAL CIVICS™, with our Grand Jury Awake™ project, will clear up the public's confusion caused by private impostor groups calling themselves grand juries, but who seat themselves. With our American Militia 2.0™ project, we similarly seek to remove the stigma attached to the very word militia by private armed groups who are unaccountable to their elected town or county governments.

As you will learn in Chapter 9, We The People in the U.S. Constitution stipulate that each State must appoint Militia officers and provide for training. But no State is doing so; in fact, many State legislatures are in high violation of the Second Amendment and becoming more lawless each session. Given this lawlessness by the servants in state palaces, groups of armed men for over 40 years have been operating as private vigilante groups, creating a massive hobbyist and re-enactment demographic that often uses the term 'militia'.

As I am explaining in our newest book, Time to Start Over, America, which I am writing simultaneously with this book in your hand, our American Militia 2.0™ project can bring together all those who are ready to serve *constitutional* Militia duty in their community and State, as the Founding Fathers intended. Our county Militias should be much like America's local Volunteer Fire Departments. TACTICAL CIVICS™ is committed to restoring squeaky-clean, law-abiding, all-American, locally-controlled constitutional Militia for a new sense of community, liberty and security that is of, by, and for The People Themselves.

Second: We finish ratifying the first right in our Bill of Rights, breaking the U.S. House into small districts. In Chapter 7, you will learn more about this amazing gift left to us by the Founding Fathers. All we have to do is finish that chore; 'Our First Right' in the original Bill of Rights is already ratified by 11 states so it only needs 27 more.

It was the first of 12 articles in the original Bill of Rights: keeping congressional districts small, to reduce corruption. It was the only subject on which George Washington stood before the Philadelphia convention to speak about in 1787. When we finish ratifying Our First Right, a U.S. House campaign will cost a few *thousand* dollars, not millions. This will make serving in the U.S. House appealing to countless regular, honest, hard-working Americans.

Third: Once we've broken congress down into about 6,500+ small districts represented by citizen-statesmen, we *Bring congress Home*, to be the world's first distributed legislature, now under *our* watchful eye. In this 21st century, while over 40% of American businesses are using telecommuting and online meetings, why do we allow our arrogant, corrupt servants in D.C. to remain huddled together in the most ruthless, corrupt city-state on earth, while we pay their bills? It's *insane.*

See Chapter 8 for a fuller analysis, but the Bring Congress Home Act stipulates that they get just one modest office per member of congress and it must be in their district. We limit them to two terms, House or Senate and *no* benefits; they can pay their own way like most of *us* have to. We cut congressmen's salaries to half of what they pay themselves now, and we annually audit their operations, as any employer should.

Fourth: As you'll read in more detail in Chapter 9, we then deploy our Indictment Engine™ mobile app, to track and arrest legislation violating the U.S. Constitution. Its language artificial intelligence algorithms search the proposed legislation to match it against the applicable sections of the sponsor's and co-sponsors' State Penal Code sections, and the Indictment Engine™ outputs a felony presentment for each attempted crime. Those presentments can be used by the Grand Jury of the politician's home county, to pass down a criminal indictment count against the politician proposing the lawless legislation, for each such violation of his State Penal Code.

Fifth: Through our 19 Reform Laws, TACTICAL CIVICS™ will help citizen-statesmen in our new, distributed Congress scrape back all that We The People lost to D.C. organized crime over the past 160 years.

TACTICAL CIVICS™ county chapter leaders are holding meetings from coast to coast in hundreds of counties, learning the same civics contained in this book. They are spreading the same good news that we hope you will spread as a pastor after the model of the 'Black Regiment' (aka, 'Black Robed Regiment') during our War of Independence.

With county chapters from Alaska to Florida and new ones added almost daily now, TACTICAL CIVICS™ is not politics, needing majorities. It's *popular constitutionalism;* the People enforcing the Constitution for the first time, and from now on.

Since it is law enforcement rather than electoral politics, we only need half of 1% to meet our objectives and rebuild America's walls.

We are witnessing the noisy, cursing, clawing collapse of American Communism after 160 years, and of the massive Deep State and media empires who have enjoyed fat careers on the backs of a population that have never enforced our highest law.

Hundreds of thousands of complainers and Fear Porn hawkers daily spew fabricated passion on social media, pointing out evils both real and imagined. *But they never deliver solutions or actually get to work.*

What good does it do to continually complain about the gathering darkness? Even if America is collapsing – at some point we'll have to clean up and restore normal life, right? TACTICAL CIVICS™ has already *begun.*

We The People, just a remnant, are now doing our best every day, to repent our abdication and reclaim our authority and duty over government. We have the only full-spectrum action plan in this republic. No one else…no private sector startup, no one in academia, no nonprofit…has anything even *approaching* this mission.

Yes of *course* it will be difficult! Of *course* it will take years! Restoring rule of law in the largest free republic in history, when the criminals have had generations to perfect their game – what would you *expect?*

Sincere Americans must wake up, *now.* Perform your own research to corroborate our shocking assertions in this book. The hard truth is that

Americans were lied to in school and defrauded in college for over a century. We've been propagandized by the servants whose salaries and benefits we pay.

Now the good news: *this is the best time to be alive in America, and God is blessing us yet again, if the responsible remnant will only do our duty.*

CHAPTER 4

Tactical Civics™ vs Failed 'Save America' Efforts

Almost 80% of sub-Saharan Africa has cell service. An African herdsman can look up weather, learn English, and diagnose maladies that killed his fellow villagers just a decade ago. Technology puts in your hand more information than the Library of Congress. Given all the smartphone applications, it was only a matter of time before we created one to arrest D.C. organized crime. We *can* stop allowing congress to run by 19th century procedures in secret, directed by corrupt industry. That is textbook fascism, and we can end it.

In Chapter 9 you'll learn about our proposed mobile app that will allow us to monitor our congressional servants as easily as checking weather, and stop criminals cold. On social issues, for 50 years a godless urban culture forced our civilization off the rails, always in our face. They claimed this Sodom was America's future, and pantywaist pastors and Christian authors have been folding, proclaiming 'post-Christian America'. It was all a lie; the only thing 'post-Christian' in America is that the vast majority of pulpits are timid, and it must stop!

Moral and ethical life continues in America's 31,000 small towns and rural areas. In the 2016 election we defeated and shocked Progressives; we did it again even more overwhelmingly in 2020 as everyone witnessed with the huge turnouts in all of Trump's rallies including many that were not associated with his campaign; just spontaneous citizen displays of support.

Alas, the Deep Axis was ready for it this time (it was blindsided by Trump in 2016) and overthrew our federal government anyway. It's a sad thing to be under God's judgment, but as I love to say…

Repentance is always an option.

We The People *will not* allow criminals to hijack our republic like this. And we *will not* look to Trump to fix the mess resulting from *our* abdication of duty.

After two generations running from a ruthless, small minority that fights dirty and plays only offense, we in the Remnant *now go on offense, from now on.*

Forget Failed 'Solutions'

Now let's assess the top nine proposed solutions of the past: an Article V convention, nullification, secession, the TEA Party, armed revolution, anarchy, PACs and think tanks, a shadow government, and a D.C. coup.

1. A Constitutional Convention

A heated argument took place among patriotic Americans for several years. In one corner was Dr. Tom Woods and his allies at The Tenth Amendment Center arguing for nullification. In the other corner were celebrities Mark Levin, Glenn Beck, George Soros and a long line of conservatives, libertarians, anarchists, TEA Party folk, Progressives and sexual perverts, all beating the drum for an Article V convention to amend the Constitution.

A latter-day 'ConCon' movement using the moniker 'Convention of States' suggests that by using that label, a constitutional convention becomes a new thing that will not become a runaway convention, like the first and only ConCon, back in 1787. This nonsensical position is debunked by this article by veteran Article V scholar Dan Fotheringham and these articles by former JAG attorney and constitutional scholar Joanna Martin (aka 'Publius Huldah').

Watch this presentation by Robert Brown, exposing the lies being pushed by the COS movement. Then notice these hundreds of liberal organizations pushing for a convention of states to tear our Constitution apart!

The ConCon idea is silly. First: over 11,000 potential amendments have been proposed since 1789. Secondly: our servants violate the Constitution not because it needs amendment but because it needs *enforcement.* Think about it: if the criminals in government have not obeyed the Constitution we have now, why on earth do you think they will obey a new one with all the features that George Soros and the globalists and perverts want to add to it?

2. Nullification

Nullification was first proposed by Thomas Jefferson: when a state's residents disagree with a federal law, the state passes a nullification resolution to block it in that state.

Until our full-spectrum solution is in operation, we support enforcing the 10th Amendment via nullification. But long-term, it's a bad idea for three reasons.

First, it's terribly inefficient for states to spend citizens' time and money in a new rear-guard action every time Congress violates the law. Secondly, it's ineffective: a security fence around one home in a high crime neighborhood does nothing to protect the other homes in the area. Thirdly, nullification would create a constitutional hodgepodge across the republic.

3. Secession

As the Confederacy learned from the War to Enslave the States, secession is tactical folly. Small minorities in California, Texas, Colorado and other states have sought to secede or to create new states, but it will never happen.

The families who relocated to New Hampshire in the 'Free State Project' gained nothing. They still face federal and state laws, regulations, and predation by bureaucrats.

4. The TEA Party

Like a Rolling Stones 50th Anniversary concert, it was sad to see TEA Party rallies and posters and costumes for ten years while the GOP kept double-crossing its base. Mob actions and electoral politics failed to substitute for law enforcement. The TEA Party was run over by the Trump Train after it created millions of cynical, whipped political activists. For 30 years, the <u>Fear Porn</u> industry had the same destructive effect.

5. Armed revolution

Some say it's time to take arms in the streets. Oh? Who will they shoot and what will they do afterwards? You cannot enforce the Constitution by *violating* it.

Jefferson's eloquent Declaration of Independence asserted that our forefathers first exhausted all other options. We now have a Constitution, over which We The People retain every imaginable power over our lives except 17 services that we delegate to the servants. In Article I, Section 8, Clause 15 we stipulate that the Militia must "suppress Insurrections" so the duty of the Militia would be to *stop* armed revolutionaries.

6. Anarchy

Of all principles of political economy, anarchy is the most foolish. It refuses to acknowledge human nature and the lessons of history. There is not one example of a successful anarchist culture or economy anywhere on earth.

7. Conservative Think Tanks and Nonprofits

The 501c3 industry – PACs, think tanks, the NRA, Americans for Prosperity, Heritage Foundation, CATO Institute, Hillsdale College and countless others that fill your in-box asking for donations – have never reversed a single federal usurpation.

8. Shadow Government

Several shadow-government proposals have arisen over the past decade. Tim Turner's bizarre 'Restore America Plan' with its 'Guardian Elders' was updated and re-named The Republic of the United States. There are others, equally strange. Again: you can't enforce the Constitution by *violating* it.

9. Coup d'état

In 2013, Adam Kokesh planned an armed march on D.C.; it fizzled. In 2014, a retired Army major led 'Operation American Spring', a sort of 'peaceful coup' in D.C., named after Arab mob uprisings; it also fizzled. Granting benefit of the doubt to those who plan such events, again: you can't enforce the Constitution by violating it.

Words Matter

Gay makes perversion sound fun; *anti-abortion* makes pro-life people appear evil. Bureaucrats and schools (including private schools) use nonsensical vocabulary to transform our servants into our masters. It's time that We The People, the collective sovereign, detox our terms.

Two preliminaries. First, always capitalize *State;* never capitalize *federal* or offices of our servants (mayor, governor, president, congressman, senator, judge), and write *supreme Court* as the founders did. Second, popular sovereignty is *collective,* not individual. We're not each a monarch as 'sovereign citizen' cultists claim. Popular constitutionalism is the *antithesis* of anarchy. Now, ten words to detox…

Nation: America is a constitutional republic; see the Constitution, Article IV, Section 4. A 'nation' is the universal term for a population under a central government; the tyrannical system hatched by Dishonest Abe and forced on us by D.C. ever since. Unlike the Indian nations, these united States are a *republic*, not a nation.

If you're inclined to argue the semantics, nothing more summarily obliterates your case – that a 'nation' is any people sharing common culture and affinities, history, etc – than Colin Woodard's 2011 book, *American Nations: A History of the Eleven Rival Regional Cultures of North America.* I highly recommend it, though I don't share his politics.

Democracy: Calling America a democracy is as inaccurate as calling it monarchy. James Madison wrote: "Democracies have ever been spectacles of turbulence and contention; have ever been found incompatible with personal security or the rights of property; and have in general been as short in their lives as they have been violent in their death." Adams wrote: *"Democracy never lasts long. It soon wastes, exhausts, and murders itself. There never was a democracy yet that did not commit suicide."*

Government: Most people who say, *"I'm against the government!"* in truth are against organized crime. We The People are the highest level of government. So federal government is *only those who perform duties enumerated* in Article I, Section 8. Those who instead skim payroll accounts, counterfeit money, open our borders and spy on us are not government; they are *organized crime.*

Revolution: means overturning government. In our Constitution We The People create, define and severely limit government. The last thing we want to do is overturn it.

Grassroots: We The People are the highest level of government in our republic; why use the brainwashed term *grassroots* as though we are earthworms underfoot?

Voter: We constantly breathe and walk. Why don't we refer to ourselves as 'breathers' or 'walkers'? Don't say *voter;* it's not a noun.

Voting is only a small part of our citizen power and duty. Many Americans no longer vote because organized crime turned our elections into a sham. Banana republic *voters* choose puppets.

Elected leaders: Have you ever been *led* by a politician? Statesmen *represent* sovereigns, they do not *lead* us.

Elected officials: If an office is nowhere authorized by us in the Constitution, a person cannot be an *official.* 'Public servant' is a fitting term if they are honest, or 'criminal' if they are not.

Constituent: This one is worse than *voter,* tiny citizens making up one politician. We don't *constitute* servants; we *oversee* them.

Tyranny: is a term used for a corrupt sovereign who becomes ruthless. Today, our servants are financial criminals, extortionists, defrauders, embezzlers, and shameless bureaucrats. This isn't tyranny, it is simply longstanding *crime.*

Like ideas, words have consequences. Let's use accurate vocabulary as we embark on our new way of life. Galileo said, *"All truths are easy to understand once they are discovered; the point is to discover them."* This new life includes responsible *action,* not more words; duty that our fathers shirked. Just one action at a time, we will recover our lives, property, liberty, civilization, and Christian witness.

Death of a Monster

In one generation, Lincoln, Darwin and Marx hijacked America; then, five generations of Christians did nothing as government became a false god walking on earth.

Today, many people believe that the militant Left had gone berserk with 'Trump Derangement Syndrome'. But if we repent, we're actually witnessing the kicking, clawing, biting *death* of American communism that has grown like cancer for over 160 years.

Think I overstate the case? Go online and Read Karl Marx's 1848 *Communist Manifesto.* See his ten points that define Communism; by the time Woodrow Wilson was in the White House, eight of those points were federal policy, and by FDR's reign, all 10 of Marx's planks of Communism were D.C. policy.

American Communism is 160 years old; like Communism all over the world, it's dying. But it never dies quietly, so we're in for quite a ride.

It's All About Jesus

When God lifts His judgment, where *else* can restoration possibly begin than in the Church? Think about it: if it is His decree, God will not allow anyone but Christians to restore America. Spineless pastors have cowered in fear long enough. It is time for repentance in the pulpit!

TACTICAL CIVICS™ is a new way of life for an American remnant as humanity finally learns to use the Internet for self-government. *No other people can do this.* As silly as we Americans are sometimes, our Christian bedrock and our inspired, powerful Constitution make us uniquely blessed among all peoples. Just as one generation hijacked us, now by God's grace, our generation can end the long hijacking.

TACTICAL CIVICS™ is forging a network of homes, churches, small businesses, shops, farms, ranches, VFW halls, constitutional Militia units, educated Grand Jury members, and others; Christians who will not run for the hills but will instead join us in repairing the ruins of our civilization. We The People, not our servants, are the only level of government who can *enforce* the Constitution…*elementary civics.*

You can bring real impetus to our home missions outreach by learning the civics they don't teach in seminary, then teaching these key precepts by working them into your sermons, blog articles, podcasts, or other special messages. America's pastors bear the most blame for our condition, and pastors are the most influential people in the lives of tens of millions of Americans. This book is your invitation to use that influence for the glory of our King, in this perilous hour.

CHAPTER 5

Voting is Meaningless
in Failed Systems

In January 2013, a friend expressed his deep concern about the 2012 re-election of Obama, and asked what my feelings were about it. I told him that the 2012 election is immaterial; that to remain a free and happy people we must face the challenge of the 21st century – enforcing our Constitution. I suggested to him that until sovereigns meet that challenge, *voters* will continue to direct our course to Hell.

To define terms: a *patriot* is a citizen who loves the land of his birth. The Latin *patria* means land of one's birth; a small region, not a polyglot republic or empire. In American context, a patriot is a person that lives out popular sovereignty; protects, defends, and enforces the U.S. Constitution to the extent he can. A *voter*, on the other hand, is a nonsense word as we explained in Chapter 1 – but can be generally characterized as one who lives for himself, with no fixed principles other than his wallet; who believes the old political mantra of every election; *"the most important election in our lifetime!"*

To demonstrate why America's presidential elections are presently pointless, I must backtrack a century, to the election of 1912 – the second watershed in the destruction of our republic.

War, Inc: Crushing 'Insurgents' and the Constitution

But first I must mention the *first* watershed in that destruction, which as we explain in *AmericaAgain! – The Movie*, was the *War to Enslave the States*. Lincoln's war was a smokescreen for the mercantilist's divide-and-conquer tactic that has fooled us ever since. As Tom DiLorenzo explains in his book *Lincoln Unmasked,* Dishonest Abe's war killed or wounded nearly one million American men, women, and children; destroyed almost 50% of total assessed property value in America; Lincoln suspended free speech, freedom of the press, and the fundamental rule of *habeas corpus;* and hijacked the sovereignty of We

The People and our sovereign States. He also created a lawless new centralized Leviathan state with a standing military replacing the Constitutional 'Militias of the Several States', and replaced lawful U.S. money with worthless paper. In short, he hijacked our money and guns.

Until Americans grasp the devastating extent and underlying causes of that war, they cannot grasp the forces controlling American life – and our elections will be as futile as those held in Iraq or Afghanistan.

Since that watershed war, We The People have never exercised our limitless retained powers or been able to restrain our federal servant to its 17 enumerated powers. The birth of the GOP – the industrialists' chosen party – came in the generation of Darwin, Marx, and Lincoln. Since then, the average American who might otherwise be liberty-minded, has been increasingly clueless as D.C. Leviathan violates laws at will.

As brazenly criminal as Election Steal 2020 was (literally the overthrow of our government by D.C. organized crime allied with China), the end of meaningful American elections was the administration of Dishonest Abe. In the 160 years since, no presidential election could ever change our national direction for good; only for ill. TR, Wilson, FDR, LBJ, Nixon, Carter, Clinton, Bush II, Obama, Trump, and 'resident' Biden have clearly demonstrated this.

The Father of American Bureaucracy

The second reason that American elections are now immaterial is because the vast majority of federal functionaries are invisible, unelected, unaccountable bureaucrats. The father of that Marxist mess was our second most destructive president, Tom 'Woodrow' Wilson, who took office in 1912.

In that race, Teddy Roosevelt was characterized as the Progressive (which he was; he saw the U.S. Constitution as a mere inconvenience to be circumvented). TR was a man of the people who loved the wilderness, fought the corporations, and strode across the earth as a military dictator. Like Hitler with the gullible German people, TR spun visions of national greatness as he grossly violated the Constitution, sending troops to further plunder the former kingdom of Hawaii, followed by Cuba, Puerto Rico, the Philippines, Guam, the Marshall Islands, and other American 'colonies'. This plunder, including the fabricated 'Spanish-American War', was precipitated by a mysterious,

9/11-style explosion aboard a U.S. ship in Havana harbor. To learn the history of War Inc., see *AmericaAgain! – The Movie,* and read the book synopses in Appendix A, *Recommended Reading.*

Teddy lost the election of 1912 to Wilson, the Democrat contender who had the *chutzpah* to paint himself the *conservative* in the race. Though not the grinning plunderer that TR was, Wilson's deep Progressive bent is exposed in Ronald Pestritto's book *Woodrow Wilson and the Roots of Modern Liberalism.* Pestritto surveys Wilson's decades of writing and speeches conveying his lifelong goal of an all-powerful bureaucratic state, which he fulfilled beyond his wildest dreams.

Wilson followed Teddy's example, using the extremely fishy Black Tom explosion, which took a 15-year investigation to conclude that oh yes, it was Germany. The war industry needed Wilson to trick America into war. Wilson wanted to create, without a shred of constitutional authority, the FBI. One handy explosion accomplished both.

FDR used the same trick for War, Inc to play one-upsmanship to Wilson's explosion, coaxing Japan to attack Pearl Harbor (see Recommended Reading) and creating the OSS, precursor of the CIA.

Occupy Wall Street, 150 Years Too Late

Congress' financial crimes include far more than their concession to the Federal Reserve crime cartel, but let's consider that one. A Federal Reserve Note is a worthless slip of paper manufactured by the Bureau of Printing and Engraving at taxpayer expense, sold by the FED cartel to the U.S. government, who congress forces to pay face value *plus interest on each printing run.* In return, the FED gets physical gold.

No counterfeiting ring was ever so successful because no other cartel has ever enjoyed a concession from congress. It's clearly counterfeiting; per Article I, Section 8 of the Constitution, *only* congress can *only* coin gold and silver (perhaps paper if backed 100% by gold and silver in a vault). Most people think that the financial crime has gone on for a century; they blame the FED cartel alone, not realizing that *congress* is the kingpin. Few Americans also know that congress' money and banking fraud and racketeering began in 1862, behind the smokescreen of Lincoln's war.

Every Southern defender 150 years ago was an 'insurgent', like 'Iraqi insurgents' defending their own homes and towns. Lincoln's illegal national military shook the republic to its foundations. In shock,

Americans lacked the presence of mind to look into congress' money crime. Although 19 other countries abolished slavery during the same period without firing a shot, the bankers' plan – the *War to Enslave the States* – turned Americans against one another in equal, offsetting halves first as North-South and later as Donkey-Elephant:

The Occupy Wall Street movement had no idea that Wall Street had run this divide-and-conquer strategy against the 99% for *150 years*.

Tom Wilson's Legacy: D.C. Bureaucracy

An ardent supporter of Dishonest Abe, Tom 'Woodrow' Wilson rightly believed that *The War to Enslave the States* was the dawn of a new, omnipotent Leviathan State. During his reign, Wilson did more damage to our republic than any president since Lincoln.

He supported the 62nd congress' plan to pass the 16th Amendment, setting up the second-largest financial crime in history, later misrepresented as creating an income tax on individual wages. He supported the 63rd congress' passage of the 17th Amendment, stripping the State legislatures of the power to elect their U.S. senators, and a key aspect of our constitutional republic. He abetted congress' largest financial crime by signing its Federal Reserve Act of 1913. He promised he would keep us out of Europe's first war, then had the suspicious Black Tom explosion as *casus belli* on behalf of the military and banking industries. His utopian 'League of Nations' became the United Nations, a nest of foreign spies based in New York City, financed by American taxpayers.

Wilson's goal was a bureaucratic superstate; he envisioned professional bureaucrats as capable of attaining utopia: the state as savior, with enlightened ones like himself leading commoners. A century later – after LBJ, Nixon, Carter, two Bushes, Clinton, Obama, Trump and now 'resident Biden' – we live under Leviathan of our own making. Wilson's perverse, upside-down civics had been earlier depicted in a tyrant's plan of government modeled with great pride by a Jewish lawyer from Ohio, a Freemason by the name of N. Mendal Shafer.

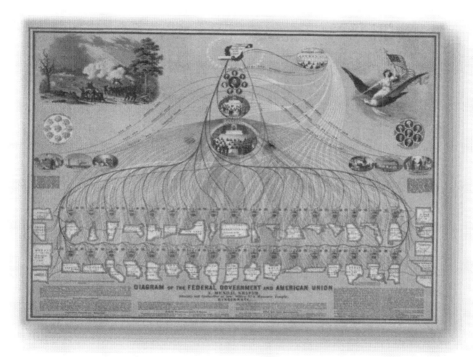

Blaming Presidents for congress' Crimes

But we must not give Wilson more credit than he is due. Americans often credit our presidents with things they never did, and we blame presidents for crimes committed by the other two branches during that administration.

As an example: whenever the subject of worthless fiat money arises, most people pin the blame on Wilson's signing the Federal Reserve Act of 1913. True, he signed it into law; but the 62nd and 63rd congresses originated the crime of granting the exclusive counterfeiting concession to the FED cartel – and as just recounted, the true originator of the crime was the 37th Congress during the first Lincoln term.

Presidential elections are meaningless as long as We The People refuse our *higher* office. For 150 years, our presidents have done either more or less evil, but never have they done lasting good.

U.S. Supreme Court, Criminal Accomplice

Six years after the war ended, the U.S. supreme Court joined congress' crime with a series of lawless Legal Tender rulings, covering the bankers' tracks with *stare decisis* ('let prior decisions stand').

However, three illegitimate rulings, the last one handed down over 130 years ago, cannot amend the U.S. Constitution. As Stanford Law dean Larry Kramer asserts in his book *The People Themselves*, the final judge of the meaning of the U.S. Constitution has always been We The People.

The U.S. Constitution states clearly in Article I, Sections 8 and 10 that *only* gold and silver coin are lawful U.S. money. No amendment to the Supreme Law has ever been passed or ratified. This is the law, and the U.S. supreme Court violates it *often*.

Later, in the Gold Clause Cases during the next massive shock (the Great Depression), the court again ratified a crime, with FDR playing Thief in Chief – demanding the People hand over their gold to government, or else. What the federal court system refers to as 'well-settled law' is actually *well-settled lawlessness* – all three branches of our federal servant arranging, enabling, and defending multi-trillion-dollar financial crimes, corrupting American morals, crippling the productive sector with debt, and racking our economy with artificial boom-bust cycles. Imagine the sheer *nerve* of this crime perpetrated for over a century on an 'educated' population of 240 million adults: *"Pay me the face value on this counterfeit money, plus the interest I demand for loaning it to you!"*

The 'Fractional Reserve' Scam

As outrageous as its FED crime is, it is only one of congress' mega-crimes. Over a century ago, bankers created a fractional-reserve lending scam by drafting legislation and having their pets in congress pass it. FED paper violated the Constitution anyway; why not aim for the stars? Congress fashioned a scheme allowing banks to 'loan' $1000 for every $100 deposit they receive, yet *they're not actually lending a thing*.

Presidents Jefferson and Jackson warned us that American banking is corrupt from nose to tail. With no skin in the game, the banker forces 'borrowers' to put up real labor, materials, and property as collateral in trade for a bank clerk's keystrokes and a bank charter on the wall. The victims pay origination fees, points, interest, and processing costs – in exchange for *nothing but keystrokes and a journal entry.* And the gargantuan derivatives scam dwarfs the other two crimes. Learn much more about the systemically criminal nature of the banking industry from books listed in Appendix A, and in the Appendix E essay.

But enough about the money and banking aspect of D.C. organized crime. Let us return to the discussion of why as things stand now, presidential elections are meaningless.

Monster with a Monocle

The third reason that elections are futile is that ignorant votes do more harm than good. Brainwashed under the direction of our third most destructive president, a scoundrel named Franklin Delano Roosevelt, Americans during the Great Depression were transformed from diligent, liberty-minded citizens into 'voters' and 'workers' in socialist food lines, with their hands out to government. As Jim Powell's excellent book *FDR's Folly* explains, FDR was a master of deception, forcing millions of citizens into slavery to the bankers. FDR was a dear friend to Josef Stalin, who killed 20 million of his own people. FDR had the *chutzpah* to act the part of crippled, benevolent savior, and starving Americans ate it up. For the banking and military industries, Americans have been fish in a barrel ever since.

The Useless 'Voter'

Thus, while nothing compared to the shocking, cynical, brazen overthrow of our government in Election Steal 2020, the 2012 election was eerily like the 1912 election and D.C. organized crime keeps us enslaved. Eisenhower, in his 1961 Farewell Address, warned us that the Military Industrial Complex was threatening our republic; but he saw only the tip of the D.C. organized crime iceberg. To learn how the cartels control every election, read Lawrence Lessig's book *Republic, Lost.* But to see the utter, pathetic joke that our elections have become since electronic voting – both Obama 'miraculous' wins are no mystery now, after seeing how the corrupt machine works – you need only study Election Steal 2020. It's as embarrassing as it is shocking.

A more openly brazen crime was never committed. But the Deep Axis simply doesn't care anymore if we catch them in their crimes. Their lapdog media and Big Tech cover it up, just as government-owned media in China and Russia do. Election crimes *do* pay, you see, as long as We The People refuse to restore rule of law, as Tactical Civics™ teaches and organizes Americans to do, county by county. Yes, the open criminality is shocking; but *repentance is not words; it's work.*

We cannot have meaningful elections until a critical mass of Americans understand basic history and civics. Like any Russian, Afghan, or Mexican, the American voter is gullible and lazy; but unlike people of those countries, *we have the authority and duty to arrest our occupiers.*

Our founders were statesmen who considered elections to be mere furnishings in a solid home. After 150 years of attack by domestic enemies, and finally a worldwide 2019-2022 gaslighting campaign by the evil alliance of Communist D.C. and Communist China, our home is in ruins! It's insane to argue over the furnishings!

Regardless who we put in office, congress, presidents, and the U.S. supreme Court are deep-captured. No politician can ever bring real change for the better. It's up to the People to make the repairs.

Repentance and Restoration

The ill-fated circus of the Trump administration should have taught us that presidents were never meant to be our saviors. Our way ahead is in Nehemiah 9:34-38… *"Neither have our kings, princes, priests, nor our fathers kept Your law…they have not served You in their offices…in the large and fat land which You placed before them they did not turn from their wicked works. Behold, we are servants in the land that You gave to our fathers to eat the fruit and the good thereof… It yields much increase for the kings that You have set over us because of our sins. They have dominion over our bodies, and over our property at their pleasure, and we are in great distress. Because of all this, we make a sure covenant, and write it…".*

Yes; and write it. That's the purpose of this book.

As the highest human sovereign in government, will we repent before Sovereign God? Will we learn from history and put our hands to rebuilding fallen walls? Only when we return to Christian faith and our sovereign duty will American elections ever have meaning again.

CHAPTER 6

Split Them Up (Our First Right)

To take Congress out of Washington D.C., we first need a tactical preliminary action to change the makeup of Congress.

By God's grace, the framers of the Constitution left us just the weapon we need: their first Article in the original Bill of Rights. The only one that has not been fully ratified, it has been gathering dust for over two centuries. So our first action project, called Our First Right, is designed to get our State legislatures to finish ratifying it. As you'll soon see, this has been done before, by *just one man*.

The original First Amendment was designed to preclude exactly the corruption we have today: multimillion dollar campaigns with congressmen reigning over 750,000 citizens that they cannot know, much less represent.

Two years before the Bill of Rights was finalized, on the last day of the 1787 Constitutional Convention, Nathaniel Gorham made a motion to change one word in Article I, Section 2, Clause 4 of the new Constitution: "the number of Representatives shall not exceed one for every forty thousand" would now read, "...for every *thirty* thousand". Others seconded the motion, then George Washington rose to speak for the first and only time in the four month long convention, as James Madison describes on page 644 in *Records of the Federal Convention*:

When the President rose…he said that although his situation had hitherto restrained him from offering his sentiments…he could not forbear expressing his wish that the alteration proposed might take place… The smallness of the proportion of Representatives had been considered by many members of the Convention an insufficient security for the rights and interests of the People.

He acknowledged that it had always appeared to himself among the exceptionable parts of the plan…as late as the present moment was for admitting amendments, he thought this of so much consequence that it would give much satisfaction to see it adopted. The delegates passed the change unanimously.

For the next two years the State legislatures deliberated about ratifying the new Constitution. On June 8, 1789 Madison's team introduced 39 amendments. On September 25, Congress did pass the Bill of Rights, but only twelve of the 39 articles of amendment, and sent them to the States for ratification. We were taught that the Bill of Rights had ten amendments; in truth, it had twelve. But the first two were not ratified by the necessary three-quarters of the States so they remained open in the States, gathering dust…*for two centuries.*

Then in 1983, University of Texas student Greg Watson ran a campaign to get 29 more State legislatures to ratify the original Second Amendment. It stipulated that if Congress gives itself a pay raise, it does not take effect until an election intervenes. After Watson had toiled away for almost ten years, in May 1992 the U.S. Archivist certified that three-fourths of the States had ratified and that 'Article the Second' of the Bill of Rights was now the 27th Amendment.

Every article in our Bill of Rights is ratified except the first and most important one. It has 11 ratification votes; it needs 38. So when we get 27 more State legislatures to ratify it, the original 'Article the First' will become the 28th Amendment. If a college student could get this done, so can we. Since Congress already passed the Amendment, Washington D.C. can't stop us and no constitutional convention is needed. Our State legislatures have a duty to ratify our full Bill of Rights so that we can finally restore the People's House.

What This Will Accomplish

Congress today spends $5.85 billion annually on operations, opulent lifestyles, imperial palace, and massive staffs. No sane employer allows employees to set their own pay, staff, benefits, and office arrangements.

Making districts small will reduce House members' power but our big payoff is that Capitol Hill will not accommodate 6500 House members and staffs, so we can split Congress up and bring them home where we, not lobbyists, control them.

Chapter 7 explains the Bring Congress Home Act, stipulating that the 6500 congressmen and 100 senators will work full-time back home in one modest office each and be limited to two terms. We do not need a term-limits amendment; they were able to limit the *size* of the House to 435 seats without an amendment. They can limit their *terms,* too.

Capitol Action Teams

Nothing can be done at any state 'palace' until we have a sufficient number of active Tactical Civics™ chapters in that state. This is Phase 1, remember!

Once we do, we will deploy Capitol Action Teams consisting of one very adept public speaker to do the press and social media events in each capital city, and a team of canvassers comprised of Tactical Civics™ county chapter members deployed from across each State, to go to each state legislator's office and make our demand on camera, to hold the vote on Our First Right, at last.

Twelve state legislatures (CT, KY, MD, NH, NJ, NY, NC, PA, RI, SC, VT and VA) already voted to ratify it, but CT failed to turn in its paperwork. So we need 27 more states out of the 38 who have not acted on it, to just vote 'yes'.

Remember basic civics. Mob action isn't for sovereigns. We specifically do _not_ want large mobs at these events. We only need many small teams to do the canvassing and our national OFR spokesman to do press events in the capital city. Our two-person Capitol Action Teams go to every state legislator and get them on video, answering one question:

"We sent you a 28th Amendment Fact Sheet and model Joint Resolution. This is a simple issue with no political downside. Will you bring to the floor the ratification vote of the original First Amendment, the First Right in our Bill of Rights?"

We make them answer yes or no; no excuses or bloviating. We get them on video. We will be firm but cordial and upbeat; this is a great thing we're offering them: equal representation for all, at last! Our teams will send materials to every state legislator once they get their email address. Appendix B is the 28th Amendment Fact Sheet, and Appendix C is the model Joint Resolution for State legislators.

Logistics and Schedule

Most State legislatures open their session in January and end by May or June but calendars vary as you see here. If you live in AR, MT, ND, NV or TX, those legislatures will not meet in 2022 so they need to push the ratification vote hard in the 2023 session if possible.

Deadlines for submitting bills and floor or committee actions don't matter; we are only telling the legislature to hold a ratification vote, period. It can happen anytime in the session, and in the first few dozen states, it has no political downside.

So simple, right? But be advised: *politicians are never to be trusted.* I have been double-crossed more often by Christian politicians than any others. Once they win a place under the granite dome, your servants are *never* on your side, no matter *what* they say. Your state capitol is no better than Capitol Hill. Recall civics from Chapter 3; a sovereign does not have to yell at servants. But politicians and their staffs have a habit of foot-dragging. They always try to appear very busy, unless a lobbyist or wealthy donor drops by. Then they will drop everything.

This is not typical 'political activist' nonsense. It is the crucial first step in the most powerful popular sovereignty transformation in history. Next chapter introduces Tactical Civics Good Guys™, to help thousands of citizen-statesmen become the most historic Congress in history, and explains how we Bring Congress Home, forever.

CHAPTER 7

The Bring Congress Home Act

"If we lose freedom here, there is no place to escape to. This is the last stand on Earth. And this idea that government is beholden to the people, that it has no other source of power except to sovereign people, is still the newest and most unique idea in all the long history of man's relation to man... Whether we believe in our capacity for self-government or whether we abandon the American Revolution and confess that a little intellectual elite in a far-distant capital can plan our lives for us better than we can plan them ourselves". (Ronald Reagan, Oct. 1964)

Washington D.C. is earth's most corrupt and powerful city-state, working for 534 billionaires and U.S. industry. Idealistic statesmen win office, move to D.C., receive orientation, and then are surrounded by veteran staffers, other unelected D.C. bureaucrats, D.C. law firms, and industry and special interest lobbyists.

By turning the tables, We the People demonstrate to the world that Americans truly are self-governing; that we still have a Constitution that we enforce, even if it means incarcerating incumbents in congress. That shouldn't be necessary after Our First Right transforms the entire congressional election process. After the States ratify it, the next congressional election will be for approximately 6,500 representatives in compact, local congressional districts rather than 435 huge, gerrymandered fiefdoms for industry. I suspect that when we ratify the 28th Amendment, most incumbents will suddenly need to *"devote time to my family so I'm not running for re-election"*. Good riddance; that's what we've needed for decades.

Losing Our Royalty Fetish

Because we have been ignorant of civics for generations, we have had a childish attitude toward presidents, a caricature of I Samuel 8, when Israel's judges had become corrupt:

"And it came to pass when Samuel was old, that he made his sons judges over Israel. Now the name of his firstborn was Joel; and the name of his second, Abiah. They were judges in Beersheba. His sons walked not in his ways, but turned aside after money, and took bribes, and perverted judgment."

That describes the average federal judge or politician.

The people told Samuel that they wanted a king to rule over them. Samuel warned them that kings would take 10% of their substance and would make their lives difficult:

"But the people refused to hearken unto the voice of Samuel; they said, 'No, but we will have a king over us, that we may be like all the other nations'".

Like the British, too many Americans are unwilling to govern themselves and instead seek monarchs like Barack and Michelle, or like Donald and Melania with their Arab sheikh-style opulent lifestyle, to rule over them. We liked the Trumps; our point is that the gold-plated first couple made Americans gawk like British subjects, and far too many Americans have a fascination with celebrity as it is.

If we accept or even demand celebrity of our public servants, we have no right to oversee them or even to vote. Productive Americans are losing ground against bloated bureaucracy, supported by wealthy predators at the top and growing hordes of parasites at the bottom.

Tactical Civics Good Guys™

It is time to wake up, repent, and take our lives back. The whole world awaits such hope; a model of what can be done. It must begin with repentance, followed by duty. Imagine: every two years, one out of 50,000 of us can take responsibility to represent the others, obeying and supporting the U.S. Constitution as the oath of office demands, and co-sponsoring our reform laws. Surely there are a few hundred thousand intelligent, patriotic Americans who will accept our Good Guys™ challenge after we ratify Our First Right.

If you're honest and of average intelligence, you're far superior to the average member of congress today, and it will hardly be a sacrifice. Half of today's congressman's salary is $90,000 and you won't have to move to D.C. or keep a second home.

The new U.S. House of Representatives can fulfill the Founding Fathers' dream for The People's House: serve for two or four years, then return to regular life. No career in politics. No rich, famous narcissists and showmen. Just citizen-statesmen representing self-governing citizens.

The one in 50,000 citizens will have simpler duties than the mayor of a city. Any competent adult can read the Constitution and obey it better than today's D.C. incumbents do. Self-government is just a matter of applying morality and common sense to the issues. Largely, it requires plain fiscal discipline, to shut down unconstitutional agencies, bureaus and programs. That's impossible for a politician seeking a lifelong career, but a no-brainer for any productive American.

No one expects perfection in a congressman, either; just honesty and common sense. But even if you don't feel called to the Good Guys™ challenge to serve in congress from your community, surely you know at least one person of character and integrity in your town that you can nominate and support to take the challenge.

Time for a Mass Extinction Event

Why do we despise politicians? Because whether local, state or federal, they speak lies, cut deals, and daily huddle with one another in a world of make-believe, spending our hard-earned money like drunken sailors at a magic ATM machine. Our servants in congress runs earth's most powerful city-state as organized crime, for the benefit of a bewildering list of powerful industries and groups.

So We the People believe we can't win because we can't get to the billionaires. But we only need to get their puppets, who are the control mechanism of our Constitution. When we take congress out of that corrupt city-state to work from our own communities, *D.C. organized crime loses its grip on productive America's payroll accounts.*

One statesman out of every 200 politicians – statesmen like Ron Paul – were considered gadflies, painted by lapdog media as curmudgeons because they remind us that congress is violating the Constitution. Because they appeal to honesty in a city of liars. Trump did the same thing, but he tried to do it all alone and take the credit. But as you now know, ending D.C. organized crime is the job of We The People!

Our first reform law is the *Bring Congress Home Act* or 'BCHA'. Something like the 2013 resolution called HR287 to bring congress home to work from their district offices via *telepresence*, which is common tech today, with thousands of participants able to meet by desktop, laptop, tablet or even smart phone.

The BCHA stipulates that all members of congress will work full-time back home in one modest office each, with staff of two for a congressman or six for a senator; limited to two terms, congressmen making half their present salary since districts will be 1/14 as large, and they receive no benefits or pensions. *Our congress should be short-term public service, not a career.*

What About Cost?

Even with 6500 congressmen, with their small new staff and only one small office each, the BCHA will decrease congress' $5.85 billion annual operations budget. But much more importantly, we will save *trillions of dollars* in pork and illicit agencies and projects.

As Chapter 8 explains, the Indictment Engine™ will let you see your servants' proposed legislation on your mobile device *before* it is passed rather than having to lobby to nullify or overturn it *after* it has wrecked your life or killed your business.

The Transition

Our first 'big congress' will do what all past ones have done: set up their office and staff in their district, but then instead of moving to D.C., they will simply meet at a large D.C. venue on January 3 (of 2025, for instance) for one item only: enact the BCHA. The president signs it and makes history, then they go home to their lease office and telepresence system. Trump would *certainly* sign it, if he runs again in 2024 and the criminal cartel that stole the last election is not allowed a repeat of that crime. Just imagine; that will *gut* D.C. organized crime.

Organized Crime on the Potomac

There are more than 100,000 lobbyists in D.C.; that city-state's network of businesses and contractors will resist reform with all their might. So, We The People must break the battle down into 3,141 county-level skirmishes, where we outnumber the criminals by hundreds-to-one. Our plan is full-spectrum, long-term, lawful, peaceful, practical, and designed to last as long as the Constitution does. Our current task is building county chapters and getting the word out that We The People are now in charge of our servants, and need to bring them home. Then it all becomes public relations and citizen perseverance.

This sketch below does not include most of D.C. organized crime in a city-state of self-serving industries, law firms, think tanks, nonprofit foundations, event managers, hotels, caterers, restaurants, and special-interest organizations who will fight to the death to keep their cheese. But if it's Washington D.C. vs. America, *my money is on America.*

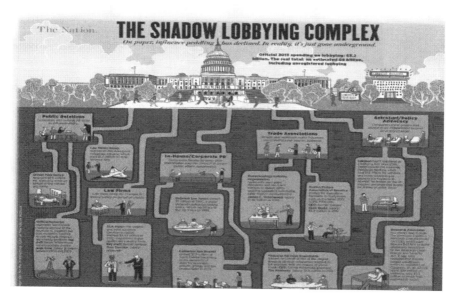

Some Days the World Just Changes

Despite their wealth and power, *Pharaohs did not have flush toilets, cars, or air conditioning.* By the grace of God and over 66,000 hours of R&D by 45 volunteers, in the fullness of time, mankind's inventions will again change the world. Tactical Civics™ with Our First Right, the BCHA, and our Indictment Engine™ will be the most powerful acts of popular constitutionalism since those American shopkeepers and planters changed the world in 1776.

It's time to *bring congress home.*

CHAPTER 8

The People's Ancient Law Enforcement Duties

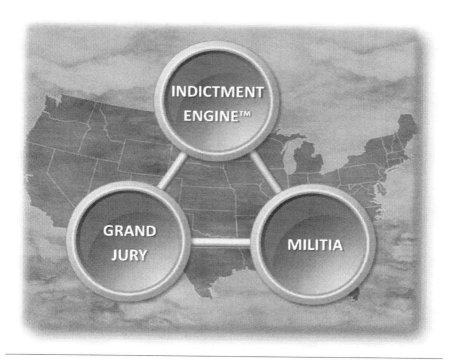

Our operating principle for TACTICAL CIVICS™ is that we will only take on one project at a time, focusing all effort on that project until we achieve it. Our ancestors did nothing for 150 years; we will not repair the ruins overnight. We crawl before we walk, and walk before we run. We have everything we need, but detoxing generations of propaganda still takes time.

In this chapter we will peek at our long-term goal: like the invention of the telephone or car, but with today's amazing tech. And possibly with another non-politician maverick president on our side; God knows.

The Tenth Amendment stipulates that the sovereign States and People retain all powers except the 17 that we delegate to DC. *It has no sovereignty in any other area of life, or jurisdiction in any other area of the world.*

Read that last paragraph again. Slowly. *Twice.*

By now you're aware that our servants have been perpetrating massive crimes for generations. *Organized Crime: The Unvarnished Truth About Government* is Thomas DiLorenzo's book exposing a century of D.C. crimes. *AmericaAgain! – The Movie* presents Congress' top seven crimes: Counterfeiting, Fraud, Grand Theft, International and Domestic Racketeering, Extortion, and Criminal Invasion of Privacy.

Yes, Organized Crime

Of the many hundreds of whistleblower books exposing D.C. organized crime operations, I recommend *War is a Racket,* the 1935 classic by General Smedley Butler, and *Theft of The Nation*, the detailed 1969 survey by criminologist Donald Cressey, describing how local, state, and federal governments 50 years ago were already operating organized crime. Cressey named mafia families in American big cities, in statehouses, and in Washington D.C.; and things have gotten *much* worse since that time. I'm not being melodramatic; our governments are operating exactly as those in Russia, Venezuela, or North Korea.

The Mask is Off

The Russia hoax, Shampeachment, Plandemic, theft of an election (the overthrow of our government) and the massive gaslighting to cover the crimes, Soviet style, demonstrate that D.C. organized crime and its minions in countless corrupt American cities will not simply disappear if we elect 'better politicians'. *Elections do not arrest criminals.*

Peter Dale Scott has published 40 books including *American War Machine*, and *Drugs, Oil, and War* and his latest book, *The American Deep State*. Peter Schweizer has published eight books, all of them *infuriating.*

We produced a 6-part podcast series in 2019-20 entitled *Who Killed America's Militia?* that is available in the Militia topic of the Discovery section of the Tactical Civics™ Training Center. In those nine hours of podcasts, we explain in detail the who, what, when, where, and why of the FBI, CIA, DOJ and other unconstitutional D.C. agencies who run interference for mafia. They make you believe, decade after decade, that things will get better someday ("Trust the Plan", the Q psyop said).

AmericaAgain! is a perpetual charitable trust whose action mission, Tactical Civics™ recruits, educates, supplies, and tactically organizes Americans to enforce the U.S. Constitution by restoring Grand Jury and Militia in every county and eventually by using the Indictment Engine™, a mobile app whose algorithms assign felony indictment target value to every bent member of Congress.

Our long-term staffing plan includes legal personnel to recruit field attorneys and support Grand Jury and Militia to superintend their state prosecutor, judge, and county sheriff as these servants learn to perform their duty at last, and support us as we learn to perform ours in Grand Jury and Militia.

State Judges Trump federal

The Constitution has been violated for generations by our servants because We the People have never *enforced* it. From now on via State criminal courts, we will.

In the Supremacy Clause (Article VI, Section 2), We The People stipulate that *the Constitution,* not federal government, is supreme. We stipulate that State judges are bound by it. But that means bound to *enforce* it as well as obey it!

Even adults with backgrounds in government or law are befuddled reading American civics for the first time. As you complete this book, if you bring this powerful truth up in a room full of law professors, you will see a few seconds of head-scratching, followed by strident defense of existing arrangements.

Our founders rejected titles of nobility for public servants, to erase all vestiges of aristocracy. The original program for attorneys was that they had no special schools; they simply read law until they could stand before the bar and be found competent to practice. The original principle for judges was that they not be lawyers like the mechanics practicing before them; simply men of wisdom and integrity.

In Article III of the Constitution, We the People create a U.S. supreme Court, then we authorize congress, which we created in Article I, to create its own inferior courts for only its federal matters. Yet, for two centuries, Americans have bowed and scraped before an arrogant priesthood of professors and judges, the most arrogant being federal judges – the servants of our servants.

Misrepresenting Marshall

John Marshall, the first chief justice of the U.S. supreme court, was an ambitious, articulate jurist. Few people outside the legal profession can appreciate how the legal industry made a single unelected man over two centuries ago, supposedly build an entire federal law guild as if he was an emperor. The industry claims that in a side-remark called a *dictum* that was not even an official part of his ruling in the 1803 case of *Marbury v. Madison*, the first chief justice built a towering artifice of jurisdiction for federal courts that we never granted them.

It's all a lie.

America's law schools for generations have put great emphasis on Marshall's ruling in the *Marbury* case. Law schools teach that Marshall transmogrified judicial review, which is *not* a strange or foreign idea, into judicial *supremacy*, which definitely *is* strange and foreign. Since about the 1870s, the law schools have used selected parts of Marshall's complex word-salad in *Marbury* to claim that the SCOTUS is supreme over congress, presidents, and *over the Constitution itself.* Before I point out this staggeringly destructive lie, let me explain the setting.

In the last days of John Adams' presidency, he and the Federalists in congress created and filled a new set of judgeships so they could keep control over at least one branch of government. Jeffersonianism was coming in like a freight train. The courts that the defeated Federalists created became known as 'the Midnight Judges' and one of them was a black-robed fellow named William Marbury.

His commission was approved by the lame duck Federalist senate, signed by lame duck Federalist president Adams, and sealed with the so-called 'Great Seal of the United States', whatever significance *that's* supposed to add. But Marbury's appointment was never delivered by the Secretary of State, who also happened to be *justice John Marshall.*

When James Madison became secretary of state in the new Jefferson administration, he found the commissions of Marbury and others sitting on his desk, undelivered. He asked president Jefferson if he should deliver them, and (obviously) Jefferson said no. Marbury sued Madison, *demanding* that he deliver his (Marbury's) commission.

We The People in Article III of the Constitution do not allow cases like that to originate in the US supreme court. But Marbury went directly to the Supreme Court with his case anyway, claiming that the Judiciary Act of 1789 (made by a Federalist congress) gave him the authority.

The case was finally heard in 1803, and chief justice John Marshall – remember, *this was the former Secretary of State who failed to deliver Marbury's commission in the first place* – decided the case! Marshall ruled that Marbury had a legal right to the position as soon as John Adams signed his commission…which *Marshall didn't deliver!* If this seems silly, you are not considering the extent of damage done by the law industry's self-dealing lie about what Marshall actually decided in the case. Here's how law professor Michael Paulsen put it in a 2003 law review article,

All in all, Marbury is rife with wrongness. It wrongly held that the Court lacked jurisdiction. It wrongly asserted that Mr. Marbury's appointment had been completed. It wrongly ignored Jefferson's power to remove Marbury, even had he been validly appointed. It wrongly proclaimed that a mandamus to compel the executive…was the appropriate remedy to right the wrong that was wrongly found. And John Marshall was wrong to have sat as a judge on the case.

As chief justice, Marshall decided wrongly. But as secretary of state, Marshall himself created the case by not delivering those commissions, so should have *recused* himself from the case. But because he chose a massively unethical course instead, the history of American law has been bent into the self-dealing, corrupt shape that we suffer today at the hands of federal judges.

Our Tyrannical, Bickering Children

In its Judiciary Act of 1789, congress gave the court power to force a president to deliver the commission by a writ of *mandamus*. That is an order from a higher court to a lower one, or to some public functionary who's required by law to do something but refuses. For instance, a judge refusing to impanel a Grand Jury when the People demand it.

Our three federal servant branches are like our children. So think of it: a writ of *mandamus* couldn't issue from one child, the supreme court, to James Madison, an officer of the executive branch, our second child… appealing to the 1789 law written by congress, our *third* child! *None* of our children have that power to direct one another. Only *we* have that authority. Pundits, legal historians and law school courses claim that the Marbury ruling gave the supreme court a new power of judicial *supremacy* but they call it judicial review. That's nonsense, and it doesn't take a law professor or even a law *student* to see it. Here's what justice Marshall actually *wrote* in the Marbury opinion; the two vital sentences in his long, confusingly-written opinion,

[T]he Constitution of the United States confirms and strengthens the principle…that a law repugnant to the constitution is void; and that courts, as well as other departments, are bound by that instrument…

[T]he framers of the Constitution contemplated that instrument as a rule for the government of courts, as well as of the legislature.

That one's *all*-important. At least in those passages, Marshall had it *right*, and all the law schools are lying through their teeth, to steal for the legal industry, especially judges, power that they've never had by law. John Marshall *never said* what the law schools and all the books about the Marbury case *claim* he said. Remember, We The People are the only human agency with the authority and duty to govern the servants. Here's how we put it in Article VI, Section 2 of our highest law:

This Constitution and the laws of the United States which shall be made in Pursuance thereof, shall be the supreme Law of the Land…and the judges in every State shall be bound thereby.

Note that we don't stipulate that *judges* shall be the supreme law of the land, or that *opinions* of judges shall be the supreme law of the land. We stipulate that the *Constitution* shall be the supreme law of the land, and that judges are bound by it! Please remember this; We The People are always the final decider of what our Constitution means. Collectively, we're the *sovereign* over it, so logically, things cannot be any other way.

The Proper View of federal judges

Should We the People defer to corrupt *servants* of our *servants?* Think logically as to jurisdiction. First, no state court was created by the U.S. Constitution; the states were the pre-existing parties. Second, the inferior federal courts are created by and serve at the pleasure of our creature congress, so must recuse themselves in any case involving a member of congress. Thirdly, since the SCOTUS is complicit in congress' largest, longest-running financial crimes and crimes of foreign occupation ('insular cases'), it must also recuse itself in all such matters. Fourthly, federal courts have no jurisdiction in State crime cases anyway.

So you see, our authority is clear. As former Stanford Law School dean Larry Kramer suggests in *The People Themselves,* when federal servants violate the Constitution, the People are superior to the U.S. supreme Court. All we needed was a mechanism to help us exercise our lawful power. Now we have one. But these things will not happen on their own; all adults in this Republic who are legal citizens *have duties!* And if your church does not teach the importance of our Romans 13 duties in this time of enemy occupation, we will remain under God's judgment.

How Our App Will Operate

The Indictment Engine™ is actually a planned combination of a software app, AmericaAgain! legal section staff work, and peaceful, perpetual citizen action to superintend servants via *tactical force-massing.*

That means a Grand Jury and Militia bring a criminal legislator under felony indictment in state criminal court on felony charges under the politician's *state* laws that coincide with the omission, commission, support for, or acquiescence in congress' violating our highest law. The legal principle *qui tacit consentit* (silence implies consent) applies to any accessory to a crime.

Our legal section prepares felony presentments against residents of your state by a fellow resident of your state who's a member of congress or your state legislature. Each time we get a county Grand Jury to hand down a criminal indictment against a legislator for a state Penal Code offense, our plea bargain deal will be like the one offered by the Saxons to King Ethelred in 1014 A.D., or by the English barons to King John in the *Magna Carta* in 1215 A.D., or by congress' IRS thugs to every 'Taxpayer'… *"Agree to our terms or go to prison with your assets seized."*

Those members of congress not yet targeted will receive the same offer, but as an immunity deal. If you cooperate, you receive immunity. Before any of that, our Tactical Civics™ Good Guys campaign will offer every candidate and incumbent an opportunity to step away from D.C. organized crime before being targeted. They stop engaging in congress' felonies and sponsor our reform laws restoring what D.C. organized crime has stolen from the American people. It's not rocket science.

Debunking Common Objections

Those who say that congress enjoys sovereign immunity from prosecution are wrong. The U.S. supreme court ruling in *Langford v. United States* is a strident reiteration of a basic premise of 1,000 years of western law – no one is above the law, especially legislators.

Those who say that the perp will file for Removal Jurisdiction in federal court when indicted by the State court, are also wrong. Title 28 U.S. Code, Section 1441 ('Removal Jurisdiction') is only available to defendants in *civil* cases; only arising under the U.S. Constitution or other federal laws; and only when there is 'diversity of citizenship' (plaintiffs and/or defendants are from different states).

Neither the SCOTUS nor U.S. district courts have jurisdiction over a criminal defendant who is a resident of a state that indicts him for violating its State Penal Code, when all plaintiffs are also residents of that state.

Those who say that state prosecutors lack courage or honesty to indict members of congress should be aware that in 2010, the State of Texas convicted Tom DeLay for financial crimes committed while he was the second highest ranking member of the U.S. house of representatives. Moreover, every county Grand Jury can pursue corrupt or dishonest prosecutors and judges and work for *their* indictment if necessary.

Those who say that DeLay's case was insignificant, should review the State of Oklahoma's 15-count, $11 billion indictment of WorldCom CEO Bernard Ebbers, who had his assets seized and is serving out the rest of his life in prison. The Oklahoma Attorney General allowed the federal court to take jurisdiction but was prepared to re-indict if the federal court failed to satisfy Oklahoma.

Looking Ahead

At that point in the restoration process, Tactical Civics™ will only pursue one major project at a time, concentrating our chapters on one achievable goal rather than allowing proponents of each of our 19 reforms to pull in a different direction, diluting our offense as patriots have done for generations. But let's look ahead to the restored popular constitutionalism that we seek in the long term.

Restored Grand Jury

This subject is covered in much more detail in our Field Handbook #2, *Grand Jury Awake*. But basically, when We The People finally enforce the U.S. Constitution, we cause public servants to "be in subjection to the higher authorities" and we also keep the Leviathan state from growing back like a cancer.

The Indictment Engine™ will produce presentments for Grand Juries, citing specific felony counts that the targeted legislator is planning to perpetrate with passage of the legislation (s)he is sponsoring. Unfortunately, our presentments cannot also name as indicted co-conspirators the attorneys and individuals in the corporations that drafted the proposed bill, for that would make them federal cases.

Called to Duty

Most states have similar Grand Jury process. Your county clerk (elected position) randomly picks names of potential jurors from the county driver license or voter registration records, and calls you to jury duty. When you arrive, they tell you whether you're being asked to serve on a Grand or petit jury.

When you agree to serve jury duty, in Common Law countries, you become the highest authority in the legal system. No judge can countervene the jury; it has ultimate disposition. The Grand Jury has more power and discretion than a judge, as the late U.S. supreme Court justice Antonin Scalia wrote in U.S. v Williams (1992):

"Rooted in long centuries of Anglo American history…the Grand Jury is mentioned in the Bill of Rights but not in the body of the Constitution…(i)t is a constitutional fixture in its own right…it belongs to no branch of the institutional government…Although the Grand Jury normally operates…in the courthouse and under judicial auspices, its institutional relationship with the judicial branch has traditionally been…arm's length. Judges' direct involvement in the functioning of the Grand Jury has generally been confined to…calling the grand jurors together and administering their oaths of office…The Grand Jury requires no authorization from its constituting court to initiate an investigation…the Grand Jury generally operates without the interference of a presiding judge…(i)t swears in its own witnesses…the Fifth Amendment's constitutional guarantee presupposes [that the Grand Jury is] *independent of either prosecuting attorney or judge…the Sixth Amendment right to counsel does not* [apply for] *an individual… summoned to appear before a Grand Jury, even if he is the subject of the investigation…the whole history of the Grand Jury institution, in which laymen conduct their inquiries unfettered by technical rules."*

Behold the power of the People!

The Grand Jury can serve for months, but is not a full-time thing; sometimes only one day per week or less. It considers only capital cases and other 'infamous crimes', like stealing an election. The Grand Jury can make its own presentments based on any information its members discover themselves, or that is brought to them. The Grand Jury does not rule on the law at issue, nor does it determine guilt or innocence; that's for the 12-person petit (trial) jury. Grand Juries only decide whether to issue a bill of indictment to take the target to trial.

The Role of Tactical Civics™

Since the beginning of its existence over a thousand years ago, the Grand Jury has been a *secret* function, to assure the safety of Grand Jurors and so they are not unduly influenced.

The Indictment Engine™ process discovers presentment material in any proposed bill filed by the legislator. Then, our legal section will 'load the hopper' and eventually the target is brought before an informed Grand Jury. Each time we acquire a new target, we will publish it in the county and state. Members of the Grand Jury are unknown to the public, but they can see and act on our targeting package delivered to the clerk of the court, as they would do with any presentment received from a local resident or that they come up with on their own.

The Indictment Engine™ will prepare a comprehensive presentment including the text of the filed bill, names and association(s) of the individuals or corporations that drafted the bill for the politician to sponsor, and the relevant State Penal Code sections that it violates, besides violating the Constitution.

Next, the Grand Jury hands down the bill of indictment. To assure the case is not hijacked by a corrupt or timid prosecutor, our members in that county's Tactical Civics™ chapter will put public pressure on the prosecutor's office. If corrupt, *they* are the next Grand Jury target!

The People's Panel

A team of editors at Tactical Civics™ is producing a reprint edition of *The People's Panel: The Grand Jury in the United States, 1634-1941* because believe it or not, Richard D. Younger's 1963 masterwork is the only history ever written about the Grand Jury in America. A fascinating, encouraging read, Mr. Younger presents story after story of American Grand Juries breaking crimes high and low, including those perpetrated by politicians and 'law enforcement'.

For 300 years, everyday Americans stopped crime in government, as the English people had done since 997 AD. But as Younger explains, increasingly over the past century, the legal industry and state legislatures went to work like termites to kill the People's ancient power of grand inquest. Thank God for Richard D. Younger. His magnificent book will inspire our county chapters to get our Grand Jury Ordinance passed in their counties, restoring the most powerful, direct control that the American People have over criminals.

Restored Militia

At this point, another aspect of our Tactical Civics™ trifecta is vital: well-regulated Militia. Our new book, entitled *Time to Start Over, America* introduces our American Militia 2.0™ project. We make it clear that our organization is not Militia; we simply educate, brief, and support Americans who want to steer clear of questionable 'militia movement' groups and start a lawful, clean-sheet, constitutional Militia unit in their community or county.

We offer Tactical Civics™ Affiliate membership to gun stores, training centers and sporting goods and tactical gear distributors. We want to make Militia duty fun, cool, and popular again; Militia duty needs to become as patriotic here as it has been for centuries in Switzerland.

We The People have a constitutional duty, and America already has the world's largest and most active firearms and shooting culture. Now, we just add a supportive Tactical Civics™ county chapter that works to also restore Grand Jury. If we persevere in true repentance and this kind of 'works meet for repentance', God will restore our land.

Although Trump claimed to be a 'law and order' president amidst unprecedented lawlessness and violence across America, he simply did not understand that law enforcement is a local and state function, *not* the job of presidents or their bureaucracies. And he obviously also did not know what we teach in our 6-part *Who Killed America's Militias?* podcast series: the 'department of justice' is an *illegal* agency nowhere authorized by us in the Constitution, that began a century ago as a part-time job for one man. That agency shouldn't even exist, but Trump was extremely gullible to believe it would stop D.C. organized crime.

'Gun Rights' Dinosaurs

I was a member for decades, but I dropped my membership after noticing that the 150-year-old NRA has never even *attempted* to restore constitutional Militia. Like most 501c3 organizations, it's a money-mill.

If it ever allowed a real solution to the crisis it pretends to want to solve, you stop donating every month for the latest 'attack on your gun rights'. Like all Fear Porn, it's a simple business model: milk five million members for donations while playing Whack-a-Mole with an endless covey of threats rising out of the brambles from your pals in congress.

What is the only law enforcement that we stipulate in the Constitution? *Militia.* And what is the first duty of the Militia? *"To execute the Laws of the Union".* So constitutional Militia working in tandem with Grand Jury in every community will be the most powerful law-enforcement, border-and-riot-control force imaginable. See the problem for NRA's revenue stream? *It was never about the guns,* but the authority and duty of the People ourselves to stop crime, riots, and illegal aliens!

When we split congress into 6,500 tiny units far from lobby-land and NRA's imperial headquarters, it will sink into the tar-pit like the cruel dinosaur it is.

Pantywaist Pastors or People's Power

Every State has the legal duty to provide for a true Citizen Militia, per Article I, Section 8, Clause 16 of the U.S. Constitution; but the state palaces now try to disarm us instead, so now we go to our counties to cure the violation. As your county Tactical Civics™ chapter pushes our county Grand Jury ordinance through your county board, the formative new Militia unit pushes through its Constitutional Militia Ordinance. Then, the county board will recognize the Militia unit and appoint officers nominated by the unit's members. At that point, whether the county government begins providing training or not, that Militia unit becomes true, constitutional Militia in America for the first time in well over a century.

Judgment begins at the Church. God's judgment has perfectly just and fair reasons, and one of them is our clear abdication of our Romans 13 duty, as we will explain next chapter. Any pastor who fears leading his flock back to our long-abdicated Romans 13 responsibilities is causing repentance to tarry. Think of the sheer numbers: with over 375,000 Christian congregations in America, the body of Christ can absolutely destroy the criminal cabal. But only after sincere repentance; and that can only be sparked from your pulpit. *No pastor in our Republic under this ongoing existential attack, has a plausible excuse for failing to stand up in this hour.*

In most efforts of Tactical Civics™, an 81-year-old woman can do as good a job as an 18-year-old man. Wisdom trumps testosterone in arresting crime; We the People serving in Grand Jury are the most powerful actors in our criminal justice system.

No other people on earth have this, even theoretically – and until the advent of the Internet and social media, We the People could never make it real. *Now we are fools if we do not.* This is the most exciting time to be alive in America.

Do not run from this challenge! Speak to a few select men in your church; challenge them to take up the duty and offer some space in the church as a regular meeting place. Allow your congregation's members to join hands in this civic duty. Tactical Civics™ has every step laid out. We give daily support to every one of our nearly 250 county chapters. We The People in the body of Christ can repent before a holy and righteous God, turn from our wicked, slothful ways, seek His face, and God will hear from heaven, forgive our sins, and heal our land.

Some Days, the World Just Changes

After the Potsdam Conference ending World War II, the city of West Berlin became an oasis of liberty surrounded by communist East Germany. Germany itself was divided into communist east and democratic west, but Berlin fell fully within the communist side so it was cut in half, the western half of town being free, the eastern half communist.

Life on the two sides was as different as night and day, but the one bright spot in the bleak life of communist East Germany was West Berlin. If you ever visited as an East German, you got a taste of real food, real tea and coffee, real cigarettes, clothing, appliances, everything. A black market developed for all of those things – and for airline tickets out of West Berlin to destinations in the free world. For years, every communist dreamed of taking that flight from West Berlin to freedom. But even that hope was extinguished, literally overnight.

If you woke up in Berlin on August 13, 1961 you discovered that overnight, Soviet forces had constructed a high fence between East and West Berlin. Topped by sharp concertina wire, it closed off all escape to West Berlin. If you had a family, job, or fiancé in West Berlin, that morning ended the relationship. Telephone lines into West Berlin were cut, so you could not even inform your family on the other side.

For 28 years, the Berlin Wall changed the world of all East Germans. But like communism itself, their ruthless artifice could only remain standing by force or fraud. *Then Ronald Reagan spoke six words.*

His challenge, *"Mr. Gorbachev, tear down this wall!"* sparked the imagination of Mikhail Gorbachev and kindled East German hearts. The world changed back again. Tasting liberty at last, the German people destroyed and carried away every chunk of the Berlin Wall almost as quickly as the Soviet crew had erected it.

God turned a page of history for the Germans when Ronald Reagan spoke those six words. God also turned a page of history for us, as a brash casino owner and real estate developer was made president by millions of conservatives. But as tens of millions began idolizing him as he lifted himself up at every event, God also allowed him to be cheated out of re-election that he fairly won. God's judgment is impartial:

For the LORD will not cast off his people, neither will He forsake his inheritance. But judgment shall return unto righteousness: and all the upright in heart shall follow it. Who will rise up for me against the evildoers? or who will stand up for me against the workers of iniquity? Shall the throne of iniquity have fellowship with thee, which frames mischief by a law? They gather themselves together against the soul of the righteous, and condemn innocent blood. But the LORD is my defense and my God, the rock of my refuge. He shall bring upon them their own iniquity, and shall cut them off in their own wickedness; yea, the LORD our God shall cut them off.

Psalm 94 has always been a major inspiration for the staff at AmericaAgain!. We believe that God is raising a repentant Remnant to cut off those who 'frame mischief by a law'. We the People *can* enforce our U.S. Constitution from now on. But we must stand for King Jesus, not King Trump (or any other human potentate); that was never our system of faith, or of government.

If we repent in responsible action, the LORD will end His judgment of the abdicating, evading Church. The corrupt city-state and federal law guild greedily held their place at the head of the table in American law, exactly as powerful crown and guilds once held Medieval Europe in serfdom…

Until they didn't.

CHAPTER 9

The Greater Magistrate is We The People

The framers of our Constitution knew the Scriptures. The memories and traditions were still fresh in their minds, of being subjects of the British throne, and they were also intimately familiar with the command in Romans 13:

Let every soul be subject to the higher powers. For there is no power but of God; the powers that exist are ordained by God. Whosoever therefore resists the power, resists God's ordinance; and they that resist shall receive to themselves damnation. For rulers are not a terror to good works, but to the evildoer. Would you wish to not have fear of the power? Do that which is good, and you shall have praise from the same, for he is the minister of God to you for good. But if you do that which is evil, be afraid; for he bears not the sword in vain. He is the minister of God; an avenger to execute wrath on him that does evil. (Rom 13:1-4)

The magnificent law they wrote, the highest and most authoritative human law in this Republic, in opening with the words, *We The People...do ordain and establish this Constitution...,* set out the most liberating, powerful, unique human law in the history of this planet. Having won their war for our independence from the tyrant monarch across the Atlantic, those men took their wish lists and went for broke, crafting a written Constitution for our blessed, unique Republic.

These states are a unique republic because as Chapter 1 explained, We The People grant ourselves in our highest law the most powerful, liberating authority that men have ever granted themselves: the duty to govern our governors. We give ourselves authority to assure that the servants we create through that Constitution will obey it or we "execute the Laws of the Union"; that's Romans 13 law enforcement. Among all governments ever created by men, only in this Republic of sovereign States are the People themselves the actual Big Boss, by law, forever.

But only if we know the Constitution and enforce it as Romans 13 says that God ordained us to do as the collective 'higher powers'. God ordained that our original founders should arrive here in Jesus' name, and He inspired our systems of law, economics, ethics, government and family structure for at least the first 250 years of this experiment. Those are our spiritual roots.

We The People (collectively, not individually as anarchists) are, in the words of the 16th century German confessions, *Greater Magistrate* above our federal, state, county, and local governments; the *lesser* magistrates. Our *servants*. We elect and pay them to perform *only* the functions that we enumerate in our constitutions and city/county charter documents.

Again, we're not suggesting that every *individual* American is sovereign in our system of government. Only *collectively*. Those who peddle the 'sovereign individual' fantasy have no foundation under their feet. They have no examples; no history, law, tradition or custom. And they have *no Constitution.*

On the other hand, the Romans 13 command, *be subject to the higher powers* applies to each of us individually, as it does to every public servant. Yes, even the international crime family don, Resident Biden, and the treacherous Roberts, the chief robe of that black robe set which has for generations been lining its own high nest as it steadily chipped away at our Rule of Law.

To sit in the Big Boss position of the Greater Magistrate, you must do it as a member of either your county Grand Jury or Militia. Only in those two primordial law enforcement institutions of Western civilization do you occupy the office of the Big Boss in your county. And only during good behavior (i.e., only when that Grand Jury or Militia are not making it up as they go along).

Our mission to America is called Tactical Civics™ because this new way of life restores basic civics and teaches Americans tactics that comprise Popular Constitutionalism. We show you what the Constitution requires of you as an American – especially when you serve in Militia and Grand Jury. We show you the lies we have been programmed in, and the powerful truth and solemn duties in the Constitution. Soon, you have enough good news and solid foundation to tell others in your circle of contacts, giving them hope.

Until a critical mass of Americans take responsibility and learn, train, and muster for duty, the Greater Magistrate that God ordained for our Republic will stay sound asleep or hiding in a corner while the lesser magistrates and criminals of every description take turns running the tables on one another.

Big Boss is Clueless

The conventional wisdom programmed into every American by government schools, Marxist colleges, the treacherous Deep State, and 20 million career government employees is that that voting is the extent of the People's power to seize or reform criminals in public office.

Others, like the clever 'Q' psyop, just tried to keep us in our cages by assuring us that DOJ attorneys or some other lesser magistrates, will start indicting felons in congress…soon! They said for years… *'Trust the plan!'* This conventional wisdom is taught by every political party, law school, Political Science course, and 'reform' book, course, national speaker, think tank, or website.

But it's not what we read in the plain language of the Constitution, is it?

No indeed; in that law, We The People do not authorize any FBI, DOJ, police, or sheriffs. We don't even *mention* any of those. And the only place we mention an army (Article I, Section 8, Clauses 12-16), We The People limit it to two years' existence, then these 'armies' raised by Congress must go back to their duties as State Militias (but I am not suggesting that I believe the huge war industry will be shut down soon).

Believing the nonsense fed to us in government schools and colleges staffed by Marxists, atheists, and unionists, We The People have allowed our servants and lesser magistrates to create their own lawless fiefdoms, in open violation of the Constitution.

So. The bedrock of our Constitution is: We The People, in Grand Juries and in Militias duly established, task *our own selves* as the *Greater Magistrate.* We're supposed to *ordain,* as we stipulate in America's highest law.

But we don't, because we're busy playing golf, or keyboard warrior. Or paying for a fancier house than we need. Or…well, you get the idea. So here we are, the collective Big Boss, just doing as commanded by every petty, blue-light bureaucrat in D.C. or in our state palace, county palace, city palace, or school district palace. The criminals are so sure of themselves, they even get us to pay for every agency, bureau, program, regulation, fancy building, vehicle fleet, junket, or fat pension package they design for themselves. No matter how unconstitutional — in other words, *criminal* — all these things may be. And taxpayers keep paying.

When Will Pastors Stand Up?

In 2020-21, at Trump's insistence and the imperious commands of dozens of rubber-sword emperors in state palaces, Americans by the tens of millions became masked zombies and took dangerous, unproved 'vaccinations' just to keep their jobs, buy groceries, eat at a restaurant, or go to any public venue. Can't be different than the flock. Must comply. To grasp the audacity of the criminals, read Dr. Joseph Mercola's *The Truth About COVID-19: Exposing The Great Reset, Lockdowns, Vaccine Passports, and the New Normal.* Even more shocking is Robert F. Kennedy Jr's, The Real Anthony Fauci: Bill Gates, Big Pharma, and the Global War on Democracy and Public Health.

This was (and at this writing, still is) the most chilling, astounding mass gaslighting operation in history. The overthrow of a government, an economy, and a civilization – and most Americans do nothing. Why? Because they don't have sober, trust, inspiring men of God showing them the seriousness of this overthrow, and the lawful, peaceful, practical, long-term way forward.

If you're reading this book, you're likely one of those pastors who stood against the gaslighting and attempted shutdown of worship in America. But you still could only take *local* action. Now, Tactical Civics™ allows the active, responsible patriots in your congregation to become part of a coast-to-coast network of county chapters with the *only* long-term, full-spectrum solution on the national scene today.

The so-called 'Masters of the Universe', today's Big Tech gatekeepers of the public square, will cancel and destroy the career of any truth-teller on the Internet. But they don't control your church – *do they?*

The latest of three massive racketeering and attempted coup operations has been the most effective. Democrats and Communist Chinese are much smarter than conservatives are. And all governors love power trips; it's why they became governors. Meanwhile, the Higher Magistrate remains clueless of our authority and *duty* to arrest this ongoing hijacking of an entire civilization and economy. The 9/11 debacle was experiment #1; this was experiment #2, and actually far more chilling in terms of mass reconditioning of a formerly self-governing People, into fearful, compliant zombies.

It's bizarre. How foolish can the collective Greater Magistrate be? I'm not sure yet; my fellow Americans continually shock me. Trump surprised me, too; either he's on the enemy's side with Bill Gates and the vaccine industry, or he was simply ignorant. But how could the latter explanation be true? His staff knew very well the several inexpensive, effective antidotes for the China virus.

Yet Trump still pushed that monster Fauci on us, and pushed Bill Gates' and Big Pharma's vaccine on hundreds of millions of Americans. And his fans accepted it.

God's judgment is a tough place to live, but repentance is always an option. We pray for a great wave of real repentance in American hearts. In our American system of government, repentance must include learning your Greater Magistrate duties, and performing them. So let's review some civics.

Nullification and Interposition

After the ratification of our Constitution, James Madison and Thomas Jefferson posed two contesting principles on how to respond to our federal servants when they violate the supreme Law that We The People laid down, and by which we created those servants' offices. Jefferson favored *nullification* by the States of any lawless federal act or pronouncement. Fans of nullification still abound today; but two facts stand in the way of Jefferson's preferred solution.

First, each of the 50 States is running a unique racket in its state palace. Some have grown much longer in the tooth than others (often corresponding to how Roman Catholic the State's population is) but all are running rackets for people and industries with money. So it is beyond naïve to think at this hour of the day that *any* of the 50 state palaces will begin operating as servants, with We The People their boss. So the first problem with nullification is that the crooks in state governments just won't do it.

Secondly, if each of the 50 States make up their own response every time our *federal* servants become outlaws, we'll have worse coast-to-coast confusion than what we already have. Nullification won't fix the mess; it will add to it.

James Madison favored another principle, called *interposition,* which is this idea: when federal servants go rogue, the State must interpose between the bad guys in federal government and the People who are targeted by the bad guys. Other than pointless resolutions and other political tomfoolery, it has never worked.

As a practical matter, exactly *who* in the State would do the interposing, depended on the nature of the threat from federal rogues. The interposition force might have been an attorney and his staff from the state palace. (Have you ever seen a state attorney general preen in front of the camera? It's as theatrical as when governors or sheriffs do it.)

Or it might have been, as Alexander Hamilton posited in the 28th Federalist, the State military who would interpose. According to We The People in our highest law, that is we ourselves, serving in the Militia of our State.

Madison's analysis of the despised Alien and Sedition Acts provided justification for such ultimate interposition. As Christian Fritz writes,

The people of the states "as co-parties to and creators of the constitution" could exercise their ultimate authority by amending the Constitution or finding other ways to express their constitutional understanding. Madison later conceded that the resolutions and his Report lacked specifics about "what mode the States could interpose in their collective character as parties to the Constitution." However, given "the object and reasoning" of those documents, specifics were "not necessary." "It was sufficient to show that the authority to interpose existed, and was a resort beyond that of the Supreme Court of the United States." If the sovereign people invoked their ultimate right to intervene, how they did so was their "own choice."

Madison knew that We The People had totally open options, because he led the committee that drafted and finalized the Bill of Rights.

Incidentally, there are 12 articles, not 10, in the 'Bill of Rights'. Our original First Right is still not fully ratified. The original Second Right was not finally ratified by three-fourths of the states until 1992…a 203-year-long ratification process!

So. Back to our law enforcement options. In the original 'Article the Twelfth', what we know today as the Tenth Amendment, We The People stipulate,

"The powers not delegated to the United States by the Constitution, nor prohibited by it to the States, are reserved to the States respectively, or to the People."

Or in modern language: *We The People, as the Big Boss, retain every power imaginable, except those that we delegated to the servants in our Constitution. What powers those may be, and in what form, and how executed, <u>is entirely up to us</u>.*

Aim High, Go Low?

Some pastors today claim that the Magdeburg Confession's 'Doctrine of the Lesser Magistrate' is how Madison's interposition idea works out today. To them, when your *high*-level lawless servant attempts to take the People's rights, the People's only recourse is to get a *lower*-level servant to stand between the People and the bad guy!

The first serious problem with this idea of lesser magistrates doing our job for us, is that it references the Magdeburg Confession of 1555 instead of the U.S. Constitution which is America's highest law today.

The second problem with this so-called doctrine of the lesser magistrate is that too many people, especially pastors who even dare preach about our murderous, lawless, ruthless civil government, always change the subject from our servants perpetrating criminal acts, to the servants just taking our rights.

No mature parents beg their rebellious, bratty 6-year-old for their rights; they lay down the law in the home. Societies only hold together as long as everyone plays by the same set of rules. We The People need to *enforce* our Constitution, just as we stipulate in that law. It's our *duty* to future generations and to God; *rights* have nothing to do with it.

Pulpit CEOs Are to Blame

Virtually every famous pastor in America being ignorant of basic American civics, it would be useful for seminaries to require a semester of true civics in the curriculum. Charles Finney once said,

"If Satan rules in our halls of legislation, the pulpit is responsible for it. If our politics become so corrupt that the very foundations of our government are ready to fall away, the pulpit is responsible for it."

I have begged and pleaded with Joe Farah, Chuck Baldwin, John McArthur, Hugh Hewitt, Bill Bennett, John Hagee, Max Lucado, Dinesh D'Souza, John Whitehead, Rick Warren, Os Guinness, Charles Stanley, Chuck Swindoll, Dave Ramsey, James Dobson and dozens more who made their names into national brands. But they do nothing and say nothing in support of our mission to wake and teach Americans to do their chores. No Christian leader can use the excuse "It's not my ministry," nor can he plead ignorance. Satan rules in our halls of legislation, and *you* are responsible for it.

Referring to a January 20, 2020 armed march in Richmond, VA by over 15,000 Americans including a great many self-proclaimed 'militia' members against an attempted gun grab by Governor Ralph 'Blackie' Northam, one pastor framed the problem like this,

The fundamental divide in America right now can be characterized as a difference over the nature of rights. What are rights? How are we to understand them? When we understand that, and not until then, we can understand gun rights. … The legislature cannot have the authority, and does not have the authority, to alienate the rights of the people from the people. Any attempt to do so is, by definition, a lawless attempt.

See? There's that silly talk about *rights* again. I challenge pastors to stop being so lazy in their civics. The American People still hold pastors in high regard. Sheep *believe* their pastor's teaching, even when it's nonsense. Programming by incompetent shepherds is even more effective than corrupt government, in keeping Americans from our duties to enforce the law.

NRA Seminary

The problem is that 'Lesser Magistrate' pastors are posing the wrong questions and framing the wrong issues because apparently, they don't know the basic principles of American civics. By simply espousing a nonsense principle, *as the NRA has done for almost 150 years,* you can have your followers and fans chasing their tails for five lifetimes. The NRA, countless think tanks and conservative groups, and America's pastors, by teaching their followers to get the U.S. Constitution exactly backwards, allow massive criminal activity by our servants to continue for yet another generation, along with the flow of donations.

Take the fiery Chuck Baldwin, who decamped from a good gig in Florida to a safer good gig in Montana. For decades, I followed and listened in rapt attention to Chuck. Then I noticed that he was preaching great sermons while avoiding *duty,* just like the National Rifle Association, one of the largest, longest-running hoaxes in American history, second only to Congress' FED cartel and IRS heists, or the myth that Abraham Lincoln was a great president.

Anyone who doubts the truth about Congress' tax scam should read my free PDF book, *A Tax Honesty Primer*. I sent (14) IRS operatives home, empty-handed over a decade and they left me alone after that. Apparently, they agreed that being a law-abiding Nontaxpayer is lawful; merely inconvenient for their embezzlement operation.

And anyone who doubts that Lincoln was the hijacker of lawful American money, Militias, and our Constitution, should review Chapter 2, then read one or more of the six books and one website linked there, exposing the true character and treachery of Dishonest Abe and the elites' *true goal* in that war.

Next, I will shift our spotlight from backwards civics in pulpits to feckless, destructive American academia where within just two generations, History, Government, Political Science, and Constitutional Law courses became palpable malpractice. Colubrine professors lead students down blind alleys, always away from the central fact of American civics: *We The People are the Greater Magistrate.*

It is long, long overdue that We The People begin executing our authority and duties, before it's too late.

Before I move on to illustrate academia's similar malpractice, one last illustration of a pastor retrenching; trying to apply 16th century German law to our constitutional Republic. He writes,

One of the things that happened in the Reformation is that in various countries, the Protestants came into conflict with the magistrates who were wanting to suppress the reform efforts. Places where this conflict could be seen in high relief were France, the Netherlands, and Scotland. And when the magistrates took to the sword and stake, one of things that resulted was a theology of Protestant resistance…a three-step theology of resistance. The first was prophetic denunciation of the civic evil. When the magistrate is defying God, then courageous men in the pulpit should be authoritatively naming what is happening, and denouncing it…

A fat lot of good 'courageous men in the pulpit' have done! Yet, this pastor continues digging himself in:

The second stage is for the believers to flee the persecution. Jesus said to do this — when you are persecuted in one city, flee to the next…

By which I can only assume he will soon lead an exodus to Canada? Yet he digs:

The third and final stage is to take up arms defensively…it is not permissible to undertake a revolution whereby the rebels seek to overthrow the existing authority. But taking up arms defensively is an option. And stating that you will refuse to comply if required by the tyrants to is also an option…

That is the logical and ethical equivalent of parents taking up defenses against their bratty children, telling them that they, the parents, refuse to comply with the brats' demands. Finally, this 'Reformed' pastor reaches his teacher's desk, invoking Calvin to twist American civics into 16th century German shape:

In his magisterial Institutes, John Calvin gave us another layer of protection against lawless anarchy. He taught that when the supreme ruler is resisted, it should be undertaken by the lesser magistrate, and that the people…should resist tyranny from the central government by means of submission to local authorities who are fulfilling their oath of office. Every lesser magistrate has the obligation (not the right, the obligation) to disobey unlawful orders from above. And, when they do this, the people have an obligation to rally behind them.

The governor wants to seize as many weapons as he can, and this is where we see Calvin's doctrine of the lesser magistrate on display… At this time of writing, over 90% of Virginia's counties have declared themselves to be Second Amendment sanctuaries. They have said to the state government that they will not comply with the usurpation of this unjust law.

Oh, Thou Pretty Resolution!

Actually, by passing toothless, non-binding political 'resolutions' (a very different thing from a binding city or county law, called an ordinance), 90% of Virginia's county governments simply took the quickest route to dispersing the crowds in late 2019 and early 2020, before the Communist Democrat machine found in its China Virus hoax a much more effective way to keep citizens from meeting in public or private, or even going to work or school; and of course the perfect excuse for manufacturing *millions* of fake mail-in ballots. These crimes will be exposed eventually, but don't hold your breath. Still, do we Christians have to be *this* gullible? We homeschoolers, at least, certainly do not.

Blind Men in Pulpits

My harsh point here, brother, is this universal practice by American preachers, twisting Romans 13 into a refutation of American civics. They preach and write as though we do *not* actually have a written

Constitution; as though We The People do *not* clearly stipulate in that highest law that collectively, we are the top level of government and 'the higher authorities'! Is the Constitution incomprehensible, truly?

The preacher I quote above simply refuses to grasp that 'submission to authorities' is not what the Greater Magistrate is supposed to do when the lesser magistrates turn to lives of crime:

And so this means that the rally in Virginia's capital — and which included a number of Virginia sheriffs — was not simply a mob. It was more than a crowd. It was not simply a protest. These were citizens were assembling in their state capital, declaring their intention of submitting to the existing authorities…They were citizens in submission to the law and to their authorities…

He even unwittingly plugs Tactical Civics™:

Some might complain…[about] *a gun rights rally like this…* [but] *this is how it is to be done. We should all do it more…everyone take note. This is how it is to be done. As it happens, in order to respond as an informed citizenry, the citizens have to be instructed, taught, catechized. They have to know what their rights are, how they are to be protected, and what the response should be whenever they are threatened. But this requires civics classes…*

Back to Grade School

As I've reiterated from the beginning of this chapter, American civics (specifically, the law enforcement that We The People stipulate in the U.S. Constitution) is *not* about citizens' *rights;* it clearly stipulates our *authority* and *duties* as the Greater Magistrate. Imagine, our haughty servants dismissively label as mere 'general public' the collective highest human authority *over* the U.S. Constitution.

Honestly, should I have to point out to pastors the unique foundation of American civics right in the opening three words of our highest law? Yet these excellent men, these stalwart teachers of Scripture, *refuse* to grasp it, though I've instructed and pleaded with them for years (in the aforementioned pastor's case, over 20 years). It stings that he ends his discombobulated civics lesson with such pathetic irony:

It requires Christian leaders to write about this stuff. And it requires, when they write about this stuff, that they get it right. When that starts to happen, we can then be — as the meme has it — the America that Hong Kong thinks we are.

This from a man who founded his own church, denomination, and Christian college.

Don't be put off by my tough treatment of blockhead pastors. Like you, I stumble behind our King, Jesus Christ. Of all the people Jesus spoke and preached to, the only group He was truly tough on were lofty, sniffy religion-men. If a pastor is teaching dangerous, backwards civics in such a perilous time as ours, and is shown the solution to the thing he is railing against, he has the duty to make the solution clear to his flock (and online fans). We The People have authority over the hired help, and we must learn to lawfully and properly exercise it *now*, before it is too late. *That* is reformation, you of the 'Reformed faith'!

Preening, Puzzled Professoriate

This is not to say that pastors are the only demographic group working for the enemy while preaching holiness and light in the public square. It is now generally accepted that American education from kindergarten to graduate school has been deep-captured by godless Marxism, now having haughtily removed its mask. Parents who send their children into those places will reap the whirlwind for sending their children to Pharaoh for training.

I will not waste space even dignifying the openly godless, destructive practices of K-12 and post-secondary teachers today; there are many books on the subject. I will only illustrate one example of dozens I could cite, of professors *supposedly* on 'our side' of American civics.

Christian Fritz teaches at the University of New Mexico School of Law. His book *American Sovereigns: The People and America's Constitutional Tradition Before the Civil War,* is a classic case of hundreds of pages of academic blather that misses basic civics. In a 2012 article about Interposition and Nullification, Fritz writes:

Political arguments frequently use history for justification. Invariably, such efforts are less about taking the past on its own terms than the desire to make symbolic historical references that resonate with modern audiences in order to achieve particular political objectives, whether liberal or conservative.

A fine kettle of fish; a professor pointing out one of the daily tactics of every member of his guild! He knows who's boss, but not what to do:

Who were "the people" that underlay the national constitution, and how could that sovereign act, and be recognized in action?... Madison's views about the constitutional implications of governments resting on a collective sovereign were easily overlooked then just as they are today.

Indeed; overlooked by law school professors writing about American constitutional history. But like the pastor above, Mr. Fritz doggedly keeps digging his students a trench.

We are no admirers of Alexander Hamilton; yet in his 28th Federalist we see the basic principle: whether the federal or state servants ran afoul of the Constitution, We The People would simply employ the non-offending servant, state or federal, to bring the other one back in line:

The obstacles to usurpation and the facilities of resistance increase with the increased extent of the state, <u>provided the citizens understand their rights and are disposed to defend them</u>. The natural strength of the people in a large community, in proportion to the artificial strength of the government, is greater than in a small, and of course more competent to a struggle with the attempts of the government to establish a tyranny. But in a confederacy the people, without exaggeration, may be said to be entirely the masters of their own fate. Power being almost always the rival of power, the general government will at all times stand ready to check the usurpations of the state governments, and these will have the same disposition towards the general government. <u>The people, by throwing themselves into either scale, will infallibly make it preponderate. If their rights are invaded by either, they can make use of the other as the instrument of redress</u>. [Underlined emphasis mine.]

Mr. Fritz walks to the water's edge repeatedly, always refusing to drink:

The right to monitor the constitutional operation of government was a central issue of American constitutionalism after the adoption of the Constitution in 1787. The struggle over that right revealed a fundamental disagreement among Americans over the puzzle at the heart of the new federal system: <u>What did rule by a collective sovereign mean under a national constitution when the people who held this sovereignty were also the sovereign of their individual state governments</u>? [Underlined emphasis mine.]

So, America's sovereign over *federal* servants somehow would *not* be sovereign over its *state* servants? How could sovereignty be parsed thus? He is puzzled, as if two servant cohorts under a collective sovereign are somehow mutually exclusive. It makes no sense; yet he continues to weave himself into confusion over the exercise of sovereignty:

In America, the people were the sovereign. A half-century after Americans established their governments on this principle, the concept remained as elusive as it was when it first energized the Revolution … For purposes of the national government, all agreed that the people were the sovereign, but how could they exercise their sovereignty? …

As the Constitution's sovereign creator, the people were not subordinate to their creation, the national government. *The people had a final authority. The Constitution was merely "a description of those powers which the people have delegated to their Magistrates, to be exercised for definite purposes." For Madison… the sovereign who gave life to the Constitution did not limit its own powers as the sovereign in adopting the Constitution. …Simply because there were physical difficulties in manifesting an authentic action by that collective sovereign did not preclude the power of that sovereign to act on constitutional questions.* [Underlined emphasis mine.]

In his 400+ page book *American Sovereigns,* Mr. Fritz surveys different events in early American history when We The People attempted to *amend, change, or ignore* the Constitution; but never have we attempted to *enforce* it. He constantly reiterates that We The People are the sovereign in this Republic, yet he never suggests action. Like far too many pastors in our day, the professor talks a great deal *but never acts.*

Summary

At this point, I'd forgive you for considering me a pompous ass. But this particular application of truth can bring an end to America's self-destruction. If one knows the truth on a tactically and strategically vital point of life, one had better put it forth, regardless how many people are offended. Our times call for repentant men and women who realize that repentance must indeed lead to *action,* not more words.

The pulpit and university have lost their former credibility because the blind have been leading the blind into a trench for generations. So while I do not pretend to have these men's credentials, to quote Erasmus of Rotterdam, *in the land of the blind, the one-eyed man is king.*

I reiterate the most fundamental principle of American civics, putting Romans 13 in the unique context of America's rule of law:

We The People, collectively, are the Greater Magistrate over all other levels of government.

In his career writing and speaking about constitutional law and history, Mr. Fritz has never cited a single case in over 230 years where We The People *enforced* the law by which we created those lesser magistrates. That is because we, the Greater Magistrate, have *never once* attempted to *enforce* it. To find, teach, support, equip, and organize We The People to enforce it finally and for the rest of American history is the goal of our consciously Christ-honoring Tactical Civics™ mission.

CHAPTER 10

Republic, Republic, Republic!

Over a decade ago, 30-year veteran New York City school teacher John Taylor Gatto published a trenchant indictment of government schools entitled **Dumbing Us Down: The Hidden Curriculum of Compulsory Schooling**. But that scholar omitted one crucial point of government programming that I will bring to your attention.

Americans are ignorant of civics. We don't know how our system of government works or even what form of government we have. I'm not referring to those ditzy high school and college kids that Mark Dice interviews, who don't know third grade material. I'm talking about most presidents, members of Congress, university professors, journalists and others who should know better.

Like most adults trained in government schools, they believe that Abe Lincoln was our greatest president, a preposterous 'fact' of propaganda on which Washington D.C. has relied for 150 years that we debunked in Chapter 2. But they also can't comprehend the stipulations of We The People in our U.S. Constitution; the most basic fact of civics that these united States are a *republic*, a form of government guaranteed by We The People to each of the States in Article IV, Section 4.

You see, *country* can mean many things. If I say I live in the country, I don't live in the city; using the word 'country' doesn't settle the matter. In political economy, *nation* refers to a population living under a unitary government, and *republic* refers to a confederation of sovereign states each with its own government but unified for only limited purposes. Read the Constitution; that's us, and this isn't rocket science. The average fourth grade homeschooler can grasp and remember it but senators and presidents apparently can't.

To those who play semantics with the Biblical term *nation,* I only agree that America is a *republic* of nations, as Colin Woodard explains in his book *American Nations: A History of the Eleven Rival Regional Cultures of North America.*

These united States of America have been a republic for 227 years. In the constitutional law sense, America has never been a *nation*, even if Founding Fathers used the word because it was handy. If you think our American *republic* is no big deal, you have no idea. Watch Europe over the next few years under the same worldwide 'Great Reset' attack, and you will begin to appreciate the value of our Christian civilization, our constitutional rule of law, and the guarantee that We The People make to every sovereign State in Article IV, Section 4:

The United States shall guarantee to every State in this Union a Republican Form of Government...

James Madison, Father of the Constitution and the unimpeachable authority on such questions, explained this clause of the new constitution in Federalist #39: *Each State, in ratifying the Constitution, is considered as a sovereign body, independent of all others, and only to be bound by its own voluntary act. In this relation, then, the new Constitution will, if established, be a federal, and not a national constitution."*

But our ignorance of civics is not limited to Americans not knowing what form of government we have by law. They also do not know that We The People are the *highest level of government*, standing over our U.S. Constitution as its *creators, interpreters, and enforcers*. For generations, government schools and even private, Christian, and so-called classical schools have trained Americans to demote ourselves with words like *voter* and *grassroots*.

Once you recognize our duty and authority as America's collective sovereign, you should never again use the word *nation* to refer to our *republic*. You should also stop using propaganda phrases such as 'elected leaders' and 'elected officials' to refer to lawless servants. We elect them to represent us and to scrupulously obey the Constitution. Instead, they serve themselves and the elite, violating our highest law every day, many times per day. And just listen to them; they're *proud* of it.

If an employer referred to his employees or servants as "my elected leaders" (since he does have to hire them from a pool of candidates), how long would it take for the hired help to take that hapless employer captive? Those 'elected leaders' set their own working conditions, staffing, salary, benefits, luxury travel – and send their IRS thugs after the taxpayers to fund it all.

Mr. Gatto and many others have pointed out the seminal part played by the government schools in destroying our republic. We have swallowed and regurgitated a great deal of destructive foolishness, and the ruins are generations deep. There is work to be done. By the grace of God, over 50 years, America's growing army of homeschoolers have been training a remnant to take up our duties and authority that our ancestors abdicated. With this book, I pray that God will move the pastoral remnant to begin teaching their flocks to do the same.

As Europe flies apart under the same Deep Axis forces that overthrew our government in November 2020 and January 2021, America is pushed to the gates of Hell with Millennials pushing for Communism, smiling all the way, courtesy of government schools to which their parents send them every day. God's judgment is not *supposed* to be fun. It is supposed to drive us to sincere repentance.

Unlike complaining 'save America' groups and websites that merely quote Founding Fathers and ask for more donations, Tactical Civics™ chapters are repentant Americans in hundreds of counties from Alaska to Florida, beginning to prayerfully rebuild the fallen walls of our...

REPUBLIC!

CHAPTER 11

The Fear Porn Industry

Like the horror film genre, the Fear Porn industry is a perverse kind of entertainment that excites the limbic system of the brain, inciting daily cycles of anxiety, fear, and anger. Like all pornography, it is false, cruel, and destructive; but it produces great revenues because Americans are predictable consumers.

Over the past generation, many young Americans came to love horror films. In the same way, millions have become addicted to conservative talk and pointless 501c3 groups, making Fear Porn potentially worse for America's future than open communism. Some of these stars admit that they are entertainers; most of them do not, and most listeners cannot discern that conservative talk is just that: *talk*.

During my lifetime, Americans transmogrified from an industrious people with time only for factual news – into self-obsessed consumers, seeking entertainment in place of news. Today, a factual news report won't garner market share; too many limbic systems have been conditioned to want fear, anxiety, and rage, which have become like a drug for millions of conservatives.

Does this describe you or your congregants? Be honest; do you or they spend time on social media to argue, knowing that we don't improve a thing that way? Do you daily listen to talk show hosts, knowing that nothing they say *ever* improves anything?

How the Industry Operates

Consider whichever passionate hero you listen to (or read) every day. Having invented the market, Rush Limbaugh removed his mask years ago; he readily admitted to being a GOP shill and an entertainer. But don't you ever wonder who will give himself a heart attack first, Mark Levin or Alex Jones, from all his screaming?

Conservative radio, TV and Internet 'news' shares an entertainment market with ABC, MSNBC, CNN, FOX, et al. And the political parties.

And the non-profits. Here's the drill: keep the folks hopping mad. Fear and loathing brings audience, who buy your brand-name tea, or your precious metals merchant's stuff, or your colloidal silver, water filters, and emergency food – or they will run their credit card for your latest 'money bomb' campaign or Holy Land cruise.

Joe and Liz Farah milked their huge audience for $274 million in gross revenues from Farah's 2009 *Send Congress a Pink Slip* campaign that did nothing to stop Obamacare. In fact, those *billions* of tiny pink slips only went to the Capitol Hill dumpsters. Joe knew that it was impossible to physically deliver them. But the campaign was a huge success for Farah's Fear Porn empire with the largest aggregate following of any Christian online corporation – yet, *today he still begs for donations.*

How long can you milk a sheep? Decades, apparently, as Farah, Limbaugh, Beck, Hannity, Levin, Jones, and countless other Fear Porn vendors have demonstrated.

Joe, Sean, Glenn, Mark, Mike, Alex, Dennis, Laura, Michael – as well as NRA, GOA, Cato Institute, Heritage Foundation, Hillsdale College, and many other 501c3s comprising 'conservatism' today are only *conservative* in the sense of *conserving their golden goose.* It's just business. Media moguls, talk stars and 501c3 donation mills are businessmen in a Fear Porn market that daily mines a rich, growing demographic vein: productive, disgruntled patriots. And the most insidious aspect is that *their pot only grows larger as the destruction of our civilization grows.*

The same is true of the politics industry. Oh yes; it's an industry just like WWF: the GOP needs the Democrat party and vise-versa, to remain profitable. Politics junkies pay to see a fight. Similarly, the world of Fear Porn (conservative talk, media, and non-profits) always need a crisis: mass murder, potential war, economic woes, organized crime in government, BLAntifa riots, natural disasters, rise of the police state – the Fear Porn industry gives you what your limbic system demands every day.

Theirs is a business model of moral turpitude; they mentally condition you to inaction and cynicism, so you *never take action* on solutions. They can only grow their revenues as long as you keep tuning in so their book sales, advertising and product sales revenues, and brand presence grow.

American Christians Have Been Here Before

You would think that gullible Americans learned their lesson after decades of public exposure of charlatans Kenneth Copeland, Benny Hinn, Creflo Dollar, Kenneth Hagin, Marilyn Hickey, Joyce Meyer, Joel Osteen, Oral Roberts, Pat Robertson, and others. But when P.T. Barnum said *"there's a sucker born every minute"*, he was too conservative.

Don't get me wrong. It's a free country and you can do as you like with your money; that's none of my business. My point is that under God's judgment, no amount of listening or donating to Fear Porn will ever restore America. Real repentance and citizen action would put the entertainer out of business.

No entertainer or think tank can restore our civilization and Republic. Popular constitutionalism is actual restoration by *citizens*.

The Gun Lobby and Non-Profit Industry

Fear Porn is not limited to radio, TV, and the Internet. For instance, the NRA and GOA will never restore the citizen militia of the several States, as demanded by law. Your dues to them is wasted on political fireworks, nothing more.

Besides repeating what you have already heard, when have you ever seen any nonprofit (Heritage Foundation, Cato Institute, et al) actually sponsor action for reform? Like government agencies, conservative think-tanks reform *nothing*. They produce monographs and studies, and sponsor expensive conferences that at the very most are reactive, but will never restore what we already lost. They scare you, to stir the same political pot that attracts the stars of conservative talk; the goal of Fear Porn is to keep you angry, afraid, and buying or paying to fight 'crises'. In time, all this pointless donating with no improvement will make you cynical, but by that point the 501c3 has already hooked your children or grandchildren after making a pile from *your* purchases and donations.

First Step in Recovery: Own It

Listening to the talkers or reading WorldNetDaily or Infowars every day will never render you part of a solution. You can go to the WND or Infowars site and learn how to buy gold and ammo, hide in the boondocks, feed yourself, and kill the hungry neighbors pounding at your door when collapse comes. You can sign up for any of the NewsMax pop-up ads, and receive a *"super-special, eye-opening, life-changing report, FREE!"* – along with a gazillion pieces of junk mail for the rest of your life. Fear Porn stars will never lead any action process for citizens to become a unified force, then to enforce and restore our Constitution. Have you ever seen a celebrity even *attempt* it?

The same applies to your social media addiction. Face it, no amount of posting patriotic quotations or pictures will change anything.

Did Glenn Beck's or Mark Levin's first five 'final solution' plans work out for you, or did you finally get the picture that building ratings and ad revenue is what the stars were really after? Levin is not as blood-spittingly angry as he used to be. He has changed his radio show persona into a TV show persona. *An act.* Even when 'angry', Mark is actually quite *happy* with his millions in ad revenue.

Do you wonder how they can drum up a new cauldron of righteous indignation again tomorrow, and the next day, and the next? Well, that's entertainment; it's the celebrity's talent. After Limbaugh made his first $50 million, he was able to start having fun as his former anger mysteriously cooled. The others learned the routine: put in your early years of righteous anger, then your estate will grow apace by keeping your audience on the hook.

Over 1,500 local American radio stations now play nothing but wall-to-wall conservative talkers with their wall-to-wall advertisements. God rest his soul, Rush Limbaugh single-handedly saved AM radio, then gave birth to an incredible cash cow for the entire genre.

Passive listening – even if you *scream* at your radio – changes nothing. It's not the kind of life lived by sovereigns. The problem is not all the perverts and criminals; it's our passive couch-potato refusal to perform the duties of free Americans and true followers of Jesus Christ. Even the Fear Porn industry creating the pig-in-a-python useless talkers and hearers is part of God's judgment. *But repentance is always an option.*

A Destructive Feedback Loop

Yes, *your* repentance. These performers should be *ashamed* of themselves for doing this; but when you listen to them and pay them, *you* are half of the feedback loop that makes Glenn cry, makes Mark scream as though he's about to have a heart attack, and makes the veins in Alex's neck and forehead pop out as he almost turns clinical. In his divorce lawsuit his ex-wife accused him of being full of anger; Alex admitted that his anger was all an act.

Fear Porn addicts have told the Fear Porn celebrities what they like. As is true of horror movie fans, they've told them that they *want* the ranting, the tears, the never-ending fear and loathing. Understand the sin here, fellow Christian: as with adultery, alcohol or drug abuse, or pornography and masturbation, you give yourself over to gradual self-destruction. Of *course* the drug dealers, liquor stores, and porn industry *love* you! But you *can* stop this, fellow American. You *can* grow up and take responsibility.

Don't suggest that I'm barking up the wrong tree. The conservative talk and non-profit industries are *not* solutions. To start regaining what we have lost, we must tune out Fear Porn, repent, and get to work.

Some Exceptions

There are exceptions. Mike Church, on his eponymous radio show for years taught history, civics, and the Constitution to his audience even though it meant smaller market share. He was a 'Re-Founding Father' in the conservative talk industry. The same goes for Tim Brown, former editor of Freedom Outpost, now with Sons of Liberty and several other news sites. Other exceptions include Mark Goodwin at Prepper Recon and Jim White at Northwest Liberty News. Best of all was the late Joyce Riley, who on her *Power Hour,* dug deep every day for real solutions and grilled her radio guests for facts, not infomercials, and urged her listeners into action.

Some Bridges Need Burning

If you think I'm attacking potential allies of Tactical Civics™, truth is *never* bad policy. They'll never promote a solution like our mission because ending the crimes they harp about every day would kill their golden goose. Besides the exceptions mentioned, if my assessment is wrong in the case of a rare conservative talker, (s)he will support our home missions work.

But I won't hold my breath; the conservative talk and 501c3 Fear Porn industry is holding American Christianity back as the Reagan presidency did. And it is *more dangerous,* because addicts can claim it's a solution, though in 40 years it has not been.

Tobias Stockwell posted this article, the best explanation I've ever seen, of how the Internet is transforming our minds, actions, and society.

Now, Turn It Off

The only real answer to the Fear Porn industry is: *turn them off.* Show this analysis to your addicted friend who spends hours per day listening to conservative talkers – or who spends just as much time posting futile arguments, quotations, pictures, or cynical jokes on Facebook or on Fear Porn site comment threads. Wasting thousands of hours.

Cynicism and venting at the radio or on social media only makes you *more* cynical. Cynicism and paranoia have already taken millions of patriots out of the fight. From Joe Farah to the NRA and Heritage Foundation and Hillsdale College, cynical Americans now expect them to sell products and beg for donations while bringing the latest atrocity or crisis, with no improvement, world without end.

Finally, the Fear Porn-weary consumer gives up and loses hope for life and for America. More importantly, he spurns his duties more than ever. That was Satan's plan all along. But God will always respond to a contrite heart. Repentant American, turn off the talk and take up works meet for repentance.

CHAPTER 12

Allegiance to *What?*

I do not recite the Pledge of Allegiance.

This gets me in a trouble with some of my fellow Americans. If you want to be despised by otherwise good, patriotic Americans, just tell them that you don't recite the pledge. But here's the irony: Americans' childhood programming was like that of any Soviet or Chinese citizen, rendering us ignorant of our history and what the D.C. machine did to us over five generations.

As we explain in the segment from 8:14 to 8:47 in *AmericaAgain!- The Movie*, the Bellamy Pledge was developed by a fascist/socialist to program America's children. If you are interested in the birth of the Bellamy Pledge, you can find more history here.

In his article entitled *What's Conservative About the Pledge of Allegiance?*, Gene Healy of the CATO Institute analyzes Bellamy's pledge and asks why any constitutionalist should chant a pledge to Washington D.C.?

Well, because Americans, like Chinese and Russians, are programmed to be ignorant of true history. For instance, you now know that Dishonest Abe and Karl Marx were pen pals and mutual admirers, and that Lincoln was the original hijacker of our Constitution, as explained in Chapter 2 with its links to six books. As hard as that will be to really detox, give it a few months. Truth is always good for your health; it increases your EQ (emotional intelligence).

For six generations, Americans have been cheated in school. With the exception of homeschoolers, every generation alive today is a victim of fascist conditioning that began 160 years ago. Marxist Obama wrought destruction on our society but did not launch American communism; *Abe Lincoln did.* 'Resident' Biden is the sickening end of a long coup.

By Woodrow Wilson's administration a century ago, seven of the ten points of the Communist Manifesto were D.C. policy; today it's all ten. We demonstrated in Chapter 10 that in Article IV, Section 4 of the Constitution we guarantee a perpetual *republic* of sovereign States, not a unitary *nation.* A vital distinction; centralized power is dangerous! So I refuse to pledge allegiance to the D.C. city state and the 'nation' it demands that our States become.

Tactical Civics™ seeks to help the remnant rebuild America's walls as in the Book of Nehemiah. First we pray in repentance, then we graduate from middle school pep rally attitudes we've had for election cycles and political parties. Both parties are criminal players in a cruel theater.

Tactical Civics™ is a new *way of life* for self-governing Americans. Not an event, not election cycles, and not politics. One of the first goals is, we detox the communist programming in schools, colleges, universities, and agencies reinforced daily by the media. As Mark Twain said,

"No country can be well governed unless its citizens as a body keep religiously before their minds that they are the guardians of the law and that the law officers are only the machinery for its execution, nothing more."

It's time to repent our sloth, gullibility, and misplaced allegiance. Time to learn basic civics and take responsibility. This book is designed to present true history and civics to empower you as no generation of American pastors has been, since the Black Regiment. As Jesus said of Himself and His gospel, *"You shall know the truth, and the Truth will make you free".* Because it's true in civil affairs too, I do not recite the Bellamy Pledge. Instead, I pledge allegiance to Christ and the Constitution. From now on I hope you will, too.

CHAPTER 13

Support Our Troops?

My first wish is to see this plague of mankind, war, banished from the earth. **General George Washington**

I hate war as only a soldier who has lived it can, only as one who has seen its brutality, its futility, its stupidity. **General Dwight D. Eisenhower**

Even now, the families of the wounded men and of the mentally broken and those who never were able to readjust themselves are still suffering and still paying...There are only two reasons why you should ever be asked to give your youngsters. One is defense of our homes. The other is the defense of our Bill of Rights and particularly the right to worship God as we see fit. Every other reason advanced for the murder of young men is a racket, pure and simple. **General Smedley D. Butler**

The world has achieved brilliance without wisdom, power without conscience. Ours is a world of nuclear giants and ethical infants. We know more about war than we know about peace, more about killing than we know about living. **General Omar Bradley**

A staccato six-year string of gaslighting operations run by D.C. and many state palaces. The overthrow of our government by election theft, with cynical GOP and Democrat legislators carrying on business as usual. Big Tech is a team of broad-shouldered thugs filling the alley so that Americans cannot pass, but must simply accept the daily lies.

Not since Lincoln's *War to Enslave the States,* have Americans been faced with this level of attack by 'our' government. This is not kinetic war, but the warfare of the future. Still refusing to repent in a meaningful way, America is in social upheaval and a true constitutional crisis. What we need is sincere repentance followed by rational, county-by-county constitutional law enforcement. The Founding Fathers designed a system of law and order; of national defense that can be back in place in an amazingly short period of time in your county. Repentance must precede anything else.

This detox book would not be complete without addressing a very unpopular subject. As every politician and Country Western singer knows, the quickest way to success is to 'support our troops'. But to restore our rule of law, we must return to the law itself, and enforce it — even if that means roasting a lawless sacred cow: the war industry.

Most of the U.S. military is illegal, according to the Constitution. This chapter will provide basics and point to more resources. Every assertion herein is true. Any veteran reading this: it will make you furious — and then challenge you to *not* hang your head in shame but be a leader right here at home, rather than a hired killer abroad.

I hope to shock you awake and truly test your allegiance to the Constitution. Christ said that no man can serve two masters; every former or current military employee or family needs to choose their allegiance: the Constitution, or their industry? Every American should support our troops, but that means two mutually exclusive things:

   1) the U.S. Constitution defines 'our troops' as the Militias

   2) military industry employees claim 'our troops' means *them*

Verify this in the U.S. Constitution (Article I, Section 8, Clauses 12-16), the only references besides the Second Amendment that relate to national defense; go to Appendix G if you want to confirm it.

Constitutional Definition of 'Our Troops'

Our troops are defined in the U.S. Constitution as only a Navy (clause 13) and Militia *"to execute the Laws of the Union, suppress Insurrections, and repel Invasions"* (clause 15).

Representative Elbridge Gerry, on August 17, 1789 in debate on what later became the Second Amendment, wrote:

"What, sir, is the use of a militia? It is to prevent the establishment of a standing army, the bane of liberty. Whenever Governments mean to invade the rights and liberties of the people, they always attempt to destroy the militia, in order to raise an army upon their ruins."

Clause 12 stipulates that Congress can only fund Militia ground operations for two years at a time, whereas Clause 13 suggests that the Navy can be full-time to defend our shores.

So forget the Second Amendment and the century-old Dick Act; citizens owning and bearing *military grade* arms — semi-auto, selective-fire, and fully automatic is not only a right stipulated in the Second Amendment, it is a *duty* of every citizen in Militia, as stipulated in Article I, Section 8, Clause 15 of the Constitution. The *Posse Comitatus* Act and the 1903 Dick Act only reiterate what the Constitution had already guaranteed, and what God had granted from the beginning.

As for the Coast Guard, that branch logically extends from the Navy and provides invaluable lifesaving service to Americans and others in U.S. waters every day. Air Force and space-based defense might even be said to be a modern-day equivalent of the US Navy defense perimeter concept of the 18th century. The Constitution has to be amended to make them legal, but in principle they're a defense shield; a high-tech extrapolation of the founders' intentions for the Navy: defending our coasts.

But this is not true of the U.S. Army or Marines; the idea of a standing army on American soil or plundering foreign lands for industry would have been anathema to every Founding Father. The Citizen Militia of the several States was the only armed force that they ever intended on American soil. The founders passionately believed that free citizens in Militia would keep America free, but paid government troops would destroy our republic. But I am *not* against military employees. Let me repeat, *I have absolutely nothing against military employees.*

As I will explain below, I believe that most members of the United States armed forces are among the most honorable, dedicated Americans alive. But an even greater number of courageous, honorable Americans have never been in the military industry. We consider most military employees a valuable asset to the republic, though a few of them are sociopaths looking for a legal way to kill, even as some gang members satisfy that lust.

As horrible as their deployment(s) may have been on their spirit and mind, the military veteran can become a vital resource in America's near-term future. He can restore the righteousness of the duty he believed he was performing for his country. Read on.

Our Troops: arming for national defense NOW

Obama claimed to have taught constitutional law, so he had read Article I, Section 8, Clause 15 many times. He knew that the American people buying millions of firearms and tens of billions of rounds of ammunition while he was in the White House, were responding to his idiotic threats exactly as Clause 15 and the Second Amendment indicate that Americans should.

Like a giant organism, We the People respond as antibodies against a looming threat to our lives, liberties, property, and way of life. During the 'Obamanation', Americans bought millions more firearms and billions more rounds of ammunition. The problem is, we are still doing no more than that, so we are not meeting the Founding Fathers' plan for law enforcement, insurrection control, border security, and national defense: the Militias of the Several States.

Civics & History Resources

First, anyone who still does not know how the military industry has evolved into possibly our greatest domestic threat, needs to learn some facts about the industry's history from 1890 to 2013. Consider Stephen Kinzer's book *Overthrow: America's century of regime change from Hawaii to Iraq*. No matter how much you may love employees of that industry; no matter how you may think it is 'defending liberty', by remaining ignorant of 20th century history, you support exactly what the Founding Fathers hated and warned against. Kinzer demonstrates that not a single foreign action/invasion by the U.S. military has ever been conducted for the national defense of these sovereign States of America. *Not one.*

Andrew Bacevich formerly taught at West Point and was a decorated officer in Vietnam. His book *The New American Militarism* explains that the military built since Lincoln's time is *antithetical* to everything the Founding Fathers fought for.

The smallest book on this subject but possibly the best, is a classic written by the most highly-decorated U.S. Marine in history, General Smedley Butler. In his classic little booklet called *War is a Racket,* the repentant old war-horse writes…

"I helped make Mexico…safe for American oil interests in 1914. I helped make Haiti and Cuba a decent place for the National City Bank boys to collect revenues in. I helped in the raping of half a dozen Central American republics for the benefit of Wall Street.…I helped purify Nicaragua for the international banking house of Brown Brothers in 1909-12. I brought electricity to the Dominican Republic for American sugar interests in 1916. In China, I helped to see to it that Standard Oil went its way unmolested." (pg. 10)

Secondly, presidents cannot initiate wars. As James Madison, Father of the Constitution, wrote…

"The declaring of war is expressly made a legislative function. The judging of the obligations to make war, is admitted to be included as a legislative function. Whenever, then, a question occurs whether war shall be declared, or whether public stipulations require it, the question necessarily belongs to the department to which those functions belong—and no other department can be in the execution of its proper functions, if it should undertake to decide such a question."

Some Troops Plunder, Others Keep Us Free

In my lifetime I've witnessed this domestic enemy that President Eisenhower, a former 5-star general, warned about. He dubbed it the 'Military-Industrial Complex' and it is *huge* business for overseas industries of every kind.

When I was a child, those U.S. troops (unknowingly) defended the Rockefellers' rubber plantations and offshore oilfields in Vietnam; but for the past century the U.S. troops also provided free mercenary forces for the petrochemical industry in Central and South America and the Middle East. It is a perfectly symbiotic relationship: while providing free mercenary services for U.S. industry overseas, the war industry is a massive business in itself. Its supply train is long, wide, and complex, affecting almost every sector of industry.

For much more on this subject, read any book by Peter Dale Scott, especially *American War Machine* and *The American Deep State*. It will make your blood boil to learn how the Deep State fools millions of patriotic Americans into working *against* the U.S. Constitution and for their industry profits. (The criminal operations of the CIA and NSA are also covered in great detail in many of Scott's books, but that subject is beyond the scope of this chapter.)

Contrary to the military industry's propaganda, U.S. military employees deployed overseas and every foreign military base operated by that industry is illegal and has nothing to do with keeping us free.

Not only that, but the war industry, beyond destroying the lives of countless American veterans and their families, have made large parts of Southern Iraq, Afghanistan, Kuwait, and Saudi Arabia uninhabitable for the rest of history, by firing over 1,300 tons of depleted uranium munitions in those areas.

If you want to learn the horrific extent of the cancers, deformities and other maladies just from the depleted uranium treachery, watch this full-length documentary _Beyond Treason_, by the late Captain Joyce Riley, founder of The Power Hour.

Resources for Those Suffering From PTSD

For a detailed analysis of how we are taught to kill other human beings, read the book _On Killing_ by Lt. Col. Dave Grossman, explaining why we are naturally unwilling to kill, except in self-defense or the defense of home or family. The Founding Fathers designed our military around the Citizen Militia, a purely defensive force, because this is the only ethical national defense. Americans are now programmed from early childhood by the 'entertainment' and computer gaming industries to love the act of killing. The war industry uses this programming to 'deploy' you to kill in homes and neighborhoods on the other side of the world, with no declaration of war. This is not only illegal; your moral soul fights it all the way.

One last book, by psychotherapist Edward Tick, is _War and the Soul: Healing our Nation's Veterans From Post-traumatic Stress Disorder._

That's the bad news. It is America's dirtiest big secret and it has been making life a living hell for America's vets. They're only human; having killed others has made them want to kill themselves. For God's sake, _they must seek help._

Drugs are all they get from the VA; they want to get people processed. The spiritual need is greater than anything – and their training can become a profound blessing for their fellow Americans and a meaningful new career for the vet.

I've shaken a veteran's foundations with truth: they were defrauded by their employer. They believed their indoctrination, as Major General Butler said: _war is a racket._ To live the rest of life with restored sanity they must face the truth, learn how they were abused – and then forgive themselves. Let me repeat that: the first thing a vet must do is forgive himself. God knows our heart; we all sin, sometimes worse than others. But what they did in ignorance, having been defrauded by a ruthless industry, God will never hold against them. They should go to God in repentance for any lives they took, and know that God is in the business of forgiveness.

A group called Oath Keepers tries to convince military employees not to turn against their sovereigns, the American people. I think we must do much more than keep public servants with firearms from abusing citizens. The Army and most of the operations of the U.S. Marines are technically unconstitutional, as I demonstrated. But vets were paid by the taxpayers to 'defend the Constitution from enemies foreign and domestic', and that is still in their DNA.

Eight of the past ten presidents and their congresses have cut deeply at the Constitution's roots. Bush II, Obama, and *Resident* Biden were finally the bridge too far. Their open disdain for the sovereign People and the Constitution placed We The People on high alert. Yet we are unprepared to defend the Republic. Trump did what Reagan did; added fuel to the war industry fires and waved the flag, with no interest in the Constitution's stipulated limits on federal military. Every politician and country singer knows that if you wave the flag and 'support the troops', you will be popular. Like Reagan, Trump played that card constantly.

Tens of millions of Americans have fine firearms, even almost military-grade equipment. But most of us could not serve effective Militia duty to save our souls. Americans need Militia training and by law, our state is supposed to provide it. But not a single state does. Veterans, especially those with recent or specialist training, will be among the most valuable citizens in this Republic. If they're still a federal employee, they should *retire*. Then they can serve this republic as never before.

Restoring the Citizen Militias

We should have Militia units recognized in every county by ordinance, meeting the intent of Article I, Section 8, Clause 16 of the Constitution, because the states are derelict. I discuss this in detail in our new book, *Time to Start Over, America*. This is not a debatable political issue; it is the highest American law. We The People must now get our county governments to do what state governments refuse to do. Lunatic social justice warriors and Antifa fascists in the streets as well as jab tyrants and ballot-creating, ballot-destroying felons need to be arrested and brought to justice. This demands Militia units in every county.

In *Time to Start Over, America* I explain that the 'militia' movement is *not* constitutional Militia and explain American Militia 2.0™, our education and briefing program and model county ordinance.

Some of the officers must be tactical firearms trainers; others might train members in logistics, communications, emergency response, first aid, survival techniques, anti-terrorism drills, riot control and suppression, emergency infrastructure, heavy equipment operations, and the like. Within a few months, those who are called and interested, like Volunteer Fire Department duty, will have the first constitutional Militia in their community in over 150 years.

Our sovereign States abdicated their duties because We the People first abdicated ours. To restore the 'Homeland Security' of our Founding Fathers, the first step is Tactical Civics™ chapters pushing through the County Grand Jury Ordinance, with the associated Militia unit pushing through the County Militia Ordinance. We will brief you on every step.

Military veteran, stop hanging your head in shame. I've been tough on you not because I don't appreciate your sacrifice, but because you've been fighting for the wrong cause, unwittingly violating the rule of law you swore to defend. Please consider helping your fellow citizens by using the leadership skills you learned at their expense to now rebuild the Founding Fathers' constitutional homeland security. The greatest military veteran stories are yet to be told, and yours needs to be one of them. Frustrated American men are waiting to be trained to do our duty as citizens. Will you stand in the gap of history?

There are over 70 million armed citizens in these sovereign States. According to the Constitution, *all of us* are the U.S. military and have a duty for Militia. In the present environment of domestic enemy occupation, every county Militia should be the visible arm of the county Grand Jury, to execute its subpoenas, search warrants, and arrest warrants. Vastly increased border security is another immediate need, along with arrest and detention of federal operatives who are illegally busing and flying hordes of illegal aliens into the American interior, as if they are literally working for lawbreaker countries and foreign enemies!

These are not kinetic military actions, and most or all of these duties can be done with sidearms. But there is much for our troops to do, right now. By working wisely and diligently at this critical time in history, we can *all* keep America free, by the grace of God.

CHAPTER 14

Constitutional Sheriffs?

Teaching fake history as truth is even more dangerous than 'reporting' fake news. For instance, besides teaching that the sheriff is the highest constitution enforcement officer in each county, KrisAnne Hall doesn't cite legal history correctly, either. She says,

'The Declaration of Independence is the Sixth liberty charter in the long history of British law. It catalogues the grievances of the colonists and lay out [sic] the principles upon which they separate from Great Britain. It is rooted in the principle of sovereignty – that no one is naturally the ruler of another. This principle is at the heart of individual liberty. Walk through this foundational document and learn the precise foundation that was laid for our future. See that the singular principle of liberty permeated all of our founders' motivations. Arm yourself with the truth that you need to counter the dispersion's [sic] about our Republic's origins.'

With all due respect to a lovely and popular lady on the TEA Party speaking circuit, KrisAnne continues wrongly citing the provenance of our Anglo-American rule of law, as we've informed her for years.

The True Origins of our Rule of Law

Our Anglo-American liberty charters actually originated in the *Compact of Ethelred* in 1014 A.D.; the English people forced Ethelred to meet their demands in order to be reinstated to the throne after being run off the island by Sweyn Forkbeard.

For the first time, kings could not do as they pleased. The people actually loved Ethelred, the same king who founded the Grand Jury institution in 997 A.D. and the first general call for Militia in 1014 A.D. Anyway, the rest of our Constitution's genealogy is...

#2 *Charter of Liberties* (1100 A.D.)

#3 *Magna Carta* (1215 A.D.)

#4 *Provisions of Oxford* (1258 A.D.)

#5 *Declaration of Arbroath* (1320 A.D.)

#6 *Mayflower Compact* (1620)

#7 *Petition of Right* (1628)

#8 *Grand Remonstrance* (1641)

#9 *English Bill of Rights* (1689)

#10 *Declaration of Independence* (1776)

Those were all established by Englishmen, over there and over here. Then the two purely *American* entries in the ancient lineage of our Anglo-American rule of law...

#11 Articles of Confederation (1781)

#12 U.S. Constitution (ratified 1789)

It would be perfectly correct to also include such charters as the Fundamental Orders of Connecticut, the Northwest Ordinance, and a few others. Like our People's ancient law enforcement institutions, Grand Jury and Militia, our rule of law was born in England, but now exists *only* here in America. Our rule of law is called *Anglo-American,* but the English people allowed it to crumble on their side of the Atlantic.

It All Belongs to the Crown

KrisAnne is still teaching her fans/customers, and former sheriff Richard Mack (founder of the group CSPOA, Constitutional Sheriffs and Peace Officers Association) is still teaching his fans/customers that the sheriff is the highest constitutional enforcement officer in America. They are both lovely people, but *that is a dangerous falsehood.*

You can learn the true history of sheriffs in our books and articles in the Tactical Civics™ Training Center but in brief, the sheriff *cannot* be the highest constitution enforcer, because...

A) We don't authorize *or even mention* sheriffs in the Constitution;

B) The *shire reeve* was the king's tax collector/enforcer; and

C) Today's sheriffs *still perform that same duty in every county.*

Think about this. However beautiful your sheriff's speeches may be, We The People cannot actually *own* property in this Republic because sheriffs and tax collection lawyers make it impossible. Like all communists, even after we pay off the mortgage, we can only *rent* our home or farm from bureaucrats living high on the hog...on our backs.

You think you own the farm or home that you paid off? Try not paying the next property tax bill! The sheriff will sell it at a foreclosure sale on the courthouse steps and put your family on the street. It was *never* your property because *private property doesn't exist anymore in America.* Corrupt politicians and bureaucrats with lovely offices, buildings, and vehicle fleets embezzle all property in America. The so-called owners have no voice in the transaction. *That's life under God's judgment.*

One duty of the friendly, neighborhood sheriff is to assure that you pay bureaucrats their pound of flesh for the privilege of living in a home. Another major activity of the sheriff is running his mouth about being a 'constitutionalist' during re-election campaigns.

In Times of Universal Deceit

...telling the truth will be a revolutionary act. That was one of George Orwell's zingers, and it fits our lawless era beautifully. This plain truth sounds harsh today, after all the political speeches you're accustomed to hearing at school board, city council, and county board meetings.

We are certainly no scofflaws at Tactical Civics™; our mission educates, supports, and organizes the repentant remnant of the People to again exercise our authority and *duty* of law enforcement in every county. Even the deeply Marxist or atheist counties. *Law is law!*

This is basic history and civics that every homeschooler can learn, but government schools certainly cannot teach or they'd have to stop taxing Americans through the nose to pay for opulent new school buildings, bureaucrat goodies, salaries, fleets, and travel junkets.

Americans complain about corruption, but it only exists because we have been lazy and ignorant. Now, by the grace of God, some of us are reforming ourselves. I am not very popular for teaching hard truth to lazy people. But truth *followed by repentance in action* is the only way to restore our land, which as I've said many times in this book, is under God's judgment.

When comparing 'save America' organizations, the first consideration should be: *does the organization offer a comprehensive, long term plan of action with projects on the ground to execute on the plan...or is it all just more talk?*

The second consideration: *what is the background of the organization's founder; could they have a former career bias?* For instance, KrisAnne Hall's prior career was a state assistant prosecutor. Richard Mack's prior career was county sheriff. My prior career was architectural engineer with side jobs as cattleman, homebuilder, missionary pilot, and private school founder. I never took a dime from taxpayers, and I never will.

I don't wish to besmirch a fellow Christian (Hall) or even a Mormon (Mack), but every few days, I hear our mission compared to theirs, and that's *preposterous.* They are teaching the *opposite* of history as *fact.* And presentation style aside, truth is terribly important just now.

CHAPTER 15

'Rights' is Wrong

If upset parents of lawless (even criminal) children, pout and insist to the children, *"I have rights!"*, would that make sense?

Our Three Ugly Babies

As soon as you turn 18 years of age, if you wish to take responsibility for government, you become one of 'We The People' – and collectively, we are the 'parent' of government. We gave birth to our federal government in an era of relative honor and morality, but in the past 160 years it became a lawless, wicked, massive monster. Still, the basic relationship of sovereign-to-servant is set out in our highest law.

No one can deny the birth process...*We The People...do ordain*...and then following that Preamble in the U.S. Constitution come Articles I, II, and III. Our three servants, newborn and innocent.

The Anti-Federalists Were Right

James Madison seems to have been saying, *"Now, be sure to check on one another, children!"*, with his horizontal checks-and-balances, which are *absurd* today. I suppose the idea was rational back then to Federalists but the Anti-Federalists saw red flags.

I can understand Madison's confidence: bracketed by that Preamble and our open-ended reservation of powers in Amendment X, there is, *'Militia, to execute the Laws of the Union'*. What could go wrong? Most honorable, diligent folk of that time could not foresee the collapse of norms and nobility that began with Lincoln, Marx, and Darwin, and grew to full-throated D.C. treachery in this 21st century.

The so-called Anti-Federalists *did* foresee it. But because they were the political minority, they were voted down and we got this Constitution with its 'elastic clauses'. But I will say in defense of both this Constitution and of the Federalists: they assumed that We The People would always do our part as the collective sovereign; a responsible parent. Old Ben Franklin had his reservations, answering Lady Powell, *"A Republic, Madam, if you can keep it."*

It's unfortunate but understandable that the Founding Fathers used the term *rights* so often. They knew what it was to be a subject of a monarch from whom you had to beg rights. But we are only subjects of our own indolence.

Having been born in a century grown long of tooth and claw, we irresponsible parents should *never* have expected our three children to check and balance one another. Our ancestors for generations should have known better! *But they didn't.*

Well, *we* certainly know better *now,* don't we?

In this surreal, hijacked condition – I am writing this in 2022, Marxist-occupied America – everything good is called evil by Communists and atheists. They will do or say *anything* to win, and with Big Tech plastering the lies everywhere you can possibly look, the lapdog media can do exactly what it does in every other Communist country: lie with total impunity, and no one can do a thing about it.

At this point, they don't even bother to hide their crimes. While we won't stoop so low, we do need to watch our language when it comes to civics. Remember the definition of civics: *Who is Boss?*.

This is crime gone wild; to put it bluntly, Communists and atheists will steal your words, twist and harden them, gut you with them, then decapitate you and urinate down your windpipe. The forces of evil are determined that American Communism not die.

And we're determined to kill it.

The overthrow of our laws, creating 'sanctuary' cities and states openly violating our laws, the gaslighting of the entire population, shutting down businesses, schools, churches, stealing elections and then salting every area of government with Communist occupiers are only some of the many crimes of late-stage American Communism.

We *need* to kill it. Pastor, you have no choice but to begin telling hard truth to soft people, or the time will come when even a small remnant will not listen. And judgment will begin at your pulpit. The time for talking in terms of 'rights' is long past.

'Rights' is Wrong

This is not a 'kinetic' war (armed conflict), but a Marxist occupation scheme that's waged with words and ideas pushed by Big Tech into every corner of American society, especially into the brains of the young. And this is the truly shocking aspect of our soft words to soft people: society's predators and parasites have been winning for generations; they lie, cheat, and are masters at gaslighting. *Yet most Americans allow them to train up their children.*

We tell the truth and play by the rules. By the grace of God, the rules are on our side. But the predators and parasites don't intend to slack off, so *neither can we.*

We The People have *authority* over the Constitution; so use *that* word.

We have a *duty* to enforce it, as we stipulate; so use *that* word.

But please, fellow Christian, never speak of *rights* again.

CHAPTER 16

Some Days
The World Just Changes

June 15, 2022 will be the 807th anniversary of the day that King John of England sealed Magna Carta, one of the most important documents in the history of western civilization.

In Tactical Civics™, you learn that an earlier law is more fundamental: the *Compact of Ethelred* (1014 A.D.), wherein the people demanded concessions of King Ethelred in order to return to his throne. Still, that day in the valley Runnymede, when John sealed Magna Carta (the image above is inaccurate; he did not sign but sealed the new law with his ring, in wax) was a day when the world changed.

America has often been called an experiment, and surely it is that. From their writings and transcribed speeches, we know that the Founding Fathers, including the framers of the U.S. Constitution, believed in an ineffable, all-powerful God and in the basic sin nature of mankind. The evidence of that belief is found in the limits and *disabilities* of servant government expressed and implied in the U.S. Constitution.

The framers' visceral distrust of governments was expressed in Ben Franklin's response as he left the Philadelphia convention when Lady Powell asked, *"Doctor Franklin, what kind of government have you given us?"*. Franklin's cogent reply was, *"A republic, madam…if you can keep it."* On the day (Sept 25, 1789) that the Constitution was finally sent to the States to be ratified, the world changed.

Losing Our Phlogiston

Around the time of our War for Independence, the consensus of the science community relative to combustion held that all matter had an indeterminate amount of an almost weightless substance called *phlogiston*. Materials like metals were supposed to be rich in phlogiston; others, like soil, were considered to have little of the substance.

Phlogiston theory stated that combustion released phlogiston from a material, resulting in the diminished weight of the remaining product. *The fire comes, the phlogiston disappears…pouf!* was combustion science in George Washington's day. Then, a Frenchman named Antoine Lavoisier wrote a treatise in 1777 that eventually earned him the title, 'father of modern chemistry'. Demonstrating that phlogiston theory was nonsense, in his treatise Lavoisier humbly proposed,

"I claim to substitute for it [the theory of 'phlogiston'] *not a rigorously demonstrated theory, but only a more probable hypothesis which presents fewer contradictions…*[it] *explains with marvelous ease almost all of the phenomena of physics and chemistry."*

Lavoisier's simple experiments burned material with and without carbon, measuring the difference in the weights of the remaining product. His hypothesis was demonstrated in the tests; material burned in the presence of carbon produced *carbon dioxide,* proving that the process of combustion did not *lose* material (so-called phlogiston), only *rearranged* it into airborne products of combustion. Lavoisier's work led to chemist John Dalton and others eventually discovering the atomic nature of matter, and beginning to understand how elements combine. But someone had to take that first radical step that 'changed the world' in chemistry and materials science, and that someone was Antoine Lavoisier.

114

Plato Had it Right

One of my favorite Plato aphorisms is, *"There are two things at which a person should never be angry: what they can help, and what they cannot."* I'm amazed at the level of anger we see from conservatives today, because we can *help* it; we can *change* things.

That's what Tactical Civics™ is all about. It's exciting even though very few people know about it yet. And do you know why?

It's a Remnant Thing

First, because these united States are a very big republic. Secondly, ever since Plato and Cicero complained about it centuries before Jesus came in the flesh, most human beings have been clueless – and quite happy to stay that way. That's not an elite statement; just a fact of life that has nothing to do with wealth or social standing. Some of the wealthiest people are also the stupidest. Ignorance is lack of information and *stupidity* is avoiding information or not acting on the information that one has, because it may change his comfortable circumstances.

If you feel angry at the stupidity of your fellow Americans, listen to Plato; give it up. As we say in our mission: be joyful in Christ, because however crazy things look presently, God's judgment is not supposed to be fun, God always has His remnant, and repentance will always bring restoration. It just takes time, diligence, and most of all, *faith*.

Some Days, The World Just Changes

I am a whale about aphorisms; little ditties that convey a vital truth about life. With respect to this new way of life, I think of Tactical Civics™ as an extended family, or a church, or a school. We are the body of Christ, attempting to glorify Him by doing the chores. And I always say that the mission will take off when God has ordained it should take off, and almost certainly not by anything we do.

While God certainly doesn't want us sitting on our hands, the mission will take off by God's amazing grace, despite our floundering around. So my aphorism is, *"Some days, the world just changes"*.

For instance, there was a time in America – a period lasting almost three generations – when the steamboat was all that stood between life and death for countless American villages and towns. In the winter, the last steamboat deliveries before the river or bay became un-navigable, iced

115

in – that steamboat brought all that you would see of the outside world until late spring.

The first steamboat whistle of late spring brought men, women and children, pig-herds and pastors, millers and matrons, running to the docks to greet their iron and thread; their fabric and rifles; their tea and coffee and sugar; their oil lamps and lumber and civilized books and magazines. No one in those generations could imagine life without the steamboats.

But! Then came the railroad to town, pushing the steamboats off the pages of history as surely as Spring pushes Winter out of our lives; as though the snows and cold had never been, and new life is everywhere. The railroads carried civilization to a whole new level.

Those steam-and-then-diesel-driven behemoths became like rolling villages on rails, transporting people and commodities and animals over mountains and across the great plains, shrinking America as the steamboats in their fixed, watery courses could never have done. The railroads were king, as summer seems to engulf all of life with its seemingly endless heat and humidity. Surely nothing could ever beat the mighty railroads?

But! Then came the automobile, with its increasing web-work of paved roads across the republic from sea to sea, and gasoline stations and tire stores and the ubiquitous American invention, the motor hotel, or 'motel'. No longer constrained by railway schedules, the traveler could go where he pleased when he pleased, stay as long as he pleased, and then move along with total liberty of travel. No official stations full of crowds; no ticket-punching officials poking their head in your room. For ease and speed of travel, nothing could supplant the automobile.

There was just one fly in the ointment, and that was, to travel beyond our shores, Americans still faced the crowds in loading areas, with their ticket-punchers and then a long, slow steamship or later diesel-burning cruise ship voyage.

But! Then came the commercial airliner; the final season, as it were, in human travel and shipping commodities. Now you can be in Europe in a matter of hours, although we still have to face the indignities of ticket-handlers, and far worse at the hands of the TSA Gestapo.

My point is, no one would think of using a steamboat for their daily needs or travel anymore because…*some days, the world just changes*. Yet back in the days of the steamboat, no one could imagine something better, faster, simpler and safer. Someone had to *invent* it and do the hard, risky work of executing on that vision. It happened in transportation, manufacturing, power generation, medicine, agriculture. Every area except government…and *that is by design.*

This seems bizarre, because government is the most crucial area of life. It impacts our lives, liberty and property more than any other area of human endeavor. Yet for two and a half centuries, one arrogant, lawless city-state, the District of Columbia, has ruled our lives as an emperor rules his subjects…since well before the steamboat era until today, in our era of space travel. *But!* then came Tactical Civics™.

Remember, though: *We The People* is not all Americans; only those who know civics and do the chores over the hired help rather than live under their lawless thumb. So before this next segment, please turn back to that infographic at the beginning of the book: We The People living above the line to *enforce* our highest law, and our public servants below the line, who take an oath to *obey* that highest law.

Two Fitting Analogies

As a former pilot, I remember experiences that you'll recall if you have flown commercial to any extent. Remember those times that your departure airport was under a solid overcast? After that lousy, dark, inclement weather, remember that feeling when the aircraft first broke out above the solid cloud deck into the dazzling, sunny sky?

Many people have a revelation the first time they experience that. As you climb to the flight levels far above the solid cloud deck, it's easy to forget all those poor folks down under that overcast, in the rain or snow several miles below. It's even easier for those on the ground to forget that it's sunny and beautiful, right then and there, just a few miles over their heads. *They can't imagine what they've never seen.*

Now back to our infographic and my analogy. When you become one of the few Americans who join the responsible remnant 'living above the line', you begin *superintending* our servants in government; enforcing the limits that We The People stipulate in the U.S. Constitution.

At the same time, all those Americans who may be just as upset as you are at the arrogant, lawless servants, have to slog it out in the ugly conditions, living below the line. Again: they can't *imagine* what they've never seen. But now picture it in your head...

By law, We The People stipulate that we operate way up above all other levels of government. But 'We The People' means only you and I and every American who dares to break through the peon programming that corrupt politicians and scheming bureaucrats have drummed into us over generations.

Mental Conditioning Trumps Physical

Tactical Civics™ Florida State Coordinator Ed Gonzalez recently reminded me of an incident that illustrates how programmed Americans are, to think and live by a rule that's imaginary; to believe a thing because...well, because *everyone* believes it.

Our Virginia and Montana teams have similar aspirations, but Ed's goal is for Florida to field our first breakthrough Tactical Civics™ chapter, that will reach membership of half of 1% of the county population, and that will enact our county Grand Jury and Militia ordinances.

I looked up the details of the story Ed told me, and it's *fascinating*. Since the 1920s, the world's distance runners had tried to break four minutes for the 1-mile run. As the 1950s dawned, several men came very close; in fact, within one second of that magic four minutes. But train and try as they might, no one could break the magic 4-minute mark. Some said that it was physically impossible for human beings.

Then on May 6, 1954 an English runner named Roger Bannister finally broke the 4-minute mark at a competitive meet at Oxford. Nobody could break that magic four minutes until Bannister's 'miracle mile' that day because the human mind overpowers even the most insanely disciplined physical conditioning.

Just weeks after Bannister broke the spell, running a race in Finland, Australian John Landy shaved *two full seconds* off Bannister's record! But far more astoundingly, and to prove my point of this illustration: once the world's runners "knew it was okay" to do so, in the 18 months after Bannister broke through the mental barrier, *40 other runners* ran the mile in under four minutes! Think of it. *Nothing* had changed other than the fact that what had seemed impossible before May 6th, became possible on that day. As of January 2022, a Moroccan runner named Hicham El Guerrouj, holds the world's record of *three minutes, 43 seconds!*

Imagine that…*seventeen seconds faster* than what was thought for almost a generation to be humanly impossible. Count to 17, and imagine a fellow breaking the tape that far ahead of the pack.

So you see, "It's impossible!" is just not true in most areas of human endeavor. Especially restoring rule of law. As hard as this seems – especially the first constitutional Militia unit – once we get one chapter and Militia unit to break through the criminals' imaginary force field, *the rest will be history.*

It's all just a mental barrier – and of course a spiritual one too. But I also believe and I know that our members agree, that the LORD has graciously granted us that great boon, to do what in the eyes of the world will appear impossible. Because not only is it possible; in fact, it is *our stipulated duty* in the law over which we're collectively the sovereign.

We can continue being like the lazy, recalcitrant child who complains that cleaning up the huge mess in his room is impossible. Or we can start doing our chores with a great attitude, and see the impossible happen. All we need to do is execute on our plan, county by county.

This is what repentance looks like in the civil realm, in this unique constitutional Republic. With no king but King Jesus, We The People – that is, a small but dedicated remnant of the American People -- are finally living *responsibly*. We're finally fulfilling the duties of America's collective sovereign over our lawless, arrogant servants.

Yes, we're just a tiny seed today, but we're living above the line. We've broken that insane mental barrier erected by five generations of liars and shameless thieves masquerading as our public servants. Their days of pillaging the earth, including our sovereign States, and doing it in our name, will now begin coming to an end, however long the process takes.

Regardless what the weather might be down below the line, We The People are finally operating up in the brilliant, clear blue skies above a 160-year-thick layer of abdication and ignorance that led to anger and hopelessness. This is our time, may it please the LORD.

APPENDIX A

Recommended Reading

When asked, *"Can you give me an essential reading list for Christians and other Tactical Civics™ members?"*, our staff could list several hundred books. But we'll be selective and explain a bit about books that I call 'vital titles'.

Besides obvious bedrock – the Bible, Shakespeare's Complete Works, *Pilgrim's Progress,* C.S. Lewis's *Chronicles of Narnia* and other great novels, this Liberty Library introduces 72 works that transformed my thinking; that shocked me at the lies I had believed all my life. This is a great reading compendium for any 14-18-year old homeschooler who plans a career in his own business or trade but also wants the equivalent of an undergraduate Liberal Arts or Political Science degree, just to get to the marrow of our civilization.

Edmund Burke's dictum, *"(t)he only thing necessary for the triumph of evil is that good men do nothing"*, keeps repeating itself because as philosopher George Santayana said, *"Those who refuse to learn the lessons of history are doomed to repeat them."* With our civilization crumbling at every turn, where will it all end? Our members know my dictum, *The tombstone of a civilization may be laid at that point where truth is no longer defended, because it cannot be known.*

The U.S. Constitution is the Supreme Law of the Land, yet D.C. organized crime considers itself untouchable. Much of the world hates us, and we can't figure out why. The rich get richer, and the productive American increasingly joins the ranks of the poor and unemployed.

In this tutorial, you learned how the Deep Axis has run our republic for at least six generations, with complete secrecy. _Regardless of elections_. To restore America, We The People must take informed, coordinated tactical action. That means first we need basic education – such as this tutorial! This is no longer available in most schools or colleges. But we need more; we need to expose the lies on which the 'culture war' is being waged, because truth _can_ be known.

This reading list makes an excellent reading program for an intensive 3-year regimen or a more leisurely 5-7 year pace. Reading the classics is fine; but our times call for more practical education. Having read all of the books listed here, an American will be in the top one-tenth of 1% of our population in American history, ethics, economics, geopolitics, political economy and more. *The Harvard Classics cannot do that.*

During the 20th century, our republic was transformed into a plundering empire populated by historically clueless 'voters' who commute to their jobs every day to pay the bills, their apathy granting legitimacy to staggering international crimes.

Since most people will not read 72 works over the next few years, I list the 16 most vital works first (15 books and an online pamphlet and white paper). Pick the work that most intrigues you, and read it with highlighter in hand; when you finish that one, read another. Move at your own pace and you will find these great books growing on you.

As you later review highlighted passages, life lessons emerge and a pattern comes together as you begin to see through media propaganda and grasp the lies that steer American policy – especially Washington DC organized crime, and its wars.

So again, set the classics aside for now. Given the duty before us, these 72 works will vault you over walls of ignorance about our history and Constitution; about money, credit, and banking; about how Israel and the Deep State used the boogeyman of communism and Islamic jihad to run America from behind the scenes with the help of megachurch pastors. You will begin to clearly see the fallen state of our Republic and the sleeping Church. These books won't make you a pencil-necked geek; *they will impart real wisdom.*

If you believe that the Internet is all we need because it is opening minds and threatening tyrants all over the world, Egyptian dictator Mubarak proved in 2011 that government can shut down a country's Internet access. It has not happened fully yet in America, but see how far Big Tech has gone in that direction already, and as Tim Wu explains in the book *Master Switch*, Big Tech can go much further still. As the movie *The Book of Eli* suggests, when civilization falls, printed books will become our most valuable treasures.

For less than the cost of two college courses, this Liberty Library will place you among that rare species: *the informed, self-governing American.*

The 15 Most Vital Books (and Two Online Resources)

The American Deep State is Peter Dale Scott's best book yet, of over 40 books published over 40+ years, exposing the Deep State. The author has spent his adult life laying a trail of primary-source evidence for the shocking, revealing assertions in his books. The Deep State refers to the banking, war, and oil industries together with the 'intelligence' industry in all its secret agencies. Every foreign war the USA has fought has been instigated by, and directly benefited, the Deep State. This shadow government is unelected, unaccountable, invisible to productive Americans, and ruthless. It first sought to hijack the Constitution through Hamilton and Clay, finally succeeding with Lincoln and ever since. _If you read only one book on the list, make it this one._

The Sovereign Individual by James Davidson & Lord William Rees-Mogg explains the shake-up of nations introduced by the Internet, much like the impact that the movable-type printing press had in medieval times. Even now, 18 years after the first edition of this book, the world's institutions have not come to grips with the Internet. But the news is daily illustrating the acceleration of revolution against wicked and bloated industries, institutions, and governments. As institutions attempt to deal with newly-liberated humanity, the authors posit that informed individuals and small businesses will win, and fascism (big governments plus industry) will lose. AmericaAgain! Trust agrees with this assessment, and the Tactical Civics™ Training Center is our antidote to anything the evil ones can throw at our civilization.

I will here clarify that we do not subscribe to the anarchist school of thought touting 'sovereign citizen' nonsense. We The People are only collectively the sovereign of this republic, and only as we operate within the stipulated bounds that we ourselves set in the U.S. Constitution.

Hamilton's Curse: How Jefferson's Arch Enemy Betrayed the American Revolution – and What it Means for Americans Today by Thomas J. DiLorenzo (2009) is a long-overdue correction of the record about Alexander Hamilton. Although a courageous hero of our War for Independence, Hamilton was a wily tactician in laying the foundation for America's corrupt banking industry, and perhaps the most destructive 'founding father'. DiLorenzo debunks the long-held legends that deify Hamilton, exposing the man for what he was: a conniving, self-absorbed con artist. In the final chapter, _Ending the Curse,_ I find nothing upon which to disagree with the author except that, like most authors offering reform proposals, he fails to offer a mechanism to *enact* his solutions.

The Problem With Lincoln by Thomas J. DiLorenzo debunks the legends offered as reasons for Lincoln's war. The author exposes why Lincoln suspended *habeas corpus,* why he imprisoned thousands of Northern war dissenters, and why he shut down hundreds of opposition newspapers. He also exposes Lincoln's real economic agenda. If you wonder why schools don't teach this, understand that the uber-wealthy love their riches more than God, and are as ruthless as they are treacherous, smiles and all.

Lincoln's Marxists: Marxism in the Civil War by Walter D. Kennedy and Al Benson, Jr. is another of those books that convinced me that I was cheated even in my expensive private education. The book exposes Union army generals that were Marxists, and the Marxist ideas that informed the Lincoln administration. I voted GOP for 25 years because I thought the GOP was the party that would conserve the Constitution. How little I knew about the history of the GOP's founding and its Red Roots! Rather than the party of individual liberty, it has always been the power center for American mercantilists and bankers.

A Century of War by John Denson; an exhaustively-documented account of how Lincoln deliberately suckered the South into war at the behest of Northern mercantilists, directly against the unanimous counsel of his cabinet. Denson omits the crucial Spanish American War – where America was transformed into a world empire – but *The War Lovers* (see below) offers that vital story.

Overthrow: America's Century of Regime Change from Hawaii to Iraq by veteran news correspondent Stephen Kinzer is the best single-volume historical survey I can find covering the U.S. government's attempts at empire. This fast-moving little book is a series of vignettes of U.S. government takeovers of Hawaii, Guam, the Philippines, Puerto Rico and countless others including botched invasions of Mexico, Venezuela, Panama, and sweet spots around the globe, all long before the present invasion of Iraq and Afghanistan. Bottom line: for 125 years, small nations and islands of the world have been mere real estate assets for American corporations and military, violating our Constitution every time.

Drugs, Oil and War by Peter Dale Scott is a more narrowly-focused explanation of how the Deep State planned and executed American foreign policy and wars since World War II. Many Americans on the left and right are finally realizing that the bankers and war industry are joined at the hip. But in this book, Scott adds the missing pieces, demonstrating how the oil industry and CIA-spawned drug cartels from Latin America to Southeast Asia, and then the Middle East, made the trap complete.

The New American Militarism: How Americans Are Seduced by War is unlike 'anti-war' books, which I do not generally care for. Andrew Bacevich is a former U.S. Army colonel, Vietnam veteran, West Point professor of history and international relations. This Christian offers a logical, historically accurate analysis of what President Eisenhower dubbed the Military-Industrial Complex. Patriotic Christians, especially active military or veterans, can discover that while the U.S. military industry outspends all other militaries on earth combined, it also opposes the positions of Washington, Jefferson, and Madison. Bottom line: veterans and civilians need to reconsider what they were taught; the Deep State programs America's military subculture to violate our Supreme Law as it directs the foreign policy of our republic.

Against Our Better Judgment by Alison Weir is only 93 pages of body text, followed by 107 pages of endnotes. With most professional academics being paid shills of the Deep State and its private foundations, a reader should not look for truth and authors' credentials to necessarily jibe. This book is copiously documented, with almost 375 references. Does Israel control Washington DC? Read, and decide.

JFK-9/11: 50 Years of the Deep State I disagree with his dismissal of Old Testament Scripture, but Frenchman Laurent Guyenot is a Renaissance man with degrees in engineering and Medieval Studies who worked in the arms industry and also authored a study on the psychological and social damage of mass pornography. In this book, Guyenot offers an even better analysis of 9/11 than Ruppert's book, in that he demonstrates the Deep State sponsorship of both the JFK assassination and the 9/11 attacks. Bottom line: the smoking gun of both Deep State actions leads to the Israeli Mossad and the CIA.

The Fourth Turning: What the Cycles of History Tell Us About America's Next Rendezvous With Destiny by William Strauss and Neil Howe is a smaller, more exciting 1998 follow-up to their 1991 book *Generations: The History of America's Future.* In this national bestseller, Strauss and Howe illustrate the historical 80- to 100-year cycle called a *saecula,* further divided into five 20-year periods/generations. The authors call each transition between these generations, a *turning.* Thus in 1998, the authors accurately predicted the fourth turning of our saecula; a crisis period from 2005-2015.

This was partially fulfilled in the Ron Paul Revolution, TEA Party movement, 'Great Recession', staggering collapse of the U.S. Dollar, and increasing mistrust of institutions leading to the election of Trump. Tracing 'heroic' generations back to pre-colonial times, the authors conclude that by 2015, Americans in the 'Baby Boomer' and 'Thirteener' generations would step up to meet the crisis. They thought they did, by electing Trump, but didn't know enough civics to realize that presidents can't do the People's job. The bottom line of this book is still correct: today's Chicken Little refrain is dead wrong, and we believe that Tactical Civics™ is the most likely contender for the major, long-term return to responsibility that Strauss & Howe predicted.

The Lost World of Genesis One: Ancient Cosmology and the Origins Debate by John H. Walton, who has a PhD in Hebrew and is a professor of Old Testament Theology at Wheaton, is one of the most liberating books I have ever read! I mean this sincerely. This book smashes the Young-Old Earth Creation debate; smashes it flat, into irrelevance, for begging the question of material origins. His thesis consists of a series of propositions, culminating in the hypothesis that the creation account in Genesis is a description of the universe's construction as a temple of God, not as material 'stuff'. A few high points...

First: There is no reason that God would have communicated 'scientifically-correct' data about His creation to simple, ancient people. In other words, no statement in the Bible conveys scientific truth that the biblical writers would not have already known.

Second: Some statements in the Bible convey cosmological and physiological notions that do not comport with science; for instance, 'domed' cosmology has no scientific merit but it worked well for primitive ancients. Some of the words translated as 'mind' in English actually mean 'entrails' in the Hebrew; people in those days (and for centuries after) believed that emotions and feelings derived from the guts. Walton suggests that God didn't correct them; there was no point, in their place and time. We would not waste our time today trying to argue that our guts are the seat of our thoughts and emotions, yet that is how Young Earth creationists and Intelligent Design apologists defend the creation account!

Third: Walton explains how the ontology of the creation account is not material but *functional*. To illustrate, he compares a chair to a corporation; a chair is 'created' by the nature of its *material* status, but a corporation is 'created' by its *functional* status; on pg. 26: *"In a functional ontology, to bring something into existence would require giving it a function or a role in an ordered system, rather than giving it material property."* Because the entities created in the Genesis account are material entities, we presume that Genesis must be a material ontology. This is a senseless assumption, as Walton explains with contextual evidence of many ancient Near Eastern creation accounts and analyzing Hebrew words like *bara*. Bottom line: the whole Origins debate is a false dilemma.

Constitutional Income: Do You have Any? by former Idaho state representative and structural engineer Phil Hart is the meticulously-documented story of how from 1909-1913, Congress conspired to create the largest, longest-running financial crime in history. Featuring facsimile copies of congressional floor debate, private memoranda, and newspaper articles of the period, this book will make every Taxpayer furious, and give ammunition to every law-abiding Nontaxpayer among today's estimated 67 million non-filers. Bottom line: all of that corruption and pork isn't magic; follow the money.

A Tax Honesty Primer is my little book and TaxHonestyPrimer.com site. Having read the Internal Revenue Code, countless court rulings and cases, seven books on Tax Honesty, and dozens of websites over two years, I then became a law-abiding Nontaxpayer in 1994. I couldn't find in one place enough information to take action and expose the corruption, so I created *A Tax Honesty Primer* as the first step in Taxpayer due diligence, so that others can avoid years of wading through tax protester theories. The book is not my opinion or 'position'; it's a compendium of easily verifiable facts, court rulings, Tax Code sections, federal regulations, jury verdicts, IRS commissioner and IRS employee statements, and well-settled law. On the site, I do not sell anything or accept donations.

Tax Honesty is wonderful defense for the self-employed (it's all but impossible if you work for someone else, especially a large company); but playing defense will never arrest Congress' crimes. Until our

Indictment Engine™ becomes our permanent citizen mechanism to arrest organized crime in Congress, at least Tax Honesty offers short-term relief. It is something like household secession from Congress' corruption.

The Official Counterfeiter is a 36-page free cartoon booklet created in 1969 by Vic Lockman; the clearest explanation I've ever read, of Congress' money and banking crimes on behalf of the corrupt banking industry.

http://scripturalscrutinydotcom.files.wordpress.com/2012/01/the-official-counterfeiter-biblical-economics.pdf

War, Oil, Drugs, Banking, and The Deep State

The Devil's Chessboard by David Talbot is the story of the Dulles brothers (Allen and John Foster), creators and evil masterminds of the CIA. As Talbot exposes the characters of these two sociopath brothers and their evil, world-shifting chicanery, you begin each chapter asking yourself how the American People failed to stop these criminals. But you cannot stop what you do not see. You begin to understand that the very existence of the CIA – like the FBI, DOJ, NSA, DIA and others – is criminal. Nowhere authorized in the Constitution, and in fact, a 'shadow government', as described in countless whistleblower books exposing the criminality of these agencies.

The Gold Warriors by Sterling and Peggy Seagraves is one of the most fascinating books I have ever read. After years and years of painstaking journalistic investigations and collecting scores of first-person testimony and actual photographs of the caves filled with gold bars and crates upon crates of gold bonds, the intrepid couple present the story of the most fascinating story in history of gold and war.

After World War II, the DC government captured and seized 288,000 metric tons of gold, plundered from Europe and China by Japan and Germany, called 'Yamashita's Gold' and 'Black Eagle Gold', respectively. How was it located, and by whom? How was it transported, and to what location? What happened to this astounding hoard of gold after the DC cabal seized it? What have congresses done about it, since this is the constitutional purview of Congress? A fascinating detective story, illustrating that Washington DC is truly the most ruthless, lawless city-state in modern world history.

The Transparent Cabal: The Neoconservative Agenda, War in the Middle East, and the National Interest of Israel by Stephen Sniegoski, is a more detailed dive into the American war industry's operations in the Middle East. If you first read Alison Weir's book, *Against Our Better Judgment* (see above), you will understand who created the modern political state of Israel, that also created a domestic PR campaign in thousands of American churches, twisting Scripture to make the case that the anti-Christian -- indeed atheistic -- political state of our day in Israel, is actually the remnant of God described in the New Testament.

Sniegoski goes much deeper into mechanics of geopolitical crime, and the DC cabal's operations. If you want to understand how and why powerful pro-Israel neoconservatives in the U.S. misled Americans and used the complicit Dubya Bush (of the Bush oil family!) to order the U.S. invasion of Iraq in 2003, and how they persuaded the U.S. Congress to give Dubya the (supposed) authority to order the invasion, read this outstanding book. Prepare to be very angry...but as with dozens of the books on this list: once you know the players and discover their massive financial motivation, the history of America's foreign wars (ALL of them) turns out to be just a series of pirate stories.

Myths, Lies and Oil Wars by William Engdahl is probably the best book if you want to learn about the theory of 'Abyssal Abiotic Petroleum Origins' (i.e., petroleum doesn't come from dead plants and dinosaurs – so-called 'fossil fuel' – but from deep in the earth and is practically limitless) and to grasp U.S. military industry geopolitics in the Middle East, Russia and China over the past few decades.

The Deep, Hot Biosphere: The Myth of Fossil Fuels by Dr. Thomas Gold was plagiarized from the Russian-Ukrainian theory of Abyssal Abiotic Petroleum Origins – the theory that there exists an enormous store of hydrocarbons upwelling from deep within the earth that can provide us with gas and petroleum for as long as man lives on Earth. In this 1999 book, Dr. Gold copied the original work of the Ukrainian and Russian pioneers to debunk the myth that petroleum had its genesis in dinosaurs and old plants. The theory is thus called the theory of 'abiotic oil' and includes three controversial, potentially earth-shattering positions:

First: Below the surface of the earth is a biosphere of greater mass and volume than the sum of all living things on all continents and in all oceans.

Second: The inhabitants of this subterranean biosphere are not plants or animals but heat-loving bacteria that survive on hydrocarbons (natural gas & petroleum).

Third: Most hydrocarbons on Earth are not the byproduct of biological debris ('fossil fuels'), but were a common constituent of the materials from which Earth itself was formed.

If all of these scientists are correct, the implications are astounding, and disastrous for the oil industry. This would also explode the environmentalist so-called 'Peak Oil' theory – which went the way of the dinosaurs in 2012 with the GAO reported that the Green River Formation alone contains more recoverable petroleum than the entire previously-known world oil reserves.

Further down in this list, I link to a white paper by J.F. Kenney, senior geologist at Gas Resources Corporation in Houston, listing most of the Russian and Ukrainian scientists that hypothesized abyssal abiotic petroleum origins' long before Dr. Gold plagiarized their work to claim in the American scientific media that it was his own. Besides the Ukrainian and Russian originators of the theory, a growing body of supporting evidence is being produced by American scientists like Jean Whelan at Woods Hole Oceanographic Institute; Mahlon Kennicutt, Professor of Chemical Oceanography at Texas A&M; Giora Proskurowski, professor of Oceanography at University of Washington, and others.

Crossing the Rubicon: The Decline of the American Empire at the End of the Age of Oil by Michael Ruppert is the only 9/11 book I include, and this will be a long synopsis because the 9/11 debacle is important – not for the tragedy itself, but because of the major shift in government and media propaganda that took place over the 20 years since that 'New Pearl Harbor'.

Erasmus of Rotterdam said, *"In the land of the blind, the one-eyed man is king"*. We needn't know everything about the 911 debacle; what we do know is more than sufficient to know it was a massive government fraud on the American people.

A fifth grader in possession of the facts grasps this general concept: powerful men and institutions have influenced governments throughout history. The 160-year pattern in America since Fort Sumter is: first we experience a catalyst attack either of unexplained origin or

130

out of proportion to the war that follows. Next, federal government and its industry allies ratchet their power; government gains new ground against its own population, then holds the new ground to gain further illicit powers. This is the one-way advance of tyranny.

Ruppert's book is the most credible of twenty-two books and three videos I reviewed over nine years relating to the 9/11 debacle. I no longer spend time on this issue; as I said above, I only include this book because that hoax catalyzed American domestic and foreign policy for the foreseeable future. The government's official story and its media hacks must be hooted off the stage!

We did a podcast in 2018 called *Collateral Damage (Beyond Treason)* discussing a report by E.P. Heidner, the only surviving member of the Office of Naval Intelligence task force that was investigating George Bush Senior's shady deal with Russian oligarchs that Heidner shows was the most likely reason for the 9/11 operation. Heidner's ONI task force's offices just happened to be located precisely where that cruise missile hit the Pentagon on 9/11. Just coincidence!

Yet it's pointless to argue about 9/11 itself; Tactical Civics™ can empower the American people to beat the predator-parasite horde at last: self-governing citizens and resurgent sovereign States can *enforce* the Constitution and arrest the long pattern of government-corporate-military corruption using a legal choke-collar on each individual member of Congress. As we work on a new long-term arrest mechanism, there's no sense arguing about one of the criminals' last in a 120-year series of frauds, since 9/11 was followed by the Russiagate-Shampeachment-BLAntifa-Chinavirus-Election Steal 2020 overthrow of anything even *resembling* legitimate government. Those who still don't get it, are beyond help.

Whoever our domestic enemies are, they use Congress for financing and legislative enablement. The typical globalist player's goal is always to become insanely wealthy, and Congress is their key. After every war, they get us arguing among ourselves for decades about who caused the fire so we won't stop to think about trapping the kingpins who hired the arsonist.

I am one of several hundred engineers, scientists, and architects who signed on at *Architects and Engineers for 911 Truth* not because I care to argue about this latest in a long pattern of war-sparking hoaxes, but because the official story is so preposterous in structural forensics, physics, and materials science. As a professional engineer having performed structural design for 28 years, I became interested in the story when I witnessed video of the collapses of WTC 1 and 2 and especially WTC Building 7, that day. To assert that the first three instances in history of fire-induced collapse of steel multistory buildings occurred in one city, in one day (one of them with no aircraft collision) is ludicrous. Of countless raging fires in steel structures around the world, some have lasted far longer than the WTC fires, yet none led to plastic collapse, much less to the pulverizing (pyroclastic-style) destruction and free-fall-velocity collapse seen thrice on 9/11 but never seen before or since. *Except in every controlled demolition.*

Occam's Razor holds that the simplest explanation is most likely; put another way, if evidence contradicts an explanation that adds a pile of unlikely assumptions, that explanation is likely not true. On the morning of July 28, 1945, a fully-fueled B-25 Mitchell *bomber* lost in fog over Manhattan slammed into the 79th floor of the *Empire State Building. The* structure sustained no lasting damage, much less did it collapse in the free-fall-velocity, symmetrical implosion failure seen in steel structures *only* in controlled demolition.

Geopolitical forces in play in the world's mega-events need phenomenal amounts of money, logistics, and coordination that only major financial players enjoy. The idea that 9/11 was done by a handful of Muslims with the U.S. defense system fully engaged, is preposterous. It is one thing to believe legends about 'Honest Abe' because you were indoctrinated in school; it is another thing to believe a ludicrous story that defies logic and evidence simply because a few in the 'truther' camp happen to be eccentric.

Just listen to the analysis we did in 2018, read Heidner's report, and apply Occam's Razor.

Bottom line: from the assassination of JFK in 1963 to the 9/11 debacle, Russiagate, Shampeachment, the Chinavirus shutdown of America, and Election Steal 2020 – the Deep State will continue to destroy our economy, flood our borders with illegals, commit murders of presidents or of thousands of civilians foreign and domestic until We The People learn to focus on *our* target: their power source and their puppet institution, *Congress.*

Churchill's Folly: How Winston Churchill created modern Iraq by Chris Catherwood, is the story of Britain's dissection of the Persian Empire into the petrodollar bloodbath we've seen ever since. Ralph Raico's *Rethinking Churchill* chapter in the book *Reassessing the Presidency* removed my blinders about the old Bulldog whose clever turns of phrase had always captured me. Bottom line: this book will teach you just what a scheming monster Churchill actually was.

Considerations About Recent Predictions of Impending Shortages of Petroleum Evaluated From the Perspective of Modern Petroleum Science by J. F. Kenney, is an online white paper that smashes the unfounded 'Peak Oil' scare trotted out along with the equally unsupported 'anthropogenic Climate Change' theory. These false prophets, ironically, helped drive oil prices through the roof for years; without a shred of evidence from petroleum science, they are useful puppets for Big Oil. The old 'fossil fuels' hypothesis originated in the 18th century; it held that petroleum miraculously evolves from decayed biological material – plants and animals – which would mean it is limited. The fossil fuels hypothesis has been replaced over the past four decades by the Russian-Ukrainian theory of 'Abyssal Abiotic Petroleum Origins' which establishes that petroleum is a primordial material that erupts from great depth and is practically unlimited in abundance, only depending on extraction technology and exploration competence. The white paper is found at http://www.csun.edu/~vcgeo005/Energy.html

It's the Crude, Dude: Greed, Gas, War, and the American Way by Linda McQuaig is a well-documented history of America's role in the game played first by the British and French in the sands of Araby. She lists individual deals, companies, sheikhs, and contracts over the past century. As bloody as we think Mohammedans are, this book proves that the Deep State, using *both* sides, causes these wars. Bottom line: we should feel sorry for any Middle East population as long as the Deep State owns Congress.

Reassessing the Presidency: The Rise of the Executive State and the Decline of Freedom is a 791-page lesson about how American history has been steered by our presidents; edited by John V. Denson. Each chapter can be read on its own to grasp a particular presidency or period. Bottom line is the book's recurring theme: as Madison and Jefferson, both presidents themselves, constantly reminded us that presidents are not to be trusted; the People must stay in control and remain always vigilant.

133

The Costs of War: America's Pyrrhic Victories is another compendium edited by John Denson. A treasure-trove for those who want to learn why our wars were fought. The book is worth buying for Raico's _Rethinking Churchill_ chapter alone; it finally puts the butcherous Bulldog of Britain in the hall of infamy alongside Lincoln, Teddy Roosevelt, and FDR. But read Denson's _A Century of War_ first.

War is a Racket is the small, powerful classic by the most-decorated officer in the history of the US Marine Corps, General Smedley Butler. He describes how the military industry – all the branches – conditions young minds to do its will, right or wrong; how he, as a decorated officer, did the bidding of banks, oil companies, sugar companies and military contractors, plundering foreign countries. General Butler spent many years after leaving the military, trying to warn America just as former 5-star general President Dwight Eisenhower did 25 years later in his farewell address when he coined the term 'Military Industrial Complex'. Bottom line: top military brass exposed the Deep State 80 years ago!

Truth is a Lonely Warrior by James Perloff is something like a Cliff's Notes version of half a dozen of the books I mention here. For lots of American history in one small book, this one is a winner.

The War Lovers: Roosevelt, Lodge, Hearst and the Rush to Empire, 1898 by Evan Thomas is the amazing story of how America was transformed from a non-interventionist economic giant into the world's foremost military plundering and invading power, knocking England from its hegemonic throne. Teddy Roosevelt was a romantic fraud; a sickly child who overcompensated by bullying the world. With his best friend, powerful warmonger Henry Cabot Lodge – and the timely help of America's most powerful newspaper man of the time – these men literally _created_ the Spanish-American War to plunder the Philippines, Guam, Puerto Rico and others. Bottom line: as the Deep State used Lincoln to hijack our Constitution and occupy America, they used Teddy Roosevelt to spawn the worldwide Military-Industrial Complex that plagues the whole world to this day.

Wilson's War: How Woodrow Wilson's Great Blunder led to Hitler, Lenin, Stalin & World War II by Jim Powell is an excellent primer on Tom 'Woodrow' Wilson, highlighting the milquetoast do-gooder's colossal blunders from Mexico to Venezuela to America joining Europe's two world wars for huge military industry profits. Reading this account of presidential incompetence that many other presidents have since displayed, I finally understood that Wilson's chief weakness wasn't incompetence so much as useful wickedness. Bottom line: how Wilson knowingly dragged America into Europe's mega-wars.

FDR's Folly: How Roosevelt and his New Deal prolonged the Great Depression is the second primer on America's world-war presidents by historian Jim Powell. As he does with Wilson, the author illustrates how mendacious, bungling and evil FDR was. The hero of my parents' generation was also a good friend of Stalin, who killed 20 million of his own people. Another Deep State tool.

Roosevelt's Secret War: FDR & World War II Espionage is the story of FDR's creation of America's intelligence industry. Author Joseph Persico says, *"Few leaders were better adapted temperamentally to espionage than FDR; (he) compartmentalized information, misled associates, manipulated people, conducted intrigues, used private lines of communication, scattered responsibility, duplicated assignments, provoked rivalries, held the cards while showing few, and left few fingerprints."* And this from an author who *likes* FDR, referring to him as a principled Machiavellian who hoped to achieve clear ends (getting America into WWII) although most Americans wanted nothing to do with it.

Day of Deceit: The Truth about FDR and Pearl Harbor is Robert B. Stinnett's copious proof showing that Pearl Harbor was no surprise to FDR, just the 9/11 that the devious president needed to prime a multi-billion-dollar war machine on both sides of the ocean. *Millions of new jobs! What's a few tens of thousands dead?* Like Persico, Stinnett is still supportive of FDR; yet by simply reporting what he found, Stinnett's smoking guns expose FDR as a puppet of the Deep State 30 years before Eisenhower coined the term 'military-industrial complex'.

The Great Oil Conspiracy: How the U.S. Government Hid the Nazi Discovery of Abiotic Oil from the American People by Dr. Jerome Corsi is much like Thomas Gold's book, building on the Ukrainian and Russian theory of Abyssal Abiotic Petroleum Origins without giving due credit to the Ukrainian and Russian scientists that developed the theory long before the rise of a German variation of the theory.

Reset: Iran, Turkey, and America's Future is another master work by Stephen Kinzer. It is likely that 99.99% of Americans have never heard of the popular revolutions against Islamic rule by the people of Iran and Turkey a century ago. The 'Young Turks' – led by Mustafa Kemal

Ataturk – succeeded, while the Persian (Iranian) people were enslaved in Mohammed's system. *Fascinating* read.

Unrestricted Warfare by Qiao Liang and Wang Xiangsui cannot be readily found in book form, but look it up online and you will find it in PDF format, over 200 pages, a 1999 publication by two Chinese politicians and military officers. Those who do not see the bigger picture (God's dealing with mankind on earth) often worry these days that China will conquer the world. Perhaps this is understandable...

First, because this 22-year-old white paper perfectly explains the Chinese bioweapon created and released, with funding and direction for gain-of-function viability research from bats to humans, by the diabolical Anthony Fauci. Late in 2019, the virus was allowed to infect a number of Chinese, who carried it from the laboratory in Wuhan province. The Chinese Communist Party took prophylactic precautions in China while allowing a few virus carriers to travel to Europe and America as human bioweapons. A brilliant, demonic strategy, perfectly fitting the thesis of Unrestricted Warfare.

Secondly, Americans should be afraid because of the sheer intellectual and strategic prowess of the two officers. A reader cannot fault the impressive and extensive knowledge of western history and culture displayed by these two Chinese military men. To read this 1999 treatise and compare it to anything published by any American author – especially an American politician or military officer – the reader chillingly understands that those Chicoms are not the boorish robots we believe they are. One wonders how many such brilliant minds exist in the Chinese Communist Party.

Read this book/paper. I read it for my own education and edification, and learned a great deal of military history, East and West, and strategic thinking, besides. All I can say is: the CCP is here already, in force. They are especially in our universities and corporations. They are brilliant, godless, and ruthless...yet with that unnerving smile and superficial graciousness that puts the target at ease, before they slip the stiletto under your ribs.

The New Empire of Debt by Bill Bonner and Addison Wiggin is the second edition of a work that traces America's past 120 years of world conquest, measuring blood and money with a mix of humor and morose fact that keeps you turning the pages to find out how stupid we can get before Congress' Deep State puppeteers bankrupt us entirely. Bottom line: illustrates exactly how America has become so hated around the world, and so bankrupt as well.

Two More on Lincoln, America's First Deep State Puppet

Forced Into Glory: Abraham Lincoln's White Dream is a 662-page shocker by Black author and history scholar Lerone Bennett Jr. This is from the back cover of this courageous African-American's book: *"Every American schoolchild knows the story of "The Great Emancipator" who freed Negroes with the stroke of a pen out of the kindness of his heart. (But) Lincoln wasn't the great emancipator…(he) was a conservative politician who said repeatedly that he believed in White supremacy. Not only that, he believed Blacks and Whites would be better off separated, preferably by the Atlantic Ocean…(his) Emancipation Proclamation…freed few if any of the slaves, and he called for the deportation of African-Americans and the creation of an all-White country."*

Bennett's scholarship is impeccable, his indictment of Lincoln, withering. Are all men created equal, as the Declaration of Independence holds? Not according to Lincoln, Bennett writes on page 315: *"Large chunks of Lincoln's debate speeches…are taken from Henry Clay's mouth…Lincoln said he had never tried to apply the principles of the Declaration of Independence to slavery or the political rights of Blacks in America. On at least fifteen occasions, he said publicly that the principles of the Declaration didn't require him or anybody else to do anything about slavery in the South and Jim Crow in the North."*

Bottom line: A racist monster was the best salesman ever in the White House.

America's Caesar: The Decline and Fall of Republican Government in the United States of America by Greg L. Durand probes more deeply than does DiLorenzo into the personal and religious aspects of Lincoln's character, using primary-sources to prove that Lincoln was a cross between Bill Clinton and Saddam Hussein: a godless butcher with a slick public persona. After you read these quotes from his friends, contemporaries, and Lincoln's own pen, you'll know that we all had a *propagandist* education.

Studies in the U.S. Constitution

The Tactical Civics™ Ready Constitution is a spiral-bound, super-handy desk copy of the U.S. Constitution with a unique design. It features Mike Holler's numbering system for each clause in the Constitution, making it easy to start memorizing where your favorite clauses are. Amendments are integrated in context where they affect the law. You can buy this handy spiral-bound edition in our Training Center. I use it every day.

Free, Sovereign, and Independent States: The Intended Meaning of the American Constitution by John Remington Graham explains the U.S. Constitution clause by clause, tracing legislative history from the kings' courts and parliaments of Great Britain to our Constitutional Convention. This ready reference on every clause in the Constitution is a masterful briefing on the origins of America's Supreme Law. Bottom line: this is the concise, historically complete explanation of every sentence in the U.S. Constitution.

The Founders' Constitution by editors Kurland and Lerner is a 5-volume massive reference set offering a more in-depth treatment than Graham's. It includes extracts from leading works of political theory, history, law, and constitutional argument that the Framers and their contemporaries used and produced. Available in paperback and CD-ROM, I find the electronic edition considerably handier. Bottom line: this is a far more in-depth background on the U.S. Constitution than Graham's book above, but Graham's work is more comprehensive regarding the provenance (legal roots) of every clause.

The People Themselves: Popular Constitutionalism and Judicial Review by Larry D. Kramer, former dean of Stanford Law School, is no dry tome filled with legal jargon. It is a refreshing look at why We The People have more lawful power than the U.S. Supreme Court. Dean Kramer discusses why it is critical that We The People begin to exercise that power peacefully and lawfully – or we will lose that power, and rule of law with it. Unfortunately, Dr. Kramer is now the president of a very liberal Silicon Valley foundation, but his thesis in this work still holds true. Bottom line: We the People have more power and authority than any U.S. supreme Court; we just never took advantage of it. *Until now!*

Founding Fathers and Roots of Our Condition

The First American Republic 1774-1789 by Thomas Chorlton is similar to an out of print book called *President Who?: Forgotten Founders* by Stanley Klos. George Washington called Payton Randolph "the Father of our country" because Randolph was the first President of the United States in Congress Assembled, and 14 presidential administrations existed prior to George Washington's! Read this one and you'll agree that most of us were cheated in our education.

The Republic of Letters: The Correspondence Between Jefferson and Madison 1776-1826 a 3-volume compendium of 50 years' correspondence between the two giants among America's founding fathers. Series editor James Smith makes segues from their correspondence to their historical context, helping the reader grasp these founders' development over their lifetimes. I learned more about Madison from these letters than from seven Madison biographies. To grasp a man's mind, read his letters.

Democracy in America by Alexis deTocqueville is a classic work of economics, sociology, and political science. Although the young Frenchman did not grasp the republican form of government guaranteed in our Constitution, he was prescient about *democracy* in America. Our founders created a representative constitutional republic of sovereign States specifically to *avoid* democracy, majority rule that always degenerates into warring mobs, grabbing for goodies from the all-knowing Nanny State.

From his limited view as a foreigner, Tocqueville accurately predicted that democracy in America would degenerate into soft despotism and 'tyranny of the majority' as Madison predicted 50 years earlier. Tocqueville said that majoritarian tyranny would spring from the confluence of two corrupting factors: dependence on government for material security, and the growing prejudices of an increasingly ignorant mass, against one another's factions and groups.

He was correct. After 150 years of government education, most Americans are European socialists, unfit to rule our passions and unwilling to oversee our servant government; instead, making it their master by begging security and provision from it.

Hull's Wall Chart of World History

Technically this is not a book, but a very long, folded pictographic chart of incredible intricacy. First published in the Victorian era, Edward Hull's superb *Wall Chart of World History: From Earliest Times to the Present* (the Dorset Press Edition if you can find it, dated 1989) is one of the most fascinating and entertaining resources I've ever used. I have bought half a dozen of them over the past 20 years, and only have one remaining. Several went to my children and grandchildren.

This wall chart is perhaps 18-20 feet long, but it folds up so that it can be read as a (large) book on your lap or table top. It's more fun to lay it out on the floor as I've done with children; you can spend hours teaching and learning world history. It is a jam-packed compendium of key people, facts, and dates in a whole new way of seeing them…as a visual flow of 'roots' from one generation to the next.

It covers all the major civilizations in the world, arranged chronologically. So you can easily see, for instance, what was happening in England, France, Germany, China, Italy, Egypt, et al, when Henry VIII was on the throne. Most people think of Henry VIII as the fellow who launched the 'Protestant' Church; but of course Martin Luther was turning the Vatican on its head at the same time and the first 'Protestant' Council took place in Augsburg.

Simultaneously, you can see that during Henry's reign, Ivan the Terrible was marauding, Michelangelo was creating his sublime works to edify mankind, the Vatican seated six successive popes, and Suleiman 'the Magnificent' had plundered and ravaged to carry the Ottoman Empire to new heights. Meanwhile, you see that Portugal had begun plundering and colonizing India, while Charles I of Spain became king…of Germany!...as China rumbled on in isolation under the Ming Dynasty.

I have never found a more powerful teaching and learning tool for world history. Buy one if you can find the Dorset 1989 edition. _Do not_ buy secular, revisionist imitations of Hull's priceless gem. There are knockoffs, but they leave out many important people and events, and add many unimportant trifles.

Economics, Money and Banking

Economics in One Lesson by Henry Hazlitt is a classic economics primer for people who would never read economics subjects but want to know how labor, money, government and credit operate in society to cause wars, inflation, depressions, and such.

The Mystery of Banking by Murray N. Rothbard, a student of Ludwig von Mises, a founder of 'Austrian School' classical economics. Rothbard shows where the bodies were buried as bankers and Washington D.C. debased and despoiled our currency and engage daily in fraud, theft, and counterfeiting. More importantly, on pages 262-268 the author provides a concise plan to restore lawful currency and banking in America that, together with the work of Professor Huerta de Soto (see below), Tactical Civics™ is using to draft our Lawful United States Money and Banking Act.

Blood Money: The Civil War and the Federal Reserve by John Remington Graham is a little booklet explaining that the Federal Reserve scam actually began generations before the Jekyll Island gang and Congress teamed up in 1910-13.

Barbara Villiers or, A History of Monetary Crimes by Alexander del Mar is a tiny book with a misleading name. Villiers was a favored mistress of an English king, for whose personal benefit coinage laws were passed. If you think this bizarre, read Rothbard's history, cited above; American monetary legislation since Lincoln's time has been the same kind of deals but with many 'mistresses'.

The Case Against the Fed by Murray Rothbard is a small book with a practical goal: to show how to shut down history's longest-running counterfeiting scam. This work forms the basic guide for the design of our proposed reform legislation, the *Lawful American Money and Banking Act.*

Money, Bank Credit, and Economic Cycles in the second English edition (2009) by Professor Jesus Huerta de Soto is the finest single volume in print on practical economics. Like the late Murray Rothbard, this author also explains the criminal nature of the fractional reserve banking scam throughout history; how all business boom-and-bust cycles have been created by the Federal Reserve crime families. Like Joseph Salerno is his book *Money: Sound & Unsound,* the author explains how the theories of Keynes and Marx are still used by central banks and the banking industry generally to defraud us. In his final chapter, Professor de Soto offers a simple, powerful plan to restore honest money and banking.

Pieces of Eight: The Monetary Powers and Disabilities of the United States Constitution by Edwin Vieira, Jr. is the definitive explanation of lawful U.S. money as stipulated in our Supreme Law, and also the definitive history of the U.S. Dollar. Out of print for about a decade, the huge two-volume hardbound set (over 1,700 pages) is available again through Amazon.com and at $200 is a bargain if you need definitive legal citations regarding U.S. money.

Unaccountable: How the accounting profession forfeited a public trust by Mike Brewster takes you from ancient clay tablets in Sumeria up to the breakup of the Big Eight, in a tale of deceit and unprofessionalism, making 'the dismal profession' a riveting read.

For background on how deeply Congress has been involved in financial crimes this century, *America Again! – The Movie* is the best start. But here are a few good resources regarding banking:

The Best Way to Rob a Bank is to Own One by UMKC Law professor and former federal bank regulator William Black explains how at the end of last century the S&L crisis was a tremor of things to come. Many more recent books expose the grifters' games today; three good ones are:

It Takes a Pillage: Behind the Bailouts, Bonuses and Backroom Deals From Washington to Wall Street by Nomi Prins

The Great American Stickup: Greedy Bankers and the Politicians Who Love Them by Robert Scheer

Griftopia: A Story of Bankers, Politicians, and the Most Audacious Power Grab in History by Matt Taibbi

If you're not much of a reader, learn how staggeringly corrupt the banking industry is (and how it controls Congress and presidents) by watching the Academy-Award winning documentary *Inside Job*. You'll never feel the same walking into your bank.

Crumbling and Corrupt Civilization

Ideas Have Consequences by Richard M. Weaver is a little classic which proposes that language, virtue, maleness, femaleness, and ancient mores have almost gone out of our world. I disagree with Weaver's somber note at the end, but this book caused me to think about truth, goodness, and beauty outside my religious categories.

Amusing Ourselves to Death by Neil Postman is the most trenchant, helpful guidebook for ridding your home of television. Written in 1985, Postman's work is in many ways an extension of the thoughts of Walter Ong in his classic *Orality and Literacy*. There are clear reasons why the American mind degenerated as it has; to know why these things happened and how they are happening still, read Postman. Then sell your televisions and start buying good books; you'll be wealthier in spirit.

The Beast on the East River: The U.N. Threat to America's Sovereignty and Security by Nathan Tabor, the founder of The ConservativeVoice.com, is the best analysis of the U.N. threat that I have read. We used this work to draft the sections of the AmericaAgain! Declaration that deal with ending our U.N. debacle.

The Master Switch by Columbia University professor Tim Wu explains several things that I had always wondered about. How did the big radio corporations of the early 20th century become big television and media empires by the end of the century? How do media content empires fit together with the distribution empires to determine what Americans see and hear? Is the Internet really the open sea of information for everyone to dip into as we imagine, or do certain entities control what we can get access to, and how it's presented? We've seen Facebook and Twitter answer that question! And of course, what about Microsoft, Apple, and Google, the 800-pound gorilla on the block, whose motto was "don't be evil"? Each corporation is more powerful than most governments on earth; we now see them working with corrupt government to be evil; controlling the content of what we think is the Internet world. The author probes all this, and more.

The Mechanical Bride by Marshall McLuhan, is a useful book on _noetics_ (knowing how we know), orality, and the impact of the written word on a world lit only by fire. This revolution of writing vs. speaking was far more fundamental to the human spirit than the modern reader might imagine. McLuhan gets a bit weighty and also more than a bit flighty at times; but if you stay with him, I think it pays off in the end.

Christians, Muslims, and Jews

A Wind in the House of Islam by David Garrison is the story of the nine geocultural variants of Islam around the world – what the author calls 'rooms in the House of Islam' – and how the Wind of God's Spirit is blowing through every one of them. Garrison spent three years travelling 250,000 miles through every corner of the Muslim world to investigate reports of Muslims turning to faith in Christ.

The researcher collected the stories of over 1,000 formerly-Muslim Christians, asking them the question: "What did God use to bring you to faith in Jesus Christ? Tell me your story." The result is an unprecedented look into the greatest turning of Muslims to Christ in history; stories of men and women who have sacrificed everything – home, family, even their lives – to follow Jesus. You hear from men and women from Africa to Indonesia and everywhere in between; how

143

God is at work through answered prayers, and through dreams and visions and through technology (Internet, satellite television, video and audio tools). The reader gains insight into each of the nine geo–cultural 'rooms' within Islam and, most importantly, learns how we can be part of the greatest turning of Muslims to Christ in history, both overseas and in our own communities.

The three main takeaways: 1) Christianity is growing today as never before on earth; 2) There is a great need for sound Biblical teaching among new converts; syncretism and pseudo-Christianity are always a danger; and 3) Most importantly, conservative Americans need to lose our hatred of all Muslims.

Similar books surveying the sudden growth of Christianity in the Middle East today are such books as *Jesus in Iran* by Eugene Bach; *Too Many to Jail: The Story of Iran's New Christians* by Mark Bradley; *Muslims, Christians and Jesus* by Carl Medearis; *The Coming Fall of Islam in Iran* by Reza Safa; *Seeking Allah, Finding Jesus* by Nabeel Qureshi and many others.

The Next Christendom by Philip Jenkins, Penn State University professor, suggests that the rapid growth of primitive and Pentecostal Christianity – both within and alongside existing traditions – is reshaping the world. 'Southern Christianity', Jenkins proposes, is Pentecostal, evangelical, and politically and morally conservative, pushing aside the cosmopolitan, unbelieving northern sensibilities that marked the senescence of European and American mainline denominations that now dismiss the basic teachings of the Bible in favor of enlightened, metrosexual life. (One caveat: Chapters 3&4 are his statistical and demographic thesis; slow, dry reading! I recommend reading the first two chapters, then jump to Chapter 5.)

Even as politically correct popes regurgitate Communism and Hollywood political correctness, the Next Christendom is draining the dying European denominations; for instance, openly challenging Anglicanism's apostasy. Jenkins posits that geopolitics, too, will be shaped by new Christians. 'Northern Christianity' and its secular political ideals are dying, as the opposite is happening in the southern hemisphere. With the gospel no longer shaped by a Eurocentric ethos and historical memory, the prophets of the 'post-Christian' world are wrong...*the Church is as alive as ever.*

Martyrs Mirror by Thielemann vanBraght is a hardbound compendium of 16 centuries of martyrs for the faith, from Christ's apostles through the 'Reformation', when believers who refused to sprinkle their babies and call it baptism were ruined, run out of town, jailed indefinitely and left to starve, drowned, or burned to death by Roman Catholics, Lutherans, and Calvinists. The purpose of reviewing these murders is to see that: a) Christians have been as savage as Muslims, for religion; b) the 'Reformation' was a *political* movement; and c) 'Reformed' folk run from these facts as Catholics run from the Inquisition. Ask me how I know this.

The Untold Story of the New Testament Church by Frank Viola explains how trying to read the Bible in the order we have it today is like re-arranging all the chapters of a novel, binding it back together, then trying to make sense of the story. Fascinating book.

Finding Organic Church: A Comprehensive Guide to Starting and Sustaining Authentic Christian Communities also by Frank Viola is a sequel to the amazing book, *Pagan Christianity?* – explaining how to gather with other believers in an organic fellowship without repeating the 501c3 lunacy of Christianity, Inc. or the opposite lunacy of most short-lived house church startups. Viola brings many years of hard experiences, as he has become a major figure in modern reformation.

The Great Christian Revolution by Otto Scott demonstrates that no matter how they may balk, even the most heathen anti-Christian in the West benefits from centuries of Christian foundation in every area of human endeavor.

Dismissing God by D. Bruce Lockerbie exposes the lives and work of the most influential writers of Abraham Lincoln's and subsequent generations. He explains how these angry humanists kicked out our moral underpinnings: Emily Dickinson, Walt Whitman, Ralph Waldo Emerson, Nathaniel Hawthorne, Herman Melville, Mark Twain, William Blake, Percy Bysshe Shelley, John Keats, John Ruskin, William Morris, William Butler Yeats, James Joyce, D.H Lawrence, Oscar Wilde, F. Scott Fitzgerald, Hemingway; the full lineup of perpetrators used by schools to *destroy* our Christian civilization.

APPENDIX B

28th Amendment Fact Sheet

Text of the 1789 Amendment

Article the First. – After the First Enumeration, required by the First Article of the Constitution, there shall be One Representative for every Thirty Thousand, until the Number shall amount to One Hundred; after which the Proportion shall be so regulated by Congress that there shall not be less than One Hundred Representatives, nor less than One Representative for every Forty Thousand Persons, until the number of Representatives shall amount to Two Hundred, after which the Proportion shall be so regulated by Congress that there shall not be less than Two Hundred Representatives, nor more than one Representative for every Fifty Thousand Persons.

Q: If we ratify this 28th Amendment with a U.S. population of 320 million, we'll have 6,600+ members of the U.S. House! Where would we put them all?

A: Which government places greater burdens on the American people – State or federal? The same 320 million Americans have 7,382 state legislators but only 535 federal ones. This is preposterous.

After ratifying the amendment, during the massive re-districting process in every state, AmericaAgain! will be pushing passage of the *Bring Congress Home Act* (BCHA) – a far more comprehensive version of HR287 filed by Eric Swalwell (D-CA) and Steve Pearce (R-NM) in 2013. Congress must move out of the 19th century.

Q: But won't the added cost be astronomical?

A: Total congressional operating budget would be approximately equal to the present $5.85 billion. Rather than the present 3-6 offices and staffs, U.S. congressmen under the BCHA would have a single office and paid staff of two. The BCHA will also end opulent perks and pensions and limit all members of Congress to two terms, either house.

Q: Doesn't the 20ᵗʰ Amendment say, "The Congress shall assemble at least once in every year, and such meeting shall begin at noon on the 3ʳᵈ day of January"?

A: Yes. People attend meetings every day via teleconference and video-conference; Congress can do the same. It's time We The People ended Washington D.C. organized crime, and we begin with the 28ᵗʰ Amendment.

Q: It has been 223 years since the last ratification vote was held on this original First Amendment; hasn't the statute of limitations run out on this process?

A: No; unless there is a ratification deadline in the body of the article, a constitutional amendment has no expiration date for ratification. The original Second Amendment was not finally ratified by the required 38ᵗʰ state legislature until 204 years after Congress passed it on to the states for ratification in 1789.

Q: If this amendment was so important, it would have been ratified when Congress first passed it.

A: It *was* ratified when Congress first passed it! See page 3 of the draft Joint Resolution; the Connecticut House of Representatives in October 1789 voted to ratify; the CT Senate in May 1790 also voted to ratify. The House sought in 1790 to alter its vote due to a transcribing error, but the Senate rejected the idea, thus technically, Kentucky's 1792 vote was the twelfth vote among 15 states, more than three-fourths of the states.

Q: With 6600+ seats in the U.S. House, we will be faced with a massive redistricting project. Given our workload on budgetary and operational matters in our state, why should the State Legislature spend time on this frivolous political issue?

A: George Washington did not speak publicly at the 1787 Constitutional Convention until the final day of that historic four-month gathering. When he finally rose to speak on the last day of the convention, Washington's first words were to urge his fellow delegates to support apportionment of representation at one congressman per 30,000 people. As a practical matter, this is very simple: no committees, reconciliation bill, or governor's signature for a ratification vote, and we provided your draft Joint Resolution. This is not rocket science.

Q. Some people argue that the amendment has a fatal flaw in the last sentence, "*there shall not be less than Two Hundred Representatives, nor more than one Representative for every Fifty Thousand Persons.*" That should say, not _less_ than one for every 50,000 persons; so if we ratify, we could have as few as 200 members in the U.S. House.

A. Read the amendment; as the 11 legislatures knew when they ratified the amendment, it is clear that the progression is 1: 30,000 then 1: 40,000 and finally 1: 50,000 people. Those who raise this objection either have ulterior motives or are ignorant of Article I, Section 2, Clause 4.

The 71st Congress, in restricting the House to only 435 districts, hijacked the Constitution. As explained on page 5 of the book *FEAR The People,* the Founding Fathers made this their first article of amendment because, as George Washington made clear during the Convention, adequate representation was paramount. It is time for our state legislatures to turn the tables on D.C., bring Congress home, and restore rule of law.

This first vital step in that process cannot be stopped by Washington D.C.; the amendment was passed by Congress, sent on to the state legislatures, and arguably already ratified once. **Now it is _your_ duty to perform!**

APPENDIX C

Ratification Vote Model Resolution

House Joint Resolution
Original Constitutional Amendment #1 (28th Amendment)

Offered by Rep. _____

WHEREAS, The First Congress of the United States of America, at its first session begun and held March 4, 1789, sitting in New York, New York, in both houses, by a constitutional majority of two-thirds thereof, adopted the following proposition to amend the Constitution of the United States of America in the following words, to wit:

"RESOLVED, by the Senate and House of Representatives of the United States of America in Congress assembled, two thirds of both houses concurring, that the following (Article) be proposed to the Legislatures of the several States, … which (Article), when ratified by three fourths of the said Legislatures, to be valid to all intents and purposes, as part of the said Constitution, viz.: (An Article) in addition to, and Amendment of the Constitution of the United States of America, proposed by Congress, and ratified by the Legislatures of the several States, pursuant to the fifth Article of the original Constitution.

"Article the First. – After the First Enumeration, required by the First Article of the Constitution, there shall be One Representative for every Thirty Thousand, until the Number shall amount to One Hundred; after which the Proportion shall be so regulated by Congress that there shall not be less than One Hundred Representatives, nor less than One Representative for every Forty Thousand Persons, until the number of Representatives shall amount to Two Hundred, after which the Proportion shall be so regulated by Congress that there shall not be less than Two Hundred Representatives, nor more than one Representative for every Fifty Thousand Persons." And

WHEREAS, on the last day of the 1787 Constitutional Convention, delegate Nathanael Gorham proposed a change in Article I, Section 2, Clause 4 of the new U.S. Constitution, to limit the size of a U.S. congressional district to 30,000 people rather than 40,000 people – and this was the only subject about which President George Washington felt strongly enough to publicly address the Convention, urging the revision to smaller districts because 40,000 was too large; and

WHEREAS, of the first 12 amendments passed by Congress on September 25, 1789 the subject amendment was placed in first position for the reason given by Melancton Smith at the New York ratifying convention: "We certainly ought to fix in the Constitution those things which are essential to liberty. If anything falls under this description, it is the number of the legislature"; and

WHEREAS in one of the Anti-Federalist letters, the prophetic 'Cato' admonished: "It is a very important objection to this government, that the representation consists of so few; too few to resist the influence of corruption, and the temptation to treachery, against which all governments ought to take precautions…" and

WHEREAS, Article V of the Constitution of the United States allows the ratification of the proposed Amendment to the United States Constitution by the Legislature of the State of _____ , and does not dictate a time limit on ratification of an amendment submitted by Congress, and the First Congress specifically having not provided a time constraint for ratification of the above-quoted Amendment; and

WHEREAS, The Supreme Court of the United States in 1939 ruled in the landmark case of Coleman v. Miller that Congress is the final arbiter on the question of whether too much time has elapsed between Congress' submission of a particular amendment and the most recent state legislature's ratification of same if Congress did not specify a deadline on the proposal's consideration; and

WHEREAS, the Legislature of the State of
_____ finds that the proposed Amendment is today even more meaningful and necessary to the United States Constitution than in the eighteenth century when submitted for adoption, given the level of corruption and lobbyist tampering resulting

in multi-million-dollar U.S. congressional elections and inability of the United States Representative to meaningfully interact with the citizens he or she is supposed to represent; and

WHEREAS, the original First Amendment was designed to avoid precisely what we suffer today: multimillion-dollar campaigns for U.S. congressmen whose districts include up to 750,000 citizens and more – a population that they can never personally know, much less represent; and

WHEREAS, the proposed amendment to the United States Constitution has already been ratified by the legislatures of the following 11 states on the dates indicated, to wit: New Jersey on November 20, 1789; Maryland on December 19, 1789; North Carolina on December 22, 1789; South Carolina on January 19, 1790; New Hampshire on January 25, 1790; New York on March 27, 1790; Rhode Island on June 15, 1790; Pennsylvania on September 21, 1791; Vermont on November 3, 1791; Virginia on December 15, 1791; and Kentucky on June 24, 1792; and

WHEREAS, the original First Amendment did actually receive sufficient votes for ratification once Kentucky's vote was recorded, due to the fact that the Connecticut House of Representatives in October 1789 voted to ratify Article the First, and the Connecticut Senate in May 1790 also voted to ratify it, and although the House sought by May 1790 to alter its vote due to a transcribing error, the Senate rejected the idea, thus technically, Kentucky's 1792 vote was the twelfth vote in 15 states at the time, the original First Amendment thus having been ratified by more than three-fourths of the states, making this present-day campaign truly a *re*-ratification of the People's original Right in the Bill of Rights; and

WHEREAS in 1993, the thirty-eighth State Legislature ratified the original Second Amendment, which had been ratified by the first State over 204 years earlier, at which time the Archivist of the United States declared it ratified as the Twenty-Seventh Amendment to the U.S. Constitution; and

WHEREAS this joint resolution only calls for the ratification vote of the original First Amendment to the U.S. Constitution under the stipulations of Article V thereof, and is not state legislation requiring committee deliberations, a reconciliation process or signature by the Governor; and

WHEREAS all due deliberation on this matter has been held on the floor of both Houses of this Legislature, it was found in the best interests of the people of _____ that the ratification vote be held without delay, and such vote having been held in favor of ratification;

THEREFORE, be it RESOLVED, BY THE HOUSE OF REPRE-SENTATIVES OF THE _____ LEGISLATURE OF THE STATE OF _____, THE SENATE CONCURRING HEREIN, that the foregoing proposed Amendment to the Constitution of the United States is hereby ratified by the Legislature of the State of _____; and be it further RESOLVED, that the Secretary of State of _____ shall transmit certified copies of this resolution to the Archivist of the United States, to the Vice-President of the United States, and to the Speaker of the United States House of Representatives with a request that it be printed in full in the Congressional Record.

APPENDIX D

Model County Ordinances

An **ORDINANCE** Providing for Citizens to Volunteer for Grand Jury and Assuring that the County Court shall Call for a Grand Jury When the People so Demand, in the County/Municipality

of_____,

in the State of_____

Short Title: County Ordinance on Grand Jury   [Revision 04]

Preamble

We, the [name of county board or commission] *of* [fill in] [COUNTY, PARISH OR BOROUGH], [fill in STATE], *in pursuance of our oaths to uphold the Constitutions of our State and of the United States, and of our duty to our community under Divine Law, hereby secure the fundamental right and authority of our Citizens to volunteer for Grand Jury service within this* [County, Parish or Borough].

Article I. Justification

§1 WHEREAS, in the preamble to the Constitution for the United States, the American People declare that, "We The People...do ordain and establish this Constitution", thus clearly establishing that The People collectively occupy the highest sovereignty over all American government; and

§2 WHEREAS, the United States supreme Court in Chisolm v. Georgia, U.S. 2 Dall 419, 454 (1793), affirmed that, "The People are Sovereign...at the Revolution, the sovereignty devolved on the people; and they are truly the sovereigns of the country...equal as fellow citizens, and as joint tenants in the sovereignty"; and

§3 WHEREAS, in Amendment X of the U.S. Constitution, we state, pari materia with the Preamble, that We The People, as well as the State governments

that We elect to represent us, retain all powers not specifically enumerated by us in the U.S. Constitution; and

§4 WHEREAS, the Grand Jury, along with the Militia, are the two ancient and pre-constitutional institutions intended and stipulated by the U.S. Constitution to maintain our rule of law and to 'execute' that and all other laws in our Republic; and

§5 WHEREAS, if our State enacts any statute that violates or is repugnant to the U.S. Constitution, that State law is null and void ab initio; and

§6 WHEREAS, no State legislature can sideline or outlaw the Grand Jury institution or impair its functionality, as it remains an independent institution of the People, pre-dating the U.S. Constitution but demanded thereby; and

§7 WHEREAS, Rule 6(a)(1) of the Federal Rules of Criminal Procedure stipulates, "When the public interest so requires, the court must order that one or more grand juries be summoned."; and

§8 WHEREAS, in times of corruption and lack of public confidence, the public must be the sole determinant of its own interest rather than public employees deciding what is the public interest; and

§9 WHEREAS, different county and state governments observe a variety of protocols allowing or disallowing the citizens to place their names on a volunteer roster for Grand Jury service;

Article II. Ordered

§1 NOW, THEREFORE, BE IT RESOLVED, that the [Board, Commission,] *of* _____ [County, Parish or Borough] *hereby orders that within this jurisdiction, any citizen and resident who has not been convicted of a felony and who applies to be placed on a standby roster for Grand Jury duty, shall be placed on that roster by the county clerk; and*

§2 For any given occasion requiring seating of a Grand Jury, all names on the volunteer standby roster shall be added to any other list used as a source of names for random jury selection, and from this aggregated list Grand Jurors shall be selected truly at random, in no particular order nor assigned to any particular case or Grand Jury target; and

§3 Each random selection session of Grand Jurors by county clerk staff shall be witnessed in person by a three-member committee of this governing body to assure that the process is uncorrupted by any staffer or potential Grand Jury target or the target's minions, contractors, or associates; and

§4 If any judge in our jurisdiction shall refuse to call for a Grand Jury venire when demanded by petition signed by a number of County residents equal to or greater than half of one percent of the number of ballots cast in the prior county election, this representative body shall seek from the State Court of Appeals or Supreme Court a writ of mandamus compelling drawing of a venire, or the appointment of an alternate judge to call for such Grand Jury to grant relief to the community; and

§5 The County shall make a page or pages available on its web site or prominently post there links, for County Grand Jury education, information, volunteer application with the County Clerk, and for Citizens to submit legitimate complaints of possible crimes, and calls for a Grand Jury if a panel is not sitting at that time.

Article III. Miscellaneous Provisions

§1 SEVERABILITY. If any section, part or provision of this Ordinance is declared unconstitutional or invalid by a court of competent jurisdiction, then it is expressly provided and it is the intention of the [name of county board or commission] in passing this Ordinance that its parts shall be severable and all other parts of this Ordinance shall not be affected thereby and they shall remain in full force and effect.

§2 EFFECTIVE DATE. This Ordinance shall take effect immediately upon its passage.

ORDAINED *by the* [name of county board or commission] *of* [fill in] [COUNTY, PARISH OR BOROUGH], [fill in STATE], *this* _____ *Day of* [month] *in the Year of our Lord 20____*

_____

[Board/Commission Member]

_____

[Board/Commission Member]

_____

[Board/Commission Member]

_____

[Board/Commission Member]

_____

[Board/Commission Member]

An ORDINANCE SECURING THE U.S. CONSTITUTION and ESTABLISHING AND WELL-REGULATING MILITIA

in the County/Municipality

of_____, in the State

of_____

[Short Title, "Constitution Enforcement and Militia Ordinance"]

Preamble

We, the [name of county board or commission] *of* [fill in] [COUNTY, PARISH OR BOROUGH], [fill in STATE], *in pursuance of our oaths to uphold the Constitutions of our State and of the united States, and of our duty to our community under Divine Law, hereby establish our County as a Constitutional County, with the purpose of securing the fundamental and natural rights, powers, and authority of our Citizens, including but not limited to the right of self-defense, and defense of family and property, and hereby declare and exercise our right, authority and duty to restore and perpetually maintain the Constitutional Militia within this* [County, Parish or Borough], *for all purposes of Militia as stipulated by the People themselves in the United States Constitution.*

Article I. Justification

§1 WHEREAS, in the preamble to the Constitution for the united States, the American People declare that, "We The People…do ordain and establish this Constitution", thus clearly establishing that The People collectively occupy the highest sovereignty over all American government; and

§2 WHEREAS, the United States supreme Court in Chisolm v. Georgia, U.S. 2 Dall 419, 454 (1793), affirmed that, "The People are Sovereign…at the Revolution, the sovereignty devolved on the people; and they are truly the sovereigns of the country…equal as fellow citizens, and as joint tenants in the sovereignty"; and

§3 WHEREAS, when the Declaration of Independence, recognized in American jurisprudence as Organic Law of this republic, recounting crimes of King George III, stated that, "He has dissolved Representative Houses repeatedly…whereby **the Legislative powers, incapable of Annihilation, have returned to the People at large for their exercise",** *the American People collectively established that powers delegated by the People return to them, when the servant body to which they have been delegated abdicates, neglects, or refuses their proper exercise; and*

159

§4 WHEREAS, the Virginia Resolution of 1798 states, "in case of a deliberate, palpable, and dangerous exercise of other powers, not granted by the [Constitution], the States who are parties thereto, have the right, and are in duty bound, to interpose for arresting the progress of the evil, and for maintaining within their respective limits, the authorities, rights and liberties appertaining to them"; and

§5 WHEREAS, the United States supreme Court in Printz v. United States, 521 U.S. 898 (1997), affirmed that, "The Constitution thus contemplates that a State's government will represent and remain accountable to its own Citizens" and quoting James Madison, "[T]he local or municipal authorities form distinct and independent portions of the supremacy, no more subject, within their respective spheres, to the general authority than the general authority is subject to them, within its own sphere" and further affirmed that, "This separation of the two spheres is one of the Constitution's structural protections of liberty"; and

§6 WHEREAS, in the same case, the United States supreme Court concluded, "The federal government may neither issue directives requiring the States to address particular problems, nor command the States' officers, or those of their political subdivisions, to administer or enforce a federal regulatory program…such commands are fundamentally incompatible with our constitutional system of dual sovereignty" – which applies as surely to the county/state relationship as to the state/federal; and

§7 WHEREAS, the Second Amendment of the United States Constitution reads "A well regulated Militia, being necessary to the security of a free State, the right of the people to keep and bear Arms, shall not be infringed"; and

§8 WHEREAS, the United States supreme Court in United States v. Miller, 307 U.S. 174 (1939), affirmed that firearms which are part of ordinary military equipment, or with uses that could contribute to the common defense, are protected by the Second Amendment; and

§9 WHEREAS, the United States supreme Court in District of Columbia v. Heller, 554 U.S. 570 (2008), affirmed the individual's right to possess firearms, unconnected with service in a militia, for traditionally lawful purposes such as self-defense within the home; and

§10 WHEREAS, the United States supreme Court in McDonald v. Chicago, 561 U.S. 742 (2010), affirmed that the right of an individual to "keep and bear arms," as protected under the Second Amendment, is incorporated by the Due Process Clause of the Fourteenth Amendment against the States; and

§11 WHEREAS, Article [fill in], *Section* [fill in] *of the Constitution of* [STATE] *affirms,* [fill in actual language such as, "A person has the right to keep and bear arms for the defense of self, family, home and state, and for lawful hunting and recreational use"]; *and*

§12 WHEREAS, certain legislation which has been or may be enacted by the legislature of this State, and which has been or may be enacted by the United States Congress, may infringe on the right, duty and authority of law-abiding Citizens to keep and bear arms to fulfill their duty stipulated in Article I, Section 8, Clause 15 of the United States Constitution and Article [fill in], *Section* [fill in] *of the Constitution of* [fill in STATE]; *and*

§13 WHEREAS, any 'red flag' 'ERPO' or similar process violates the Second, Fourth, Fifth, Sixth and Fourteenth Amendments of the U.S. Constitution; and

§14 WHEREAS, the [Board, Commission] *of* _____ [County, Parish, Borough] *believes that the legitimate and justifying role of government is to secure the rights to life, liberty and property of the People as articulated in our Declaration of Independence; and*

§15 Whereas, the Congress of the United States and the Governor and Legislature of [State] *have for too long utterly neglected their Constitutional duties in support of Militia; and*

§16 WHEREAS, within its jurisdictional boundaries, the [County, Parish or Borough] [Board, Commission] *is the most efficient and lawful body to which this power and duty, incapable of Annihilation, shall have returned for its exercise,*

§17 IN ORDER to secure its Citizens' authority and duty to possess the means of self-defense and other unalienable rights, and to execute its essential and indispensable duty to organize and regulate Militia for the same and related purposes, and to honor its oath to uphold the Constitutions of this State and of the united States,

Article II. Ordered

§1 NOW, THEREFORE, BE IT RESOLVED, that the [Board, Commission,] *of* _____ [County, Parish or Borough] *hereby expresses its intent to perform within our jurisdiction the abdicated duties required of the State as stipulated by We The People in Article I, Section 8, Clause 16 and in the Second Amendment, and our intent to oppose by all lawful means any enactment that may unconstitutionally infringe the rights of its Citizens to keep and bear arms; and that*

§2 The [Board, Commission] *of* _____
[County, Parish or Borough] *hereby ORDERS that NO public funds under its control, nor time of employees, nor physical property and equipment of the* [County, Parish or Borough] *may be used to restrict or infringe Constitutional Rights, including the Second Amendment rights of our Citizens, or to aid or cooperate with federal, state, or other agencies in any such restriction or infringement of said rights; any County employee cooperating in such infringement being subject to dismissal; and that*

§3 The [Board, Commission] *of* _____
[County, Parish or Borough] *hereby ORDERS that its human and material resources SHALL be applied as necessary to oppose, resist, obstruct, and interpose against any infringement on the authority and duty of its Citizens, including the authority and duty to keep and bear arms in Militia and the right to keep and bear arms for personal and home defense, using such legal means as are recognized and expedient to deter, prevent and obstruct any other crime, including but not limited to court action, with failure of any County employee to do so within the scope of her/his employment being grounds for dismissal; and that*

§4 Searches and Seizures of Firearms and other Militia Accoutrements Under 'Red Flag' Laws.

To secure the guaranteed due process and other rights of County residents, NO search for or seizure of a citizen's firearms, ammunition, Militia accoutrements and/or related personal property, under any 'red flag', 'ERPO' or similar purported law, enactment, or regulation shall be allowed to proceed in the County. Any complaint, application, or process intended to result in such an order or action, shall be immediately transmitted to the Grand Jury for investigation of all parties and witnesses named or participating therein. If no Grand Jury is sitting, one shall immediately be impaneled for the purpose, and the information transmitted thereto; and that

§5 The [Board, Commission,] *of* _____
[County, Parish or Borough] *hereby establishes that it shall be an offense to make a complaint under any "red flag", "ERPO" or similar law or purported law alleging a danger that cannot be proven beyond reasonable doubt to exist, with each such offense punishable by a fine of no less than $1,000 or one year in jail, or both. If any trespass or seizure has taken place as a result of such unprovable complaint, in addition to the specified fine or imprisonment, the individual or entity that filed the complaint leading to the 'red flag' action ('Complainant') shall within 30 days of notice pay to the Court its stipulated reimbursement to Target for all costs arising from the Action ('Damages'), including but not limited to a) Target's*

demonstrated loss of earnings; b) All of Target's property seized and not restored in like condition to that in which it was seized in the Action; c) any other damage to any of Target's property; and d) Attorneys' fees, court costs and all other costs demonstrably arising from the Action. If Complainant fails to pay the Damages within 60 days from date of notice by the Court, Damages are hereby statutorily tripled and the County Grand Jury and Militia shall seize, in ex parte action, all such property of Complainant as required to satisfy the Court's stipulated Damages payable to Target; and that

§6 The [Board, Commission] *of* _____
[County, Parish, Borough] *hereby establishes its Constitutional Militia, to include all County Citizens without criminal records or history of adjudicated mental incompetence, who are willing and able to aid in defending this community and upholding the Law; and that*

§7 The [Board, Commission] *of* _____
[County, Parish or Borough] *shall provide in the most timely way possible and in no case later than sixty (60) days from the date hereof, for the necessary staffing and public funding to restore the Militia in this County, during any and all such periods as the State Legislature shall continue in abdication and/or violation of duty as stipulated in Article I, Section 8, Clause 16 of the Constitution for the United States; and that*

§8 The [Board, Commission] *of* _____ [County, Parish or Borough] *shall administer and regulate its County Militia as follows:*

1. Nomination and Appointment of Officers.

This Body shall appoint officers nominated by their respective units and according to a uniform command structure mutually agreed on by all units in the County. Said power of appointment of officers shall revert to the State Governor during all such times as the State Legislature has ceased its abdication or avoidance of its constitutional duty for the same.

No nominee may have been convicted of a felony in any State, or may have been adjudicated mentally incompetent, or be regularly taking any drugs proven to be mentally incapacitating, and all officers must take an oath to uphold, defend, and enforce the Constitutions of this State and of the united States and all laws made in pursuance thereof, before entering upon their official duties.

2. [County, Parish or Borough] Militia Liaison and Coordination.

All units of County Militia must choose and report one officer from among all of them to serve as County Militia Liaison Officer, and one to serve in the incapacity of the first. Duties of the County Militia Liaison Officer shall be to coordinate operations among the several units, to coordinate operations with Militias of other jurisdictions and with paid law enforcement agencies, and to coordinate with the State at all times during which the State is performing its duties for constitutional Militia as stipulated by the People in the Constitution.

The County Militia Liaison Officer shall report to this Board/Commission on all Militia activities within the County and involving County Militia units, when requested by this Board/Commission.

3. Minimum Standards of Mental and Physical Fitness.

Uniform minimum standards of mental and physical fitness shall be adopted and updated as necessary by all militia units in the County; shall include freedom from any adjudication of mental incompetence, freedom from drugs proven to be mentally incapacitating, and the taking of an oath to uphold defend and enforce the Constitutions of this State and of the united States and all laws made in pursuance thereof, prior to the individual entering upon official duties, and shall be reported to this Board/Commission.

4. Arms, Ammunition and Accoutrements.

Citizens shall provide their own firearms, ammunition and tactical accoutrements, meeting uniform standards adopted by all County Militia units, and keep them in good repair. However, as funds allow, the County may provide ammunition and other equipment.

5. County Militia Training.

A uniform, minimum mandatory training program and schedule for new recruits and for existing members shall be adopted and updated as necessary by all County Militia units, and shall be reported to this Board/Commission.

6. Coordination and Cooperation With Paid Public Peace Officers.

All County Militia units shall cooperate and coordinate with existing paid municipal, County, and State public peace officers, upon the official request of these agencies, made through the County Militia Liaison Officer.

However, County Militia shall be responsible to the Citizens of the County and to the Constitutions of this State and of the united States, and shall NOT cooperate in, or permit, the enforcement of any enactment or supposed law which is null by reason of its conflict with the natural rights of Citizens or with the Constitutions of this State or of the united States. In _Marbury v. Madison (1803)_ the U.S. Supreme Court affirmed that "(a) Law repugnant to the Constitution is void."

7. Minimum Standards of Personal Grooming and Respectful Public Behavior.

Uniform minimum standards of personal grooming and respectful public behavior for Militia members shall be adopted and updated as necessary by all militia units in the County, to protect the effectiveness of members and promote public confidence in our Militia. Excessive or inappropriate use of coarse language and display of symbols associated with death, lawlessness, rebellion, or wanton violence shall not be permitted.

8. Law Enforcement Duty Coordinated With and Directed by Grand Jury.

Especially in cases in which one or more members of paid public law enforcement or other public officials are being investigated by the Grand Jury, law enforcement duty including but not limited to collection of evidence and service of search and arrest warrants, shall be a core function of this Militia, as coordinated with, and directed by, the Grand Jury of this [County, Parish or Borough].

9. Grand Jury Anonymity.

Uniform protocols shall be adopted by all County Militia units to protect and preserve anonymity of subjects of investigation and of members of the Grand Jury, particularly in investigations of public officials or paid law enforcement personnel or agencies.

10. Removals for Cause.

Violation by any Militia member or officer of his or her Oath to defend and enforce the Constitutions of this State and of the united States and all laws made in pursuance thereof, shall be punishable by removal from membership or office.

11. SEVERABILITY If any section, part or provision of this Ordinance is

declared unconstitutional or invalid by a court of competent jurisdiction, then it is expressly provided and it is the intention of the [name of county board or commission] in passing this Ordinance that its parts shall be severable and all other parts of this Ordinance shall not be affected thereby and they shall remain in full force and effect.

12. EFFECTIVE DATE. This Ordinance shall take effect immediately upon

its passage.

ORDAINED *by the* [name of county board or commission] *of* [fill in] [COUNTY, PARISH OR BOROUGH], [fill in STATE], *this* _____ *Day of* [month] *in the Year of our Lord 20*____

_____

[Board/Commission Member]

_____

[Board/Commission Member]

_____

[Board/Commission Member]

_____

[Board/Commission Member]

_____

[Board/Commission Member]

_____

[Board/Commission Member]

_____

[Board/Commission Member]

APPENDIX E

Follow the Money

The FED is a crime cartel.

Most conscientious Americans know this or at least sense it, and many books describe that operation and its history in detail. But many people still believe that the 'federal reserve' cartel of bankers is part of federal government, because congress and its counterfeiting outsourcing cartel commit fraud every day against the American People. Let me explain the fraud; it's much larger than any other felony fraud operation. In any country. In any age.

Defraud the Boss; He'll Never Notice

Textbook fraud: the FED cartel of banks came up with a very 'governmenty'-sounding name, and created a seal that appears to be that of a federal government agency, to print on its worthless paper slips. Textbook counterfeiting: they foist them on the American People in place of lawful (silver) U.S. dollars, *which are defined in our oldest federal law on money, and demanded by us, specifically, in the Constitution, our highest law.*

It should be a felony crime to thus impersonate a federal agency and defraud the citizens for *trillions* of dollars. But it's not, because the servants who we charge with writing federal laws *designed* the conspiracy and bankers have incredible clout in society. When congress wrote the 'law' creating the cartel, since it violates the U.S. Constitution, the Federal Reserve Act was never law in the first place: *'All laws which are repugnant to the Constitution are null and void.' Marbury vs. Madison, 5 US (2 Cranch) 137, 174, 176, (1803)*

This chapter will tell the back story in brief. Pastors in America should know this history; it's massively important.

First, They Needed a Distraction

Wars are always bonanzas for bankers; they create crises that predators and parasites can glom on to. The runaway collapse of the worthless paper 'Continental dollar' (inflation) after our War of Independence caused the delegates at the Constitutional Convention to have We The People grant *only* to congress the power to *only coin* money, *not* any more worthless paper: *'To coin Money, regulate the Value thereof...' (Article I, Section 8, Clause 5, US Constitution).*

The State Legislatures, Too

They put the same limit on the newly-independent, sovereign State governments that were printing paper bills and calling it money, too. The delegates had to bite the bullet and end the essentially criminal practice of runaway inflation by printing worthless papers and making their citizens honor it as money. This was anything but popular, because the shortage of silver specie and bullion at the time had farmers, merchants and of course speculators, short of funds with which to do their business.

But if potential crooks in congress couldn't counterfeit, the delegates reasoned, then neither could potential crooks in State legislatures, who were under great pressure from many demographic groups. So they added in the gold and silver clause, to end the flood of worthless 'bills of credit'...

'No State shall...coin Money, emit Bills of Credit; make any Thing but gold and silver Coin a Tender in Payment of Debts'. (Article I, Section 10, Clause 2, US Constitution).

In 1789, the States ratified the Constitution and it became our highest law, binding on all governments including the federal one that We The People created with the new law, and the State ones who were just as likely to be corrupted by bad men with big ideas. Like how to steal silver and give paper in return...and make it the law that the People must accept the crime!

Paper is illegal 'money'; rather, it is NOT *lawful money and has never been lawful money under our Constitution.*

Congress Once Was Honest

In 1792, congress passed the Coinage Act, of which Section 9 authorized the production of various coins...

'Dollars or Units—each to be of the value of a Spanish milled dollar as the same is now current, and to contain three hundred and seventy-one grains and four sixteenth parts of a grain of pure, or four hundred and sixteen grains of standard silver.'

168

Section 20 of the Act designates the United States dollar as the unit of currency of the United States...

'[T]he money of account of the United States shall be expressed in dollars, or units…and that all accounts in the public offices and all proceedings in the courts of the United States shall be kept and had in conformity to this regulation.'

That definition of a U.S. dollar has never changed. *And Section 19 of the Act established* **the death penalty** *for debasing the gold or silver coins authorized by the Act.*

For a while, America reverted to lawful, true money: gold and especially silver (you see that the only constitutional definition of a U.S. Dollar is a specified weight of silver).

Andrew Jackson had been able in the 1830s to beat back the Second Bank of the U.S., but he was not able to end the openly criminal counterfeiting operations of congress, protected after Lincoln's war by the corrupt SCOTUS.

Another Deadly Distraction

However, those bankers are shrewd, and many predators used Lincoln's war to bifurcate the American People into two equal, eternally-warring halves while they could increase their plunder and the People would be powerless to respond.

After the devastation of that *War to Enslave the States* (the only proper label for that war) in a series of preposterous opinions openly violating the Constitution, collectively known as the Legal Tender cases, the U.S. supreme court became an open, cynical co-conspirator. In the last such case, *Juilliard v. Greenman,* SCOTUS essentially ruled the Constitution void, and its opinions now the law of our land.

Finally in 1913, the banking families had their henchmen meet on Jekyll Island, Georgia and with several deeply corrupt senators fronting the deal, congress turned over its counterfeiting operations to the new FED cartel. We describe that crime in our documentary video, *AmericaAgain!- The Movie,* and of course there are a plethora of books, videos, papers, blog articles, and podcasts exposing that massive financial crime.

Death...and Taxes

The other half of congress' largest financial crime was evil genius. Since counterfeit paper 'dollars' would again lead to runaway inflation as it always did before, in 1913, the criminals in congress pushed through the 16th Amendment, creating the lawless monster that I expose in my book *A Tax Honesty Primer.*

You see, each year, congress siphons almost $4 TRILLION off of the American economy, with about half of that coming from individual payroll accounts. This sops up the excess liquidity that would accrue from printing all those fake 'dollars' (federal reserve paper notes), keeping inflation at bay.

We Have the Antidote

As you know, at Tactical Civics™, we teach this real history and economics and Constitution to adults and youth (see our 30-week tutorial for homeschoolers, suitable for ages 15 and up, or for adults). This article, however, is a vital issue that we forgot to include in the First Edition tutorial; it will be included in the Second Edition.

Even better news: Tactical Civics™ has a detailed reform law (Reform Law #18 in the AmericaAgain! Declaration) to end this largest, longest financial crime in world history. That reform law was drafted by Dr. Edwin Vieira, the foremost authority on the history of the U.S. Dollar.

His 2-volume, 1600-page work, *Pieces of Eight: The Monetary Powers and Disabilities of the United States Constitution,* is the most detailed, definitive history of our money but it does have a misleading title. The title refers to the powers that We The People grant to congress for our money, and the disabilities we impose on them, against counterfeiting. But as everyone knows, they counterfeit our money anyway.

Our proposed reform law speaks of transitioning back to a silver U.S. dollar, and some people immediately respond, "But there's not enough silver!" because they do not know the story of how the U.S. military captured over 288,000 metric tons of gold in World War II from Japan (Yamashita's gold) and Germany (the Black Eagle gold) and the U.S. government (or possibly the thieves at the FED?) are still holding that gold, which is worth over *$17 trillion* at today's market price. In our <u>Sunday night podcast of November 11, 2018</u> (just click on those words for the link) we told that story, and explained how it was the reason for the 9/11 operation. Mystery solved. One more mega-crime for D.C.; nothing new.

170

If we (gradually) monetize it and convert it to silver dollar, $5, $10 and $20 coins, and keep some of the gold for $50 and $100 coins, we will have the most valuable, stable money in the world. This was true of gold bezants, that became standard money accepted worldwide for almost five centuries.

So! The bad guys are in control for now; evil is enjoying its last days in the dark and thousands of billionaires and millions of bureaucrats are teaching their children and grandchildren to follow their lead. The only antidote is truth and rule of law. And that means **repentance**...the detailed, full-spectrum mission of Tactical Civics™.

Bancroft's Plea, and Mine

The George Bancroft essay *A Plea for the Constitution of the United States, Wounded in the House of Its Guardians* is one of those works of American history that is never mentioned or taught in schools, colleges, or law schools. For obvious reasons; it is a (supposedly) scathing indictment of congress, for openly counterfeiting the U.S. dollar using worthless paper.

If you read it, keep Tactical Civics™ in mind. I should hope that even our 11th grade homeschool readers of our High School text should be able to find the hole in Mr. Bancroft's goblet, from the stream of pearl-twisting nonsense pouring out.

The Hole in the Goblet

I can't take a thing away from Mr. Bancroft as an historian. But I think perhaps historians should not write treatises on constitutional law.

Set aside Bancroft's far-too-deferential view of congress throughout the pamphlet, and just note the *title* he gave it. Give the man an A+ for evocative articulation, but he refers to congress as the *guardians* of the Constitution? We The People not only clearly stipulate that *we* are its guardians, but I find it impossible to believe that George Bancroft, the most noted writer of American history of his generation, could not comprehend the plain words of Article I of that law, wherein We The People *create* congress, *define* it, and *severely limit* its powers.

I discovered the same lacuna in another renowned historian, Edmund S. Morgan. In his floridly-written, historically accurate, thoroughly confused book, *Inventing the People,* the renowned atheist historian could not find the constitutional law handle on *'We The People...do ordain...',* so he spent hundreds of pages in circumlocution, arriving at an hypothesis that 'We The People' is just a useless turn of phrase.

I've written many times about the book *American Sovereigns* by UNM Law School professor Christian Fritz, who comes to substantially the same conclusion by simply asking the wrong question for 425 pages. He surveys three historic occasions when mobs *demanded changes* in the Constitution; but never an occasion where the People simply *enforced* it. He clearly states, many times, that we have the *authority* to do so; but as he admits, he can't think of *how* we can do so.

Chisel Off the Nonsense (See Chisolm)

I don't know about you, but as I read the Constitution, I instantly see that *We The People* is the term for *the creator party* of the Constitution. It's right there in black letters, the opening three words.

Then in Article VI, Section 2 of our highest law, we stipulate in plain language that this law will be America's highest law over all others (supreme Law of the Land). Finally, in Amendments IX and X, the People lash everything down tight, saying that *we reserve to ourselves every power you can imagine*, that we didn't delegate to the servants in this Law.

Saints, America's highest law is not difficult to read. And it's not a joke; yet, it's being treated like toilet paper by our arrogant, lawless servants. Our generation needs to start the maturation process; start acting like the *Enforcers and Guardians* of this law, which we are!

It's in the black-letter Constitution: *We The People are the collective sovereign of this government.* This most elementary fact of constitutional law was first acknowledged to the world by chief justice John Jay in *Chisolm v. Georgia* (1793), the first great constitutional case decided by the supreme court. That case addressed the most fundamental question in American civics: *Who is sovereign, the People or the State?* The *Chisolm* court denied that the State of Georgia was a sovereign, entitled like a king to assert immunity from a lawsuit brought by a citizen. Chief justice Jay ruled that in our constitutional system, *sovereignty inheres only in The People.*

Of course, we don't need a judge to tell us that; I reiterate that We The People stipulate it in plain English, at an 8th grade comprehension level. As former Stanford Law dean Larry Kramer explained on page 248 of his masterful book *The People Themselves: "The supreme court is not the highest authority in the land on constitutional law. We are."*

172

In Times of Deceit, Honesty Looks Like Brilliance

So you see that unlike historians, at least a very few law professors get it. Here's another one, Randy Barnett at Georgetown Law School, who opined years ago:

"Chisholm is not among the canon of cases that all law students are taught. Why not? ...Constitutional law is taught by doctrine rather than chronologically...law professors follow the lead of the Supreme Court and...the Supreme Court has deemed its first great decision too radical in its implications."

In the inbred, overpopulated demographic of self-referencing, self-adulating mechanics of mendacity – courts, judges, law schools, all the lawyers who populate them, and all those who serve the lawyers – the rare honest ones among them bemoan 'the corrupt system' but they offer no solutions.

So on our original subject, America's counterfeit money, we come full circle, back to the criminals who are *supposed* to make laws but have been *violating* our *highest* law instead, counterfeiting our 'money' for 160 years and siphoning off the inflation threat by skimming America's payroll accounts through the IRS state-sponsored terror agency.

Apparently, historians and professors of law can't (won't dare?) figure out how to end all this criminality. But We The People, serving on our county Grand Juries, can show them how it's done; in fact, *it was always our job to do so.*

Let us pray – no; more than that, *let us work* – to hasten the day that we return to our chores.

APPENDIX F

Declaration of Independence

The Declaration of Independence as finally edited by Congress from Thomas Jefferson's draft, appeared on July 8, 1776 in The Pennsylvania Packet, a weekly newspaper.

The Unanimous Declaration of the Thirteen United States of America

When, in the course of human events, it becomes necessary for one people to dissolve the political bands which have connected them with another, and to assume among the powers of the earth, the separate and equal station to which the laws of nature and of nature's God entitle them, a decent respect to the opinions of mankind requires that they should declare the causes which impel them to the separation.

We hold these truths to be self-evident, that all men are created equal, that they are endowed by their Creator with certain unalienable rights, that among these are life, liberty and the pursuit of happiness. That to secure these rights, governments are instituted among men, deriving their just powers from the consent of the governed. That whenever any form of government becomes destructive to these ends, it is the right of the people to alter or to abolish it, and to institute new government, laying its foundation on such principles and organizing its powers in such form, as to them shall seem most likely to effect their safety and happiness.

Prudence, indeed, will dictate that governments long established should not be changed for light and transient causes; and accordingly all experience hath shown that mankind are more disposed to suffer, while evils are sufferable, than to right themselves by abolishing the forms to which they are accustomed. But when a long train of abuses and usurpations, pursuing invariably the same object evinces a design to reduce them under absolute despotism, it is their right, it is their duty, to throw off such government, and to provide new guards for their future security. –Such has been the patient sufferance of these colonies;

and such is now the necessity which constrains them to alter their former systems of government. The history of the present King of Great Britain is a history of repeated injuries and usurpations, all having in direct object the establishment of an absolute tyranny over these states. To prove this, let facts be submitted to a candid world.

He has refused his assent to laws, the most wholesome and necessary for the public good.

He has forbidden his governors to pass laws of immediate and pressing importance, unless suspended in their operation till his assent should be obtained; and when so suspended, he has utterly neglected to attend to them.

He has refused to pass other laws for the accommodation of large districts of people, unless those people would relinquish the right of representation in the legislature, a right inestimable to them and formidable to tyrants only.

He has called together legislative bodies at places unusual, uncomfortable, and distant from the depository of their public records, for the sole purpose of fatiguing them into compliance with his measures.

He has dissolved representative houses repeatedly, for opposing with manly firmness his invasions on the rights of the people.

He has refused for a long time, after such dissolutions, to cause others to be elected; whereby the legislative powers, incapable of annihilation, have returned to the people at large for their exercise; the state remaining in the meantime exposed to all the dangers of invasion from without, and convulsions within.

He has endeavored to prevent the population of these states; for that purpose obstructing the laws for naturalization of foreigners; refusing to pass others to encourage their migration hither, and raising the conditions of new appropriations of lands.

He has obstructed the administration of justice, by refusing his assent to laws for establishing judiciary powers.

He has made judges dependent on his will alone, for the tenure of their offices, and the amount and payment of their salaries.

He has erected a multitude of new offices, and sent hither swarms of officers to harass our people, and eat out their substance.

He has kept among us, in times of peace, standing armies without the consent of our legislature.

He has affected to render the military independent of and superior to civil power.

He has combined with others to subject us to a jurisdiction foreign to our constitution, and unacknowledged by our laws; giving his assent to their acts of pretended legislation:

For quartering large bodies of armed troops among us:

For protecting them, by mock trial, from punishment for any murders which they should commit on the inhabitants of these states:

For cutting off our trade with all parts of the world:

For imposing taxes on us without our consent:

For depriving us in many cases, of the benefits of trial by jury:

For transporting us beyond seas to be tried for pretended offenses:

For abolishing the free system of English laws in a neigh-boring province, establishing therein an arbitrary government, and enlarging its boundaries so as to render it at once an example and fit instrument for introducing the same absolute rule in these colonies:

For taking away our charters, abolishing our most valuable laws, and altering fundamentally the forms of our governments:

For suspending our own legislatures, and declaring them-selves invested with power to legislate for us in all cases whatsoever.

He has abdicated government here, by declaring us out of his protection and waging war against us.

He has plundered our seas, ravaged our coasts, burned our towns, and destroyed the lives of our people.

He is at this time transporting large armies of foreign mercenaries to complete the works of death, desolation and tyranny, already begun with circumstances of cruelty and perfidy scarcely paralleled in the most barbarous ages, and totally unworthy the head of a civilized nation.

He has constrained our fellow citizens taken captive on the high seas to bear arms against their country, to become the executioners of their friends and brethren, or to fall themselves by their hands.

He has excited domestic insurrections amongst us, and has endeavored to bring on the inhabitants of our frontiers, the merciless Indian savages, whose known rule of warfare, is undistinguished destruction of all ages, sexes and conditions.

In every stage of these oppressions we have petitioned for redress in the most humble terms: our repeated petitions have been answered only by repeated injury. A prince, whose character is thus marked by every act which may define a tyrant, is unfit to be the ruler of a free people.

Nor have we been wanting in attention to our British brethren. We have warned them from time to time of attempts by their legislature to extend an unwarrantable jurisdiction over us. We have reminded them of the circumstances of our emigration and settlement here. We have appealed to their native justice and magnanimity, and we have conjured them by the ties of our common kindred to disavow these usurpations, which, would inevitably interrupt our connections and correspondence. They too have been deaf to the voice of justice and of consanguinity. We must, therefore, acquiesce in the necessity, which denounces our separation, and hold them, as we hold the rest of mankind, enemies in war, in peace friends.

We, therefore, the representatives of the United States of America, in General Congress, assembled, appealing to the Supreme Judge of the world for the rectitude of our intentions, do, in the name, and by the authority of the good people of these colonies, solemnly publish and declare, that these united colonies are, and of right ought to be free and independent states; that they are absolved from all allegiance to the British Crown, and that all political connection between them and the state of Great Britain, is and ought to be totally dissolved; and that as free and independent states, they have full power to levy war, conclude peace, contract alliances, establish commerce, and to do all other acts and things which independent states may of right do. And for the support of this declaration, with a firm reliance on the protection of Divine Providence, we mutually pledge to each other our lives, our fortunes and our sacred honor.

New Hampshire: Josiah Bartlett, William Whipple, Matthew Thornton

Massachusetts: John Hancock, Samuel Adams, John Adams, Robert Treat Paine, Elbridge Gerry

Rhode Island: Stephen Hopkins, William Ellery

Connecticut: Roger Sherman, Samuel Huntington, William Williams, Oliver Wolcott

New York: William Floyd, Philip Livingston, Francis Lewis, Lewis Morris

New Jersey: Richard Stockton, John Witherspoon, Francis Hopkinson, John Hart, Abraham Clark

Pennsylvania: Robert Morris, Benjamin Rush, Benjamin Franklin, John Morton, George Clymer, James Smith, George Taylor, James Wilson, George Ross

Delaware: Caesar Rodney, George Read, Thomas McKean

Maryland: Samuel Chase, William Paca, Thomas Stone, Charles Carroll of Carrollton

Virginia: George Wythe, Richard Henry Lee, Thomas Jefferson, Benjamin Harrison, Thomas Nelson, Jr., Francis Lightfoot Lee, Carter Braxton

North Carolina: William Hooper, Joseph Hewes, John Penn

South Carolina: Edward Rutledge, Thomas Heyward, Jr., Thomas Lynch, Jr., Arthur Middleton

Georgia: Button Gwinnett, Lyman Hall, George Walton

APPENDIX G

Constitution *for* the United States

*This edition of the Constitution contains the exact language of the original, including archaic spellings. For ease of reference, we have added an indexing system, appearing before each clause in bold numerals. For instance, Article I, Section 8, Clause 15 reads, "**1.8.15** To provide for calling forth the Militia to execute the Laws of the Union, suppress Insurrections and repel Invasions". This system allows the citizen to quickly reference and more easily memorize the Constitution.*

We the People of the United States, in Order to form a more perfect Union, establish Justice, insure domestic Tranquility, provide for the common defence, promote the general Welfare, and secure the Blessings of Liberty to ourselves and our Posterity, do ordain and establish this Constitution for the United States of America.

Article I

Section 1

All legislative Powers herein granted shall be vested in a Congress of the United States, which shall consist of a Senate and House of Representatives.

Section 2

1.2.1 The House of Representatives shall be composed of Members chosen every second Year by the People of the

several States, and the Electors in each State shall have the Qualifications requisite for Electors of the most numerous Branch of the State Legislature.

1.2.2 No Person shall be a Representative who shall not have attained to the Age of twenty five Years, and been seven Years a Citizen of the United States, and who shall not, when elected, be an Inhabitant of that State in which he shall be chosen.

1.2.3 Representatives and direct Taxes shall be apportioned among the several States which may be included within this Union, according to their respective Numbers, which shall be determined by adding to the whole Number of free Persons, including those bound to Service for a Term of Years, and excluding Indians not taxed, three fifths of all other Persons.

1.2.4 The actual Enumeration shall be made within three Years after the first Meeting of the Congress of the United States, and within every subsequent Term of ten Years, in such Manner as they shall by Law direct. The Number of Representatives shall not exceed one for every thirty Thousand, but each State shall have at Least one Representative; and until such enumeration shall be made, the State of New Hampshire shall be entitled to chuse three, Massachusetts eight, Rhode-Island and Providence Plantations one, Connecticut five, New-York six, New Jersey four, Pennsylvania eight, Delaware one, Maryland six, Virginia ten, North Carolina five, South Carolina five, and Georgia three.

1.2.5 When vacancies happen in the Representation from any State, the Executive Authority thereof shall issue Writs of Election to fill such Vacancies.

1.2.6 The House of Representatives shall chuse their Speaker and other Officers; and shall have the sole Power of Impeachment.

Section 3

1.3.1 The Senate of the United States shall be composed of two Senators from each State, chosen by the Legislature thereof, for six Years; and each Senator shall have one Vote.

1.3.2 Immediately after they shall be assembled in Consequence of the first Election, they shall be divided as equally as may be into three Classes. The Seats of the Senators of the first Class shall be vacated at the Expiration of the second Year, of the second Class at the Expiration of the fourth Year, and of the third Class at the Expiration of the sixth Year, so that one third may be chosen every second Year;

1.3.3 and if Vacancies happen by Resignation, or otherwise, during the Recess of the Legislature of any State, the Executive thereof may make temporary Appointments until the next Meeting of the Legislature, which shall then fill such Vacancies.

1.3.4 No Person shall be a Senator who shall not have attained to the Age of thirty Years, and been nine Years a Citizen of the United States, and who shall not, when elected, be an Inhabitant of that State for which he shall be chosen.

1.3.5 The Vice President of the United States shall be President of the Senate, but shall have no Vote, unless they be equally divided.

1.3.6 The Senate shall chuse their other Officers, and also a President pro tempore, in the Absence of the Vice President, or when he shall exercise the Office of President of the United States.

1.3.7 The Senate shall have the sole Power to try all Impeachments. When sitting for that Purpose, they shall be on Oath or Affirmation. When the President of the United States is tried, the Chief Justice shall preside: And no Person shall be convicted without the Concurrence of two thirds of the Members present.

1.3.8 Judgment in Cases of Impeachment shall not extend further than to removal from Office, and disqualification to hold and enjoy any Office of honor, Trust or Profit under the United States: but the Party convicted shall nevertheless be liable and subject to Indictment, Trial, Judgment and Punishment, according to Law.

Section 4

1.4.1 The Times, Places and Manner of holding Elections for Senators and Representatives, shall be prescribed in each State by the Legislature thereof; but the Congress may at any time by Law make or alter such Regulations, except as to the Places of chusing Senators.

1.4.2 The Congress shall assemble at least once in every Year, and such Meeting shall be on the first Monday in December, unless they shall by Law appoint a different Day. [Changed; see 20th Amendment.]

Section 5

1.5.1 Each House shall be the Judge of the Elections, Returns and Qualifications of its own Members, and a Majority of each shall constitute a Quorum to do Business; but a smaller Number may adjourn from day to day, and may be authorized to compel the Attendance of absent Members, in such Manner, and under such Penalties as each House may provide.

1.5.2 Each House may determine the Rules of its Proceedings, punish its Members for disorderly Behaviour, and, with the Concurrence of two thirds, expel a Member.

1.5.3   Each House shall keep a Journal of its Proceedings, and from time to time publish the same, excepting such Parts as may in their Judgment require Secrecy; and the Yeas and Nays of the Members of either House on any question shall, at the Desire of one fifth of those Present, be entered on the Journal.

1.5.4   Neither House, during the Session of Congress, shall, without the Consent of the other, adjourn for more than three days, nor to any other Place than that in which the two Houses shall be sitting.

Section 6

1.6.1   The Senators and Representatives shall receive a Compensation for their Services, to be ascertained by Law, and paid out of the Treasury of the United States.

1.6.2   They shall in all Cases, except Treason, Felony and Breach of the Peace, be privileged from Arrest during their Attendance at the Session of their respective Houses, and in going to and returning from the same; and for any Speech or Debate in either House, they shall not be questioned in any other Place.

1.6.3   No Senator or Representative shall, during the Time for which he was elected, be appointed to any civil Office under the Authority of the United States, which shall have been created, or the Emoluments whereof shall have been encreased during such time; and no Person holding any Office under the United States, shall be a Member of either House during his Continuance in Office.

Section 7

1.7.1   All Bills for raising Revenue shall originate in the House of Representatives; but the Senate may propose or concur with Amendments as on other Bills.

1.7.2   Every Bill which shall have passed the House of Representatives and the Senate, shall, before it become a Law, be presented to the President of the United States; If he approve he shall sign it, but if not he shall return it, with his Objections to that House in which it shall have originated, who shall enter the Objections at large on their Journal, and proceed to reconsider it.

1.7.3   If after such Reconsideration two thirds of that House shall agree to pass the Bill, it shall be sent, together with the Objections, to the other House, by which it shall likewise be reconsidered, and if approved by two thirds of that House, it shall become a Law.

1.7.4 But in all such Cases the Votes of both Houses shall be determined by yeas and Nays, and the Names of the Persons voting for and against the Bill shall be entered on the Journal of each House respectively. If any Bill shall not be returned by the President within ten Days (Sundays excepted) after it shall have been presented to him, the Same shall be a Law, in like Manner as if he had signed it, unless the Congress by their Adjournment prevent its Return, in which Case it shall not be a Law.

1.7.5 Every Order, Resolution, or Vote to which the Concurrence of the Senate and House of Representatives may be necessary (except on a question of Adjournment) shall be presented to the President of the United States; and before the Same shall take Effect, shall be approved by him, or being disapproved by him, shall be repassed by two thirds of the Senate and House of Representatives, according to the Rules and Limitations prescribed in the Case of a Bill.

Section 8

1.8.1 The Congress shall have Power To lay and collect Taxes, Duties, Imposts and Excises, to pay the Debts and provide for the common Defence and general Welfare of the United States; but all Duties, Imposts and Excises shall be uniform throughout the United States;

1.8.2 To borrow Money on the credit of the United States;

1.8.3 To regulate Commerce with foreign Nations, and among the several States, and with the Indian Tribes;

1.8.4 To establish an uniform Rule of Naturalization, and uniform Laws on the subject of Bankruptcies throughout the United States;

1.8.5 To coin Money, regulate the Value thereof, and of foreign Coin, and fix the Standard of Weights and Measures;

1.8.6 To provide for the Punishment of counterfeiting the Securities and current Coin of the United States;

1.8.7 To establish Post Offices and post Roads;

1.8.8 To promote the Progress of Science and useful Arts, by securing for limited Times to Authors and Inventors the exclusive Right to their respective Writings and Discoveries;

1.8.9 To constitute Tribunals inferior to the supreme Court;

1.8.10 To define and punish Piracies and Felonies committed on the high Seas, and Offences against the Law of Nations;

1.8.11 To declare War, grant Letters of Marque and Reprisal, and make Rules concerning Captures on Land and Water;

1.8.12 To raise and support Armies, but no Appropriation of Money to that Use shall be for a longer Term than two Years;

1.8.13 To provide and maintain a Navy;

1.8.14 To make Rules for the Government and Regulation of the land and naval Forces;

1.8.15 To provide for calling forth the Militia to execute the Laws of the Union, suppress Insurrections and repel Invasions;

1.8.16 To provide for organizing, arming, and disciplining, the Militia, and for governing such Part of them as may be employed in the Service of the United States, reserving to the States respectively, the Appointment of the Officers, and the Authority of training the Militia according to the discipline prescribed by Congress;

1.8.17 To exercise exclusive Legislation in all Cases whatsoever, over such District (not exceeding ten Miles square) as may, by Cession of particular States, and the Acceptance of Congress, become the Seat of the Government of the United States, and to exercise like Authority over all Places purchased by the Consent of the Legislature of the State in which the Same shall be, for the Erection of Forts, Magazines, Arsenals, dock-Yards, and other needful Buildings;—And

1.8.18 To make all Laws which shall be necessary and proper for carrying into Execution the foregoing Powers, and all other Powers vested by this Constitution in the Government of the United States, or in any Department or Officer thereof.

Section 9

1.9.1 The Migration or Importation of such Persons as any of the States now existing shall think proper to admit, shall not be prohibited by the Congress prior to the Year one thousand eight hundred and eight, but a Tax or duty may be imposed on such Importation, not exceeding ten dollars for each Person. [Nullified; now obsolete.]

1.9.2 The Privilege of the Writ of Habeas Corpus shall not be suspended, unless when in Cases of Rebellion or Invasion the public Safety may require it.

1.9.3 No Bill of Attainder or ex post facto Law shall be passed.

1.9.4 No Capitation, or other direct, Tax shall be laid, unless in Proportion to the Census or enumeration herein before directed to be taken.

1.9.5 No Tax or Duty shall be laid on Articles exported from any State.

1.9.6 No Preference shall be given by any Regulation of Commerce or Revenue to the Ports of one State over those of another: nor shall Vessels bound to, or from, one State, be obliged to enter, clear, or pay Duties in another.

1.9.7 No Money shall be drawn from the Treasury, but in Consequence of Appropriations made by Law; and a regular Statement and Account of the Receipts and Expenditures of all public Money shall be published from time to time.

1.9.8 No Title of Nobility shall be granted by the United States: And no Person holding any Office of Profit or Trust under them, shall, without the Consent of the Congress, accept of any present, Emolument, Office, or Title, of any kind whatever, from any King, Prince, or foreign State.

Section 10

1.10.1 No State shall enter into any Treaty, Alliance, or Confederation; grant Letters of Marque and Reprisal;

1.10.2 coin Money; emit Bills of Credit; make any Thing but gold and silver Coin a Tender in Payment of Debts;

1.10.3 pass any Bill of Attainder, ex post facto Law,

1.10.4 or Law impairing the Obligation of Contracts, or grant any Title of Nobility.

1.10.5 No State shall, without the Consent of the Congress, lay any Imposts or Duties on Imports or Exports, except

what may be absolutely necessary for executing its inspection Laws: and the net Produce of all Duties and Imposts, laid by any State on Imports or Exports, shall be for the Use of the Treasury of the United States;

and all such Laws shall be subject to the Revision and Controul of the Congress.

1.10.6 No State shall, without the Consent of Congress, lay any Duty of Tonnage, keep Troops, or Ships of War in time of Peace, enter into any Agreement or Compact with another State, or with a foreign Power, or engage in War, unless actually invaded, or in such imminent Danger as will not admit of delay.

Article II

Section 1

2.1.1 The executive Power shall be vested in a President of the United States of America. He shall hold his Office during the Term of four Years, and, together with the Vice President, chosen for the same Term, be elected, as follows

2.1.2 Each State shall appoint, in such Manner as the Legislature thereof may direct, a Number of Electors, equal to the whole Number of Senators and Representatives to which the State may be entitled in the Congress: but no Senator or Representative, or Person holding an Office of Trust or Profit under the United States, shall be appointed an Elector.

2.1.3 The Electors shall meet in their respective States, and vote by Ballot for two Persons, of whom one at least shall not be an Inhabitant of the same State with themselves.

2.1.4 And they shall make a List of all the Persons voted for, and of the Number of Votes for each; which List they shall sign and certify, and transmit sealed to the Seat of the Government of the United States, directed to the President of the Senate.

2.1.5 The President of the Senate shall, in the Presence of the Senate and House of Representatives, open all the Certificates, and the Votes shall then be counted. The Person having the greatest Number of Votes shall be the President, if such Number be a Majority of the whole Number of Electors appointed;

2.1.6 and if there be more than one who have such Majority, and have an equal Number of Votes, then the House of Representatives shall immediately chuse by Ballot one of them for President; and if no Person have a Majority, then from the five highest on the List the said House shall in like Manner chuse the President. But in chusing the President, the Votes shall be taken by States, the Representation from each State having one Vote; A quorum for this Purpose shall consist of a Member or Members from two thirds of the States, and a Majority of all the States shall be necessary to a Choice. [Changed; see 12ᵗʰ Amendment.]

2.1.7 [Removed; see 20ᵗʰ Amendment.]

2.1.8 [Removed by the 20ᵗʰ Amendment.]

2.1.9 In every Case, after the Choice of the President, the Person having the greatest Number of Votes of the Electors shall be the Vice President. But if there should remain two or more who have equal Votes, the Senate shall chuse from them by Ballot the Vice President.

[Changed; see 12ᵗʰ Amendment.]

2.1.10 The Congress may determine the Time of chusing the Electors, and the Day on which they shall give their Votes; which Day shall be the same throughout the United States.

2.1.11 No Person except a natural born Citizen, or a Citizen of the United States, at the time of the Adoption of this Constitution, shall be eligible to the Office of President; neither shall any Person be eligible to that Office who shall not have attained to the Age of thirty five Years, and been fourteen Years a Resident within the United States.

2.1.12 In Case of the Removal of the President from Office, or of his Death, Resignation, or Inability to discharge the Powers and Duties of the said Office, the Same shall devolve on the Vice President, [Changed; see 25ᵗʰ Amendment.]

2.1.13 [See 25ᵗʰ Amendment]

2.1.14 and the Congress may by Law provide for the Case of Removal, Death, Resignation or Inability, both of the President and Vice President, declaring what Officer shall then act as President, and such Officer shall act accordingly, until the Disability be removed, or a President shall be elected.

2.1.15-18 [See 25ᵗʰ Amendment]

2.1.19 The President shall, at stated Times, receive for his Services, a Compensation, which shall neither be encreased nor diminished during the Period for which he shall have been elected, and he shall not receive within that Period any other Emolument from the United States, or any of them.

2.1.20   Before he enter on the Execution of his Office, he shall take the following Oath or Affirmation:—"I do solemnly swear (or affirm) that I will faithfully execute the Office of President of the United States, and will to the best of my Ability, preserve, protect and defend the Constitution of the United States."

Section 2

2.2.1   The President shall be Commander in Chief of the Army and Navy of the United States, and of the Militia of the several States, when called into the actual Service of the United States; he may require the Opinion, in writing, of the principal Officer in each of the executive Departments, upon any Subject relating to the Duties of their respective Offices, and he shall have Power to grant Reprieves and Pardons for Offences against the United States, except in Cases of Impeachment.

2.2.2   He shall have Power, by and with the Advice and Consent of the Senate, to make Treaties, provided two thirds of the Senators present concur; and he shall nominate, and by and with the Advice and Consent of the Senate, shall appoint Ambassadors, other public Ministers and Consuls, Judges of the supreme Court, and all other Officers of the United States, whose Appointments are not herein otherwise provided for, and which shall be established by Law:

2.2.3   but the Congress may by Law vest the Appointment of such inferior Officers, as they think proper, in the President alone, in the Courts of Law, or in the Heads of Departments.

2.2.4   The President shall have Power to fill up all Vacancies that may happen during the Recess of the Senate, by granting Commissions which shall expire at the End of their next Session.

Section 3

2.3.1   He shall from time to time give to the Congress Information of the State of the Union, and recommend to their Consideration such Measures as he shall judge necessary and expedient;

2.3.2   he may, on extraordinary Occasions, convene both Houses, or either of them, and in Case of Disagreement between them, with Respect to the Time of Adjournment, he may adjourn them to such Time as he shall think proper;

2.3.3 he shall receive Ambassadors and other public Ministers; he shall take Care that the Laws be faithfully executed, and shall Commission all the Officers of the United States.

Section 4

The President, Vice President and all civil Officers of the United States, shall be removed from Office on Impeachment for, and Conviction of, Treason, Bribery, or other high Crimes and Misdemeanors.

Article III

Section 1

The judicial Power of the United States, shall be vested in one supreme Court, and in such inferior Courts as the Congress may from time to time ordain and establish. The Judges, both of the supreme and inferior Courts, shall hold their Offices during good Behaviour, and shall, at stated Times, receive for their Services, a Compensation, which shall not be diminished during their Continuance in Office.

Section 2

3.2.1 The judicial Power shall extend to all Cases, in Law and Equity, arising under this Constitution, the Laws of the United States, and Treaties made, or which shall be made, under their Authority;—to all Cases affecting Ambassadors, other public Ministers and Consuls;—to all Cases of admiralty and maritime Jurisdiction;—to Controversies to which the United States shall be a Party;—to Controversies between two or more States;— between a State and Citizens of another State,— between Citizens of different States,—between Citizens of the same State claiming Lands under Grants of different States, and between a State, or the Citizens thereof, and foreign States, Citizens or Subjects. [Changed by the 11th Amendment.]

3.2.2 In all Cases affecting Ambassadors, other public Ministers and Consuls, and those in which a State shall be Party, the supreme Court shall have original Jurisdiction. In all the other Cases before mentioned, the supreme Court shall have appellate Jurisdiction, both as to Law and Fact, with such Exceptions, and under such Regulations as the Congress shall make.

3.2.3 The Trial of all Crimes, except in Cases of Impeachment, shall be by Jury; and such Trial shall be held in the State where the said Crimes shall have been committed; but when not committed within any

State, the Trial shall be at such Place or Places as the Congress may by Law have directed.

Section 3

3.3.1 Treason against the United States, shall consist only in levying War against them, or in adhering to their Enemies, giving them Aid and Comfort. No Person shall be convicted of Treason unless on the Testimony of two Witnesses to the same overt Act, or on Confession in open Court.

3.3.2 The Congress shall have Power to declare the Punishment of Treason, but no Attainder of Treason shall work Corruption of Blood, or Forfeiture except during the Life of the Person attainted.

Article IV

Section 1

Full Faith and Credit shall be given in each State to the public Acts, Records, and judicial Proceedings of every other State. And the Congress may by general Laws prescribe the Manner in which such Acts, Records and Proceedings shall be proved, and the Effect thereof.

Section 2

4.2.1 The Citizens of each State shall be entitled to all Privileges and Immunities of Citizens in the several States.

4.2.2 A Person charged in any State with Treason, Felony, or other Crime, who shall flee from Justice, and be found in another State, shall on Demand of the executive Authority of the State from which he fled, be delivered up, to be removed to the State having Jurisdiction of the Crime.

4.2.3 No Person held to Service or Labour in one State, under the Laws thereof, escaping into another, shall, in Consequence of any Law or Regulation therein, be discharged from such Service or Labour, but shall be delivered up on Claim of the Party to whom such Service or Labour may be due. [Made obsolete by the 13th Amendment.]

Section 3

4.3.1 New States may be admitted by the Congress into this Union; but no new State shall be formed or erected within the Jurisdiction of any other State; nor any State be formed by the Junction of two or more

States, or Parts of States, without the Consent of the Legislatures of the States concerned as well as of the Congress.

4.3.2 The Congress shall have Power to dispose of and make all needful Rules and Regulations respecting the Territory or other Property belonging to the United States; and nothing in this Constitution shall be so construed as to Prejudice any Claims of the United States, or of any particular State.

Section 4

The United States shall guarantee to every State in this Union a Republican Form of Government, and shall protect each of them against Invasion; and on Application of the Legislature, or of the Executive (when the Legislature cannot be convened), against domestic Violence.

Article V

Section 1 The Congress, whenever two thirds of both Houses shall deem it necessary, shall propose Amendments to this Constitution, or, on the Application of the Legislatures of two thirds of the several States, shall call a Convention for proposing Amendments,

Section 2 which, in either Case, shall be valid to all Intents and Purposes, as Part of this Constitution, when ratified by the Legislatures of three fourths of the several States, or by Conventions in three fourths thereof, as the one or the other Mode of Ratification may be proposed by the Congress;

Section 3 Provided that no Amendment which may be made prior to the Year One thousand eight hundred and eight shall in any Manner affect the first and fourth Clauses in the Ninth Section of the first Article; and that no State, without its Consent, shall be deprived of its equal Suffrage in the Senate.

Article VI

Section 1 All Debts contracted and Engagements entered into, before the Adoption of this Constitution, shall be as valid against the United States under this Constitution, as under the Confederation.

Section 2 This Constitution, and the Laws of the United States which shall be made in Pursuance thereof; and all Treaties made, or which shall be made, under the Authority of the United States, shall be the supreme Law of the Land; and the Judges in every State shall be bound thereby, any Thing in the Constitution or Laws of any State to the Contrary notwithstanding.

Section 3   The Senators and Representatives before mentioned, and the Members of the several State Legislatures, and all executive and judicial Officers, both of the United States and of the several States, shall be bound by Oath or Affirmation, to support this Constitution; but no religious Test shall ever be required as a Qualification to any Office or public Trust under the United States.

Article VII

The Ratification of the Conventions of nine States, shall be sufficient for the Establishment of this Constitution between the States so ratifying the Same.

Done in Convention by the Unanimous Consent of the States present the Seventeenth Day of September in the Year of our Lord one thousand seven hundred and Eighty seven and of the Independence of the United States of America the Twelfth In witness whereof We have hereunto subscribed our Names,

Go. WASHINGTON — Presidt.
and deputy from Virginia

New Hampshire

    JOHN LANGDON   NICHOLAS GILMAN

Massachusetts

    NATHANIEL GORHAM   RUFUS KING

Connecticut

    WM. SAML. JOHNSON   ROGER SHERMAN

New York

    ALEXANDER HAMILTON

New Jersey

    WIL: LIVINGSTON   DAVID BREARLEY
    WM. PATERSON   JONA: DAYTON

Pennsylvania

    B FRANKLIN   THOMAS MIFFLIN
    ROBT MORRIS   GEO. CLYMER
    THOS. FITZ SIMONS   JARED INGERSOLL
    JAMES WILSON   GOUV MORRIS

Delaware

    GEO: READ   GUNNING BEDFORD jun
    JOHN DICKINSON   RICHARD BASSETT
    JACO: BROOM

Maryland

    JAMES MCHENRY   DAN OF ST THOS. JENIFER
    DANL CARROLL

Virginia

    JOHN BLAIR   JAMES MADISON jr

North Carolina

    WM. BLOUNT   RICHD. DOBBS SPAIGHT
    HU WILLIAMSON

South Carolina

    J. RUTLEDGE   CHARLES COTESWORTH PINCKNEY
    CHARLES PINCKNEY
    PIERCE BUTLER

Georgia   WILLIAM FEW   ABR BALDWIN

In Convention Monday, September 17th, 1787.

Present

The States of New Hampshire, Massachusetts, Connecticut, MR. Hamilton from New York, New Jersey, Pennsylvania, Delaware, Maryland, Virginia, North Carolina, South Carolina and Georgia.

Resolved,

That the preceding Constitution be laid before the United States in Congress assembled, and that it is the Opinion of this Convention, that it should afterwards be submitted to a Convention of Delegates, chosen in each State by the People thereof, under the Recommendation of its Legislature, for their Assent and Ratification; and that each Convention assenting to, and ratifying the Same, should give Notice thereof to the United States in Congress assembled. Resolved, That it is the Opinion of this Convention, that as soon as the Conventions of nine States shall have ratified this Constitution, the United States in Congress assembled should fix a Day on which Electors should be appointed by the States which have ratified the same, and a Day on which the Electors should assemble to vote for the President, and the Time and Place for commencing Proceedings under this Constitution. That after such Publication the Electors should be appointed, and the Senators and Representatives elected: That the Electors should meet on the Day fixed for the Election of the President, and should transmit their Votes certified, signed, sealed and directed, as the Constitution requires, to the Secretary of the United States in Congress assembled, that the Senators and Representatives should convene at the Time and Place assigned; that the Senators should appoint a President of the Senate, for the sole purpose of receiving, opening and counting the Votes for President; and, that after he shall be chosen, the Congress, together with the President, should, without Delay, proceed to execute this Constitution.

By the Unanimous Order of the Convention

Go. WASHINGTON — Presidt.
W. JACKSON Secretary

Amendments to the Constitution

On September 25, 1789, the First Congress of the United States proposed the first 12 amendments to the Constitution. The original 'Bill of Rights', all 12 Articles, is displayed in the National Archives Museum. Ten of the proposed 12 amendments were ratified by three-fourths of the states by December 15, 1791. In 1992, over 200 years after the first states ratified it, Article 2 was ratified as the 27th Amendment. Article 1 has been ratified by 11 states; **Our First Right** *is our effort to gain ratification by the 27 more states required to make it the 28th Amendment: no U.S. congressional district shall contain more than 50,000 persons.*

Congress of the United States begun and held at the City of New-York, on Wednesday the fourth of March, one thousand seven hundred and eighty nine.

THE Conventions of a number of the States, having at the time of their adopting the Constitution, expressed a desire, in order to prevent misconstruction or abuse of its powers, that further declaratory and restrictive clauses should be added: And as extending the ground of public confidence in the Government, will best ensure the beneficent ends of its institution.

RESOLVED by the Senate and House of Representatives of the United States of America, in Congress assembled, two thirds of both Houses concurring, that the following Articles be proposed to the Legislatures of the several States, as amendments to the Constitution of the United States, all, or any of which Articles, when ratified by three fourths of the said Legislatures, to be valid to all intents and purposes, as part of the said Constitution; viz.

ARTICLES in addition to, and Amendment of the Constitution of the United States of America, proposed by Congress, and ratified by the Legislatures of the several States, pursuant to the fifth Article of the original Constitution.

[The following is a transcription of the first ten amendments to the Constitution in their original form. Ratified December 15, 1791 they are restrictions on the servants, but are erroneously called 'Bill of Rights'.]

Amendment I

Congress shall make no law respecting an establishment of religion, or prohibiting the free exercise thereof; or abridging the freedom of speech, or of the press; or the right of the people peaceably to assemble, and to petition the Government for a redress of grievances.

Amendment II

A well regulated Militia, being necessary to the security of a free State, the right of the people to keep and bear Arms, shall not be infringed.

Amendment III

No Soldier shall, in time of peace be quartered in any house, without the consent of the Owner, nor in time of war, but in a manner to be prescribed by law.

Amendment IV

The right of the people to be secure in their persons, houses, papers, and effects, against unreasonable searches and seizures, shall not be violated, and no Warrants shall issue, but upon probable cause, supported by Oath or affirmation, and particularly describing the place to be searched, and the persons or things to be seized.

Amendment V

No person shall be held to answer for a capital, or otherwise infamous crime, unless on a presentment or indictment of a Grand Jury, except in cases arising in the land or naval forces, or in the Militia, when in actual service in time of War or public danger; nor shall any person be subject for the same offence to be twice put in jeopardy of life or limb; nor shall be compelled in any criminal case to be a witness against himself, nor be deprived of life, liberty, or property, without due process of law; nor shall private property be taken for public use, without just compensation.

Amendment VI

In all criminal prosecutions, the accused shall enjoy the right to a speedy and public trial, by an impartial jury of the State and district wherein the crime shall have been committed, which district shall have been previously ascertained by law, and to be informed of the nature and cause of the accusation; to be confronted with the witnesses against him; to have compulsory process for obtaining witnesses in his favor, and to have the Assistance of Counsel for his defence.

Amendment VII

In Suits at common law, where the value in controversy shall exceed twenty dollars, the right of trial by jury shall be preserved, and no fact tried by a jury, shall be otherwise re-examined in any Court of the United States, than according to the rules of the common law.

Amendment VIII

Excessive bail shall not be required, nor excessive fines imposed, nor cruel and unusual punishments inflicted.

Amendment IX

The enumeration in the Constitution, of certain rights, shall not be construed to deny or disparage others retained by the people.

Amendment X

The powers not delegated to the United States by the Constitution, nor prohibited by it to the States, are reserved to the States respectively, or to the people.

Amendment XI

Passed by Congress March 4, 1794. Ratified February 7, 1795.

Article III, section 2, of the Constitution was modified by amendment 11.

The Judicial power of the United States shall not be construed to extend to any suit in law or equity, commenced or prosecuted against one of the United States by Citizens of another State, or by Citizens or Subjects of any Foreign State.

Amendment XII

Passed by Congress December 9, 1803. Ratified June 15, 1804.

A portion of Article II, section 1 of the Constitution was superseded by the 12th amendment.

The Electors shall meet in their respective states and vote by ballot for President and Vice-President, one of whom, at least, shall not be an inhabitant of the same state with themselves; they shall name in their ballots the person voted for as President, and in distinct ballots the person voted for as Vice-President, and they shall make distinct lists of all persons voted for as President, and of all persons voted for as Vice-President, and of the number of votes for each, which lists they shall sign and certify, and transmit sealed to the seat of the government of the United States, directed to the President of the Senate; — the President of the Senate shall, in the presence of the Senate and House of Representatives, open all the certificates and the votes shall then be counted; — The person having the greatest number of votes for President, shall be the President, if such number be a majority of the whole number of Electors appointed; and if no person have such majority, then from the persons having the highest numbers not exceeding three on the list of those voted for as President, the House of Representatives shall choose immediately, by ballot, the President. But in choosing the President, the votes shall be taken by states, the representation from each state having one vote; a quorum for this purpose shall consist of a member or members from two-thirds of the states, and a majority of all the states shall be necessary to a choice. [And if the House of Representatives shall not choose a President whenever the right of choice shall devolve upon them, before the fourth day of March next following, then the Vice-President shall act as President, as in case of the death or other constitutional disability of the President. –]* The person having the greatest number of votes as Vice-President, shall be the Vice-President, if such number be a majority of the whole number of Electors appointed, and if no person have a majority, then from the two highest numbers on the list, the Senate shall choose the Vice-

President; a quorum for the purpose shall consist of two-thirds of the whole number of Senators, and a majority of the whole number shall be necessary to a choice. But no person constitutionally ineligible to the office of President shall be eligible to that of Vice-President of the United States.

*Superseded by section 3 of the 20th amendment.

Amendment XIII

Passed by Congress January 31, 1865. Ratified December 6, 1865.

A portion of Article IV, section 2, of the Constitution was superseded by the 13th amendment.

Section 1.

Neither slavery nor involuntary servitude, except as a punishment for crime whereof the party shall have been duly convicted, shall exist within the United States, or any place subject to their jurisdiction.

Section 2.

Congress shall have power to enforce this article by appropriate legislation.

Amendment XIV

Passed by Congress June 13, 1866. Ratified July 9, 1868.

Article I, section 2, of the Constitution was modified by section 2 of the 14th amendment.

Section 1.

All persons born or naturalized in the United States, and subject to the jurisdiction thereof, are citizens of the United States and of the State wherein they reside. No State shall make or enforce any law which shall abridge the privileges or immunities of citizens of the United States; nor shall any State deprive any person of life, liberty, or property, without due process of law; nor deny to any person within its jurisdiction the equal protection of the laws.

Section 2.

Representatives shall be apportioned among the several States according to their respective numbers, counting the whole number of persons in each State, excluding Indians not taxed. But when the right to vote at any election for the choice of electors for President and Vice-President of the United States, Representatives in Congress, the Executive and Judicial officers of a State, or the members of the Legislature thereof, is denied to any of the male inhabitants of such State, being twenty-one years of age,* and citizens of the United States, or in any way abridged, except for participation in rebellion, or other crime, the basis of representation therein shall be reduced in the proportion which the number of such male citizens shall bear to the whole number of male citizens twenty-one years of age in such State.

Section 3.

No person shall be a Senator or Representative in Congress, or elector of President and Vice-President, or hold any office, civil or military, under the United States, or under any State, who, having previously taken an oath, as a member of Congress, or as an officer of the United States, or as a member of any State legislature, or as an executive or judicial officer of any State, to support the Constitution of the United States, shall have engaged in insurrection or rebellion against the same, or given aid or comfort to the enemies thereof. But Congress may by a vote of two-thirds of each House, remove such disability.

Section 4.

The validity of the public debt of the United States, authorized by law, including debts incurred for payment of pensions and bounties for services in suppressing insurrection or rebellion, shall not be questioned. But neither the United States nor any State shall assume or pay any debt or obligation incurred in aid of insurrection or rebellion against the United States, or any claim for the loss or emancipation of any slave; but all such debts, obligations and claims shall be held illegal and void.

Section 5.

The Congress shall have the power to enforce, by appropriate legislation, the provisions of this article.

Changed by section 1 of the 26th amendment.

Amendment XV

Passed by Congress February 26, 1869. Ratified February 3, 1870.

Section 1.

The right of citizens of the United States to vote shall not be denied or abridged by the United States or by any State on account of race, color, or previous condition of servitude.

Section 2.

The Congress shall have the power to enforce this article by appropriate legislation.

Amendment XVI

Passed by Congress July 2, 1909. Ratified February 3, 1913.

Article I, section 9 of the Constitution was supposedly (arguably) modified by amendment 16.

The Congress shall have power to lay and collect taxes on incomes, from whatever source derived, without apportionment among the several States, and without regard to any census or enumeration.

Amendment XVII

Passed by Congress May 13, 1912. Ratified April 8, 1913.

Article I, section 3, of the Constitution was modified by the 17th amendment.

The Senate of the United States shall be composed of two Senators from each State, elected by the people thereof, for six years; and each Senator shall have one vote. The electors in each State shall have the qualifications requisite for electors of the most numerous branch of the State legislatures.

When vacancies happen in the representation of any State in the Senate, the executive authority of such State shall issue writs of election to fill such vacancies: *Provided,* That the legislature of any State may empower the executive thereof to make temporary appointments until the people fill the vacancies by election as the legislature may direct.

This amendment shall not be so construed as to affect the election or term of any Senator chosen before it becomes valid as part of the Constitution.

Amendment XVIII

Passed by Congress December 18, 1917. Ratified January 16, 1919. Repealed by amendment 21.

Section 1.

After one year from the ratification of this article the manufacture, sale, or transportation of intoxicating liquors within, the importation thereof into, or the exportation thereof from the United States and all territory subject to the jurisdiction thereof for beverage purposes is hereby prohibited.

Section 2.

The Congress and the several States shall have concurrent power to enforce this article by appropriate legislation.

Section 3.

This article shall be inoperative unless it shall have been ratified as an amendment to the Constitution by the legislatures of the several States, as provided in the Constitution, within seven years from the date of the submission hereof to the States by the Congress.

Amendment XIX

Passed by Congress June 4, 1919. Ratified August 18, 1920.

The right of citizens of the United States to vote shall not be denied or abridged by the United States or by any State on account of sex.

Congress shall have power to enforce this article by appropriate legislation.

Amendment XX

Passed by Congress March 2, 1932. Ratified January 23, 1933.

Article I, section 4, of the Constitution was modified by section 2 of this amendment. In addition, a portion of the 12th amendment was superseded by section 3.

Section 1.

The terms of the President and the Vice President shall end at noon on the 20th day of January, and the terms of Senators and Representatives at noon on the 3d day of January, of the years in which such terms would have ended if this article had not been ratified; and the terms of their successors shall then begin.

Section 2.

The Congress shall assemble at least once in every year, and such meeting shall begin at noon on the 3d day of January, unless they shall by law appoint a different day.

Section 3.

If, at the time fixed for the beginning of the term of the President, the President elect shall have died, the Vice President elect shall become President. If a President shall not have been chosen before the time fixed for the beginning of his term, or if the President elect shall have failed to qualify, then the Vice

President elect shall act as President until a President shall have qualified; and the Congress may by law provide for the case wherein neither a President elect nor a Vice President elect shall have qualified, declaring who shall then act as President, or the manner in which one who is to act shall be selected, and such person shall act accordingly until a President or Vice President shall have qualified.

Section 4.

The Congress may by law provide for the case of the death of any of the persons from whom the House of Representatives may choose a President whenever the right of choice shall have devolved upon them, and for the case of the death of any of the persons from whom the Senate may choose a Vice President whenever the right of choice shall have devolved upon them.

Section 5.

Sections 1 and 2 shall take effect on the 15th day of October following the ratification of this article.

Section 6.

This article shall be inoperative unless it shall have been ratified as an amendment to the Constitution by the legislatures of three-fourths of the several States within seven years from the date of its submission.

Amendment XXI

Passed by Congress February 20, 1933. Ratified December 5, 1933.

Section 1.

The eighteenth article of amendment to the Constitution of the United States is hereby repealed.

Section 2.

The transportation or importation into any State, Territory, or possession of the United States for delivery or use therein of intoxicating liquors, in violation of the laws thereof, is hereby prohibited.

Section 3.

This article shall be inoperative unless it shall have been ratified as an amendment to the Constitution by conventions in the several States, as provided in the Constitution, within seven years from the date of the submission hereof to the States by the Congress.

Amendment XXII

Passed by Congress March 21, 1947. Ratified February 27, 1951.

Section 1.

No person shall be elected to the office of the President more than twice, and no person who has held the office of President, or acted as President, for more than two years of a term to which some other person was elected President shall be elected to the office of the President more than once. But this Article shall not apply to any person holding the office of President when this Article was proposed by the Congress, and shall not prevent any person who may be holding the office of President, or acting as President, during the term within which this Article becomes operative from holding the office of President or acting as President during the remainder of such term.

Section 2.

This article shall be inoperative unless it shall have been ratified as an amendment to the Constitution by the legislatures of three-fourths of the several States within seven years from the date of its submission to the States by the Congress.

Amendment XXIII

Passed by Congress June 16, 1960. Ratified March 29, 1961.

Section 1.

The District constituting the seat of Government of the United States shall appoint in such manner as the Congress may direct:

A number of electors of President and Vice President equal to the whole number of Senators and Representatives in Congress to which the District would be entitled if it were a State, but in no event more than the least populous State; they shall be in addition to those appointed by the States, but they shall be considered, for the purposes of the election of President and Vice President, to be electors appointed by a State; and they shall meet in the District and perform such duties as provided by the twelfth article of amendment.

Section 2.

The Congress shall have power to enforce this article by appropriate legislation.

Amendment XXIV

Passed by Congress August 27, 1962. Ratified January 23, 1964.

Section 1.

The right of citizens of the United States to vote in any primary or other election for President or Vice President, for electors for President or Vice President, or for Senator or Representative in Congress, shall not be denied or abridged by the United States or any State by reason of failure to pay any poll tax or other tax.

Section 2.

The Congress shall have power to enforce this article by appropriate legislation.

Amendment XXV

Passed by Congress July 6, 1965. Ratified February 10, 1967.

Article II, section 1, of the Constitution was affected by the 25th amendment.

Section 1.

In case of the removal of the President from office or of his death or resignation, the Vice President shall become President.

Section 2.

Whenever there is a vacancy in the office of the Vice President, the President shall nominate a Vice President who shall take office upon confirmation by a majority vote of both Houses of Congress.

Section 3.

Whenever the President transmits to the President pro tempore of the Senate and the Speaker of the House of Representatives his written declaration that he is unable to discharge the powers and duties of his office, and until he transmits to them a written declaration to the contrary, such powers and duties shall be discharged by the Vice President as Acting President.

Section 4.

Whenever the Vice President and a majority of either the principal officers of the executive departments or of such other body as Congress may by law provide, transmit to the President pro tempore of the Senate and the Speaker of the House of Representatives their written declaration that the President is unable to discharge the powers and duties of his office, the Vice President shall immediately assume the powers and duties of the office as Acting President.

Thereafter, when the President transmits to the President pro tempore of the Senate and the Speaker of the House of Representatives his written declaration that no inability exists, he shall resume the powers and duties of his office unless the Vice President and a majority of either the principal officers of the executive department or of such other body as Congress may by law provide, transmit within four days to the President pro tempore of the Senate and the Speaker of the House of Representatives their written declaration that the President is unable to discharge the powers and duties of his office. Thereupon Congress shall decide the issue, assembling within forty-eight hours for that purpose if not in session. If the Congress, within twenty-one days after receipt of the latter written declaration, or, if Congress is not in session, within twenty-one days after Congress is required to assemble, determines by two-thirds vote of both Houses that the President is unable to discharge the powers and duties of his office, the Vice President shall continue to discharge the same as Acting President; otherwise, the President shall resume the powers and duties of his office.

Amendment XXVI

Passed by Congress March 23, 1971. Ratified July 1, 1971. Amendment 14, section 2, of the Constitution was modified by section 1 of the 26th amendment.

Section 1.

The right of citizens of the United States, who are eighteen years of age or older, to vote shall not be denied or abridged by the United States or by any State on account of age.

Section 2.

The Congress shall have power to enforce this article by appropriate legislation.

Amendment XXVII

Passed by Congress Sept. 25, 1789. Ratified May 7, 1992.

No law, varying the compensation for the services of the Senators and Representatives, shall take effect, until an election of Representatives shall have intervened.

APPENDIX H

AmericaAgain! Declaration

When a government has ceased to protect the lives, liberty and property of We The People from whom its legitimate powers are derived, and for the advancement of whose happiness it was instituted, and so far from being a guarantee for the enjoyment of those inestimable and inalienable rights, becomes an instrument in the hands of evil rulers for their oppression;

When the federal republican Constitution, which they have sworn to support, no longer has a substantial existence – the whole nature of our servant government having been changed without our consent, from a restricted republic of sovereign States to a consolidated central despotism in which productive Americans are forced to work for imperious bureaucrats and government functionaries, favored industries, tyrannical and abusive Big Tech corporations more powerful than governments, and a growing parasitic population that has rendered our Republic fully Communist;

When, long after the spirit of the Constitution has departed, moderation is thrown to the wind by those in power, the semblance of freedom removed, and the forms of the Constitution discontinued as in the arrogant violation of the Second Amendment's proscription against any infringement of the right of the People to keep and bear arms (which Article I, Section 8, Clause 15 assumes is the duty of all able-bodied Americans);

When for five generations, We The People have suffered the general government's instigation, perpetration, funding, and defense of organized crime;

When, far from our petitions being regarded, citizens who show public concern for these infringements and usurpations are marked as 'terrorists' or arrested by tyrannical new city, state, and federal agencies hatched under the guises first of 'war on terror' then of a hoax 'pandemic';

When, with each new legislature, administration, and federal Supreme Court, the public servants of We The People more openly and arrogantly burden us and encroach on our privacy; on our liberty to travel freely; on our ability to enjoy our own property freely or to raise our children as we see fit; on our ability to actually own our property free and clear; to operate our farms, shops, or businesses as we see fit without posing any harm to others; on our ability to even open our small businesses, eat in restaurants or even gather in our own homes and churches! – all under the threat of a proven Chinese-engineered hoax 'pandemic'; and now have colluded in both corrupt political parties to openly, cynically steal a national election in which one candidate received easily 80 million true votes, yet was 'defeated' by a nearly senile puppet candidate whose gaslighting operation enlisted a massive, Communist-style phalanx of state-owned media (Google, Twitter, YouTube, Facebook, ABC, MSNBC, CBS, CNN, NPR, Fox News and others);

In consequence of such acts of malfeasance and abdication on the part of the servant government, anarchy threatens to dissolve civil society into its original elements, the first law of nature and the right of self-preservation, the powers reserved by We The People as stipulated in the U.S. Constitution, Amendment X, enjoins not only our right but a sacred obligation to our posterity, to enforce the specific limits of federal power as enumerated in that supreme Law of the Land, by all the lawful and necessary means provided in that Constitution, including but not limited to the Courts of our sovereign States and such federal legislative reforms as We The People may effect, to secure our welfare and happiness.

Nations, as well as individuals, are amenable for their acts to the public opinion of mankind. A statement of a part of our grievances is therefore submitted to an impartial world along with the peaceful, lawful, and legitimate enforcement steps that We The People of these United States now intend to take, to which the nations of the earth are witness.

We The People of the fifty sovereign States of America, creators of the U.S. Constitution, acknowledge the duty of every American to preserve, protect, and defend that Supreme Law. We hereby announce to a watching world our intention to restore the original form, purpose, and enumerated limits of our government, superintending from this day forward our State courts and federal servants so that we may once more secure the Blessings of Liberty to ourselves and to our posterity.

These United States have a solemn duty to serve their citizen masters by enforcing our supreme Law of the Land when one or more branches of federal government violate it. When the States neglect this duty, our Declaration of Independence establishes that this duty and the power to execute it return to the people at large for their exercise. The three branches of federal government are creatures — things created by us in the U.S. Constitution, the highest law in this Republic.

In the Constitution, We the People clearly enumerate the powers of federal government. We retain any powers not specifically enumerated therein, to ourselves and our sovereign States. Any exercise of power by government beyond those listed powers is an egregious violation of the Supreme Law.

President Jefferson said that *"in questions of powers…let no more be heard of confidence in man, but bind him down from mischief by the chains of the Constitution"*. Such "binding down" can be peaceably accomplished by binding the federal purse and by We the People and sovereign States enforcing that Law of Limitation for the first time in American history.

The present $3.9 trillion annual federal revenue – and the far larger mountain of financial derivatives that Congress allows the financial industry to create from thin air and our labor – have spawned a brood of corruptions as unlimited oceans of money always do. This ocean of illicit D.C. cash has spawned unconstitutional federal powers, cabinet departments, agents, agencies, programs, projects, offices, regulations, and financial industry 'assets' that for sheer number are impossible to list here but that threaten our liberties, property, livelihood, posterity, and public morals, making a joke of our Supreme Law.

In Federalist #28, Alexander Hamilton said that by merely exercising our power as creators of the federal government, we can prevail: *"the larger the American population would become, the more effectively we can resist federal government tyranny… Power being almost always the rival of power, the general government will at all times stand ready to check the usurpations of State governments, and these will have the same disposition towards the general government. The People, by throwing themselves into either scale, will infallibly make it preponderate. If their rights are invaded by either, they can make use of the other as the instrument of redress.."*. The mission of AmericaAgain! is to make good on the guarantees offered in the Federalist Papers to our fore-fathers.

All three branches of our federal creature have ceased to check-and-balance one another, instead colluding over the past 150 years abusing the "necessary and proper", "general welfare", and "interstate commerce" clauses to fashion a lawless, limitless system of power, pork, and perquisites warned against by James Madison, the primary author of the Constitution: *"...it is evident that there is not a single power whatever, which may not have some reference to the common defense or the general welfare; nor a power of any magnitude which, in its exercise, does not involve or admit an application of money. The government, therefore, which possesses power in either one or other of these extents, is a government without the limitations formed by a particular enumeration of powers.*

"Consequently, the meaning and effect of this particular enumeration is destroyed by the exposition given to these general phrases... Congress is authorized to provide money for the common defense and general welfare. In both, is subjoined to this authority an enumeration of the cases to which their power shall extend...a question arises whether (any) particular measure be within the enumerated authorities vested in Congress. If it be, the money requisite for it may be applied to it; if it be not, no such application can be made.

"It is incumbent in this, as in every other exercise of power by the federal government, to prove from the Constitution, that it grants the particular power exercised.

"With respect to the words 'general welfare', I have always regarded them as qualified by the detail of powers connected with them. To take them in a literal and unlimited sense would be a metamorphosis of the Constitution into a character which there is a host of proofs was not contemplated by its creators."

Congress and presidents for many generations have violated the highest law in America in precisely this blank-check manner, at a cost of tens of trillions of dollars – and at the further cost of our liberty, privacy, and rights to property and peaceful self-government. When a government of, by, and for The People stands in perennial, collusive violation of the Constitution, We The People have constitutional authority to take enforcement action. The duty of constitutional law enforcement falls on We the People, not by resisting government's lawlessness with lawlessness of our own, but by having the courts of our States bring law enforcement power to bear as our right and duty under that Law.

With respect to compliance with his "Oath or Affirmation, to support this Constitution", no public official can be allowed to be the judge of his own case, as Presidents Jefferson and Madison observed.

The nefarious practice of executive orders is nowhere authorized in Article II of the Constitution. Numerous such executive fiats are demonstrable violations of the limited powers stipulated in Article II, yet We The People have had no voice in said imperial edicts issued by presidents. The same principle holds true for treaties signed by tyrannical presidents under the noses of the American people to our detriment, without popular review before being trundled through a complicit U.S. Senate.

Every public official's oath is made to We the People; the Constitution commands that the official be bound by that oath; thus We the People have the right to enforce that oath and the power to do so as well, for no right can exist without an effective remedy, including remedy via State courts.

With the Chinese virus hoax, Congress' corrupt, imperious practices to oust a sitting president then infested State, county, and municipal governments; as U.S. Supreme Court Justice Louis Brandeis suggested in his 1928 dissenting opinion in Olmsted v. U.S.: *"In a government of laws...Our government is the potent, the omnipresent teacher. For good or for ill, it teaches the whole people by its example. Crime is contagious. If the government becomes a lawbreaker, it breeds contempt for law..."*.

Congress has perennially refused to balance its federal budgets.

The flow of illegal aliens across our borders reached epidemic proportions long ago, yet Congress refused to allow President Trump to seal the border, instead arming a ticking time bomb against our culture and civil order; saddling Taxpayers with the cost of socialist programs for politicians' future political pawns. America was a melting pot Republic with a common language, currency, culture and work ethic; now it is polyglot warring factions seeking African-America, Mexican-America, Israeli-America, and Muslim America.

The U.S. Congress was intended to be populated by citizen-statesmen for limited terms so that no lifelong political oligarchy would rule over the citizens as is now the case, with members of Congress being wealthy, insular individuals with little affinity with, or empathy for, the average citizen. Members of Congress shamelessly enjoy fat pensions, insurance policies, private spas, limousines, private jets hidden in federal budgets, and much more – paid for by citizens who never enjoy such free luxuries.

The original intent of the Constitution's framers was to balance the Legislative branch with two bodies, the House of Representatives representing the interests of the People, and the Senate representing the interests of the States. Prior to 1913, the individual State legislatures appointed representatives to serve in the US Senate who were expected to act and vote in the interest of the State or were subject to immediate recall and replacement.

During the administration of Woodrow Wilson, Congress introduced the Seventeenth Amendment, which was ratified under questionable circumstances. The new amendment stripped away a critical power of the States to control D.C. by balancing the desires of the mob with cooler heads in their deliberative legislatures. Making both houses of Congress elected directly by the People opened the Senate to even greater corruption by moneyed interests and their lobbyists.

Many socialist accretions that have drained America's private sector wealth and inflated dependent populations, could never have passed if the sovereign States had retained direct control of the U.S. Senate as designed by the framers. Repealing the 17th Amendment will restore this critical check-and-balance mechanism as our founding fathers intended when they designed the U.S. Constitution.

Because the 13th Amendment disallows slavery or involuntary servitude, national conscription for military or other national service is illegal.

In the interests of a massive industry rather than national security, the U.S. Congress has refused to cut off funding for undeclared, unprovoked foreign attacks and invasions ordered or maintained by presidents who cannot prove they serve a national defense purpose. There will always be men in the world whose goal is plunder, to amass insane wealth; such chieftains buy and trade politicians as game pieces, world without end. They amass plunder using the U.S. military as free mercenaries.

The U.S. Constitution only authorizes Congress to use military power in declared war with a Navy, or with a Citizen Militia mustered for national purposes for a maximum of two years, or to use the Citizen Militia of the Several States, with officers and training provided by the States, "to execute the Laws of the Union, suppress Insurrections, and repel Invasions". No other federal armed forces are authorized by the Constitution.

214

Thus, it is illegal for full-time U.S. military ground forces to even exist, much less to plunder foreign resources or threaten foreign people who present no threat to us, under the guise of 'democracy', 'peacekeeping', 'war on terror', or 'protecting American interests abroad'.

The only difference that the United States military industry brings to conquered lands is replacing Arab family crests or banana republic dictators' logos with U.S.-based corporate logos. While this lawless plunder continues, We the People will continue to be regarded as enemies by citizens of the world.

The majority of Americans was once Christian; most still profess Christianity at least in name. The melting-pot culture that made America the envy of the world was not theocracy, but was demonstrably the ethic of Christ, not of Mormonism, Judaism, or Islam. We The People refuse to have America become as Europe – another battleground for a 1,400-year old Islamic jihad.

The legislation labeled 'Legal Tender Act' beginning in 1862 and collusive rulings by the U.S. Supreme Court in 1871 and 1884 violated the U.S. Constitution's stipulations in Article I, Sections 8 and 10. By law, only Congress has the power only to coin gold and silver, and every State shall use only gold and silver coin as legal tender. All paper scrip – and the tens of trillions of dollars annually in derivative financial instruments – are illegal and immoral, yet enabled under the protection of Congress, whose members have overseen and acquiesced in a 150-year-old conspiracy to defraud, embezzle from, and place into servitude the citizens they pretend to serve and represent.

It is *illegal* for Congress to declare that paper shall be considered lawful money. It is *illegal* for Congress to grant a concession to a private cartel using the Federal Reserve brand to manufacture counterfeit (paper) money and to require the People and sovereign States to pay face value plus interest for the worthless scrip. Before Great Depression II falls on our heads, we declare *this will not stand*.

Congress has willfully allowed the Internal Revenue Service to perennially violate the federal tax laws, regulations, and its own operating manual, transforming Taxpayers by terrorist coercion into pack-mules to carry the financial burdens of Congress' demonstrable crimes. We refuse to allow Congress to burden future generations with an equally corrupt revenue-neutral 'fair tax', so-called, that would

215

continue to amass over four times the revenues required to fund enumerated federal powers.

It is *illegal* for Congress to allow its servants, federal judges, to hold the entire population in 50 sovereign states hostage to the 1% sexual pervert lobby. In the Constitution, nowhere do We The People empower Congress or a federal court to hold the population hostage to an immoral minority by the imperial whim of five people in robes who on June 26, 2015 in their preposterous opinion, suggested that sexual perversion would now become 'marriage' in America. *This will not stand.*

Trillion-dollar tech corporations have occupied, captured, and dominate Town Square in every American community. Every major news outlet and social medium is working in lock-step towards Communist, environmental-anarchist goals inimical to our civilization and economy, while stratospherically enriching a tiny band of monopolist billionaires at Google, Facebook, Twitter, YouTube, Microsoft, Apple, Amazon and others who declare their hatred for conservative and Christian America. Year after year, Congress held pointless hearings and promised relief that never comes. Over 150 million Americans' lives remain occupied, dominated, and driven by godless globalists. *This will not stand.*

On a Sunday night in March 2010, the Democrat members of Congress conspired to transform the IRS into an American Gestapo – finally unmasking its terror organization to enforce its unconstitutional 'health care' scheme in which Barack Hussein Obama was also complicit. Now with the GOP members of Congress fully on board with arrogant tyranny, history proves that if Congress is allowed to fully arrogate this lawless new power, it will never relinquish them. *This will not stand.*

It is illegal for Congress to allow illegal aliens to enter this country and be catered to by federal government — the exact opposite of enforcing immigration laws that every productive American expects to have enforced. Individual works of mercy and foreign missions are biblical outreach; unrestrained communism and open borders are not. The Obama administration and Congress held several hundred million productive Americans hostage on behalf of a militant, tactically shrewd lobby of a few thousand activists. Those who pay property taxes are forced to pay the education, food, clothing, medical, incarceration, and law enforcement bills of an illegal horde, invited in and catered to by a lawless, arrogant, dismissive Congress. *This will not stand.*

Now, the militant Islamist army is following the path opened by the abortionists, by militant sexual perverts, and by the illegal alien lobby. It is illegal for Congress to allow any federal judge to enforce, support, enable, or even allow any alien law-code — whether Islamic sharia or any other — to be recognized or enforced in place of the established civil and criminal laws of these sovereign States. *This will not stand.*

After our long failure to perform our citizen duties, bearing the cost of our abdication on every hand, We the People of these fifty united States intend to lawfully, peacefully begin enforcing the Constitution in each of the 3,141 counties of our 50 States against its violation by our U.S. congressmen and senators, effecting such law enforcement through local AmericaAgain! members singly and statewide in a process called Tactical Civics™ and using a mechanism called the AmericaAgain! Indictment Engine™.

We the People hereby announce our intention to draft, refine, and push through the passage of the following Legislative Action projects. As a plea-bargaining package offered to any member of Congress indicted by using the AmericaAgain! Indictment Engine™, or as an immunity package for those who have not yet been targeted, We The People will demand that members of the U.S. House of Representatives and the U.S. Senate agree in writing to enact the following:

1) The **Bring Congress Home Act**, or 'BCHA', stipulating: Whereas a general principle of constitutional law in these United States holds that no legislature can bind a subsequent one; and whereas the Apportionment Act of 1929 set a totally arbitrary 435-district limit to the U.S. House of Representatives in clear violation of the intention of Article I, Section 2, Clause 4 and also in clear contravention of the original first Article in the Bill of Rights as passed by the first Congress and sent to the States; and whereas a sufficient number of States have ratified that amendment and it has been recorded as the 28th Amendment to the U.S. Constitution; and whereas the expanded size of the U.S. House demanded by the U.S. Constitution, in light of the benefits and cost savings of modern technology and the security risk of Congress operating from one location, therefore:

Section 1. No member of Congress shall have a private office or staff located in Washington D.C..

Section 2. All members of Congress shall serve a maximum of two terms.

Section 3. No district of the U.S. House of Representatives shall contain more than 50,000 people, as stipulated in the original First Amendment passed by Congress in 1789 and recently ratified by the State legislatures as the 28ᵗʰ Amendment.

Section 4. To remain properly accountable and accessible to the sovereigns People that (s)he represents, every member of the U.S. House of Representatives shall be provided with a single office located within his/her district, paid staff not exceeding two persons, reasonable office expenses, and the hardware, software, and encryption technology and services required to conduct the business of the U.S. House of Representatives, working from his/her own district.

Section 5. To remain properly accountable and accessible to the sovereign States that the U.S. Senate was originally de-signed to represent, every member of the U.S. Senate shall be provided with a single office located within close proximity to the State capitol, also with paid staff not exceeding six per-sons, reasonable office expenses, and the hardware, software, and encryption technology and services required to conduct the business of the U.S. Senate, working from his/her own State capitol pursuant to such time as the 17th Amendment shall be repealed.

Section 6. Public funds used by any member of Congress shall be limited to the member's salary – which shall in the case of a congressman, effective immediately, be 50% of present salary; office staff, space rent and expenses; self-operated vehicle lease payment, fuel and insurance; coach-class airfare for public business; and mail costs to communicate with his/her sovereigns. An annual audit of expend-itures for each member of Congress and his/her staff and office operations shall be posted online on that member's public web page accessible to the public, no later than 60 days after the close of each congressional session.

Section 7. Beyond those listed in Section 6 above, any and all other publicly-funded expenditures inuring to the benefit of a member of Congress shall hereafter be considered illegal use of public funds, including but not limited to: pensions and insurance premiums (retroactive), foreign travel under the guise of legislative business, limousines or other special conveyances, spas, hairdressers, and club memberships.

2) The **Constitutional Courts Act**, stipulating:

Section 1. A consensus exists among the American public that the federal courts have been corrupted and are manipulated by powerful individuals and by lobbyists for industry and special interests, rendering moot the stipulated limitations placed by the People through the U.S. Constitution on its creature, federal government.

a. James Madison, Father of the Constitution, in his Virginia Resolution of 1798, and Thomas Jefferson, in his concurring Virginia Resolution, wrote that the States, as the creator parties to the U.S. Constitution, have the right and duty to judge when the U.S. Constitution has been violated by federal government; that the federal government cannot judge of its own infractions

b. In Article III, Section 1 of the U.S. Constitution, the People grant to Congress the authority to create the inferior federal courts, thus the subject matter jurisdiction of the inferior federal courts is entirely within Congress' discretion.

c. In Article III, Section 2 of the U.S. Constitution, the People grant to Congress the authority to withhold subject matter jurisdiction even from the U.S. supreme Court, using "such Exceptions, and…such Regulations as the Congress shall make".

d. In Article VI, Section 2 of the U.S. Constitution, the People stipulate, "This Constitution…shall be the supreme Law of the Land; and the Judges in every State shall be bound thereby…", which binding includes enforcement as well as obedience.

e. Every federal legislator is now performing his federal duties full-time within his or her own district, which is the jurisdiction of his State Grand Jury and State Court.

f. Therefore, pursuant to the power granted by the People to Congress in U.S. Constitution Article III, Section 2, Clause 2, after the effective date hereof, no federal court shall have jurisdiction in any case in which a member of Congress is charged by his or her own State Grand Jury with violating, or conspiring to violate, the U.S. Constitution.

g. In no such case shall removal from state jurisdiction be available to the accused, whether pursuant to 28 USC 1441, or any subsequent federal law.

Section 2. The American People stipulated in Article I, Section 8 of the U.S. Constitution, that "The Congress shall have power…to constitute tribunals inferior to the supreme Court…", and in Article III, Section 1, that the federal courts are, "such inferior courts as the Congress may from time to time ordain and establish", and in Article III, Section 2, Clause 2, that the U.S. supreme Court, "shall have appellate jurisdiction…with such Exceptions, and under such Regulations as the Congress shall make".

In 1799 in Turner v. Bank of North America (1799), Justice Chase wrote, "The notion has frequently been entertained, that the federal courts derive their judicial power immediately from the Constitution; but the political truth is, that the disposal of the judicial power…belongs to Congress. If Congress has given the power to this

Court, we possess it, not otherwise: and if Congress has not given the power to us or to any other Court, it still remains at the legislative disposal."

In Ex parte Bollman *(1807), Chief Justice John Marshall wrote, "Courts which are created by written law, and whose jurisdiction is defined by written law, cannot transcend that jurisdiction".*

The power of Congress to create inferior federal courts, necessarily implies, as written in U.S. v. Hudson & Goodwin (1812), "the power to limit jurisdiction of those Courts to particular objects".

The U.S. supreme Court held unanimously in Sheldon v. Sill (1850) that because the People in the Constitution did not create inferior federal courts but authorized Congress to create them, that Congress by necessity had power to define and limit their jurisdiction and to withhold jurisdiction of any of the enumerated cases and controversies.

The high court even acknowledged Congress' power to re-examine particular classes of questions previously ruled on by the U.S. supreme Court, as stated in The Francis Wright *(1882): "(A)ctual jurisdiction under the [judicial] power is confined within such limits as Congress sees fit to prescribe...What those powers shall be, and to what extent they shall be exercised, are, and always have been, proper subjects of legislative control...Not only may whole classes of cases be kept out of the jurisdiction altogether, but particular classes of questions may be subjected to re-examination and review...".*

In Lauf v. E.G. Shinner & Co (1938), the U.S. supreme Court declared, "There can be no question of the power of Congress thus to define and limit the jurisdiction of the inferior courts of the United States".

In Lockerty v. Phillips (1943), the U.S. supreme Court held that Congress has the power of, "withholding jurisdiction from them [federal courts] in the exact degrees and character which to Congress may seem proper for the public good".

Section 3. Therefore, Congress hereby excludes from federal court jurisdiction any and all cases involving:

    a. Taking of human life, from point of conception;

    b. Sexual practices or the institution of marriage;

    c. Healthcare;

    d. Education;

e. Official recognition or application of any foreign law or code within these united States or any of them; and

f. Claims of United States control, possession, or juris-diction over any land outside of that granted by We the People (the sovereign People and States) as stipulated in Article I, Section 8, Clause 17, U.S. Constitution.

Section 4. What constitutes due process in all courts within the united States or any of them shall be defined and determined exclusively from within the Bill of Rights and the American common law, in that order of precedence.

Section 5. In Article III, Section 1 of the U.S. Constitution, the People stipulate, "the judicial Power of the United States shall be vested in one supreme Court, and in such inferior Courts as the Congress may from time to time ordain and establish"; therefore within 12 months of the passage of this Act:

a. No 'administrative law' tribunal in these United States shall bind the citizen in any way;

b. No administrative adjudicator shall be referred to as 'judge';

c. No administrative tribunal shall be referred to, or refer to itself, as 'court'; and

d. No administrative process or tribunal shall describe its processes in terms such as 'order', 'subpoena', 'warrant', or 'the record', which are reserved for constitutional judiciary.

Section 6. Pursuant to provisions of Section 2(f) above and the proposed Return of Sovereign Lands Act, 24 months after enactment of this legislation and thereafter, it shall be a federal felony for any agency, agent, bureau, department, officer, contractor or other representative of the government of these United States of America to claim, own, maintain or operate a purported U.S. court or detention facility that is not located within the land or property stipulated in Article I, Section 8, Clause 17 of the U.S. Constitution.

Section 7. Because Federal Rules of Criminal Procedure Numbers 6 and 7 appear to create an unconstitutional barrier to the established prerogative power of the People when serving in their State Grand Jury, no federal judicial rules shall have any bearing or authority over any State Grand Jury. As U.S. Supreme Court Justice Antonin Scalia wrote in U.S. v. Williams (1992):

"(T)he Grand Jury is an institution separate from the courts, over whose functioning the courts do not preside…Rooted in long centuries of Anglo American history, the Grand Jury is mentioned in the Bill of Rights, but not in the body of the

Constitution. It has not been textually assigned, therefore, to any of the branches described in the first three Articles. It is a constitutional fixture in its own right…

In fact, the whole theory of its function is that it belongs to no branch of the institutional government, serving as a kind of buffer or referee between the government and the People…The Grand Jury requires no authorization from its constituting court to initiate an investigation, nor does the prosecutor require leave of court to seek a Grand Jury indictment…[T]he Grand Jury generally operates without the interference of a presiding judge. It swears in its own witnesses, and deliberates in total secrecy."

Section 8. As stipulated in Article I, Section 8, Clause 15 of the U.S. Constitution, the several States retain the power to enforce this legislation by appropriate State legislation and duly authorized Citizen Militia enforcement action within their respective jurisdictions.

3) The **Non-Enumerated Powers Sunset Act,** stipulating:

Section 1. Congress hereby acknowledges as unconstitutional, any and all past enactment of legislation, 'positive law' Code sections and regulations, consent to treaties, or provision of federal funds applied to executive orders that confer on federal government any power not specifically enumerated in the U.S. Constitution or reasonably inferred from the powers enumerated, notwithstanding past creative interpretations applied by all three federal branches, to the terms 'interstate commerce', 'general welfare', and 'necessary and proper', and notwithstanding any and all 'positive law' Code sections drafted, finalized, promulgated, and/or enforced by federal employees who have no direct oversight by, or accountability to, the American People.

No federal 'positive law' regulation shall create a legal duty or liability for any citizen of these United States, unless and until the agency purporting to enforce such a regulation shall have established beyond reasonable doubt that said regulation is clearly and unambiguously authorized by the People in a specific section of the U.S. Constitution.

Congress hereby acknowledges that the government of these United States is a constitutional republic form of government under the Common Law as opposed to the positive law traditions of many foreign countries, notwithstanding the massive Deep State that has created an overwhelming burden of federal regulations produced by bureaucratic careerists at staggering cost to taxpayers.

Congress hereby further acknowledges that ultimate sovereignty in our republic is inherent in the American People rather than in a bureaucracy that propagates, promulgates and defends thousands of new 'positive law' regulations annually, which are too numerous and intentionally too complex for the average American to grasp or understand, much less to oversee or diminish.

The United States Code is the Code of Laws of the United States of America (also referred to as United States Code, U.S. Code, or U.S.C.) and is a compilation and codification of all the general and so-called 'permanent' federal laws of the republic. But no law in this republic can be repugnant to the specific words and spirit of the U.S. Constitution. Any federal law which is found to be in clear violation of, or repugnant to the plain language of the U.S. Constitution is and has been null and void since its enactment.

The U.S. Code does not include regulations issued by executive branch agencies, published in the Code of Federal Regulations (C.F.R.). Proposed and recently adopted regulations are posted in the Federal Register.

Congress shall make available online, at no cost to the user, the 51 titles of the United States Code as maintained by the U.S. House of Representatives Office of the Law Revision Counsel, and the cumulative supplements which are published annually.

Section 2. The Standing Committee to Defund Non-Enumerated Powers (SCDNEP) is hereby created in the U.S. House, to bind this body to obey the U.S. Constitution as actually written.

Section 3. Upon its formation, the SCDNEP shall appropriate adequate funding for a website and appurtenant support to serve and support the Citizens' Volunteer Research Service (CVRS) as described herein.

Section 4. In appropriating funds for CVRS website and support for citizen volunteers, Congress does not suggest that it, a federal servant, has authority to create such an oversight organ for the People themselves; only that Congress seeks hereby to provide for the People's oversight function to the extent that the People themselves require and employ it.

Section 5. Congress hereby acknowledges that the American People themselves, collectively, are sovereign in this and all other matters of federal government, as clearly and unambiguously stipulated in the Preamble, in Article I, Section 8 and especially in Amendment X of the U.S. Constitution, which sections only reiterate the People's original, God-given, organic, inherent, retained power to oversee all operations and budgets of their servants in federal government.

Congress hereby acknowledges that any CVRS Work Group or Supergroup casting its vote to de-fund and terminate any regulation issued by executive branch agencies shall infer that the CVRS has determined that the regulation in question does usurp, undermine, or countermand the stipulations of the U.S. Constitution or the retained powers of the sovereign People as stipulated in Amendment X of the U.S. Constitution. Said regulation shall become null and void and of no effect, immediately upon said vote.

Section 7. Prior to being funded or observed for any future fiscal year, any federal budget request whether executive or legislative – whether submitted by an agency, bureau, department, office, power, program, code or regulatory body, service branch, or via executive order or treaty – shall be accompanied by a written demonstration that it falls within a specifically enumerated power in Article I Section 8 or Article II Section 2 of the U.S. Constitution or duly ratified Amendment thereto, or can be reasonably inferred by the American citizen of average intelligence to be a rational appurtenance thereto. Any budget request not so accompanied, shall cease to be funded at the end of the then-current fiscal year.

Section 8. Because the functions of federal government were enumerated so as to limit the reach and power of the federal servant, such that it should never be considered either the master or the provider of the People, any agency, bureau, department, office, power, program, code or regulation not specifically enumerated in the U.S. Constitution or being an unambiguously 'necessary and proper' adjunct to the powers enumerated, as can be reasonably inferred by the American citizen of average intelligence, unless proposed and ratified as a constitutional amendment adhering to Article V of the U.S. Constitution, shall be subject to CVRS review and closure.

Section 9. In light of the long history of federal legislative, executive and judicial malfeasance and treachery by stretching the 'interstate commerce', 'general welfare', and 'necessary and proper' clauses, no federal agency, bureau, department, office, power, program, statute, code or regulation shall be added to others in any omnibus bill or amendment. If not enumerated in Article I, Section 8 and requiring application of public funds, each proposed agency, bureau, department, office, power, program, statute, code or regulation shall be proposed as a discrete bill or constitutional amendment.

Section 10. To maintain the delineation between the jurisdiction of an authorizing committee and the House Appropriations Committee, House Rule XXI creates a point of order against unauthorized appropriations in general appropriations bills. While any appropriation in such a bill is out of order unless the expenditure is authorized by existing law, if the point of order is not raised or is waived and the bill is enacted, said unauthorized appropriation is treated as legitimate. This practice has been tantamount to embezzlement of public funds.

Language requiring or permitting government action carries an implicit authorization for money to be appropriated for that purpose. The 'authorization of appropriations' provision limits the authorization of a piece of legislation to the amount and/or to the fiscal years stated. Accordingly, any prior budget authorization appropriating "such sums as may be necessary", without specifying the amount, years, and specifically constitutional purpose for which such appropriations were authorized, shall receive no further funding after the date of enactment hereof.

Section 11. There is hereby authorized a national Citizens' Volunteer Research Service (CVRS) with five citizens per U.S. congressional district, comprising one CVRS Work Group, said citizens selected by each U.S. representative's staff at random from the legislator's congressional district tax and voter rolls.

No citizen selected at random to serve on a CVRS Work Group shall be compelled to serve. All CVRS members shall be volunteers, receiving no remuneration for their service to the public.

Section 12. As with a Grand Jury, all CVRS members selected shall remain anonymous, to protect the Members from lobbying pressure or threats, and from threats or retaliation by endangered government employees.

Section 13. The deliberations of each and every CVRS Work Group shall remain completely confidential within the Work Group. Divulging the name of a CVRS member or divulging in advance of publication on the 'More Constitutional Government' website, any decision of a Work Group to retain or de-fund a federal budget item – whether an agency, bureau, project, code section, regulation or project – shall be a felony.

Section 14. Each CVRS Work Group shall review individual federal codes, regulations and regulatory bodies and associated federal budget line items. Each CVRS Work Group shall review at one time only a single, discrete federal budget line item unless the powers and functions of the agencies, bureaus, programs, code sections or regulations entail several or many similar functions or areas of endeavor appearing to violate the U.S. Constitution, being neither explicitly nor implicitly authorized therein.

Section 15. In such cases, an entire federal agency, bureau or regulatory entity shall be reviewed and voted on for defunding and closure by a CVRS Supergroup, which shall consist of twelve (12) CVRS Work Groups located in twelve (12) states, with two Work Groups from each region (Northeast, South-east, Midwest, South Central, Southwest, Northwest).

Such draconian action by a 'mere' 60 citizens compares favorably to countless coercive actions impacting over 320 million citizens yet imposed by a single federal judge or at most by five justices of the U.S. supreme Court. As set out in the U.S. Constitution, the collective sovereignty of the American People is superior in authority to that of the People's servants, be they legislative, executive or judiciary, particularly when servants have violated the Constitution or occupy an office nowhere authorized by the People through that supreme Law.

Section 16. Each CVRS Work Group shall have 60 days to research, assess, and recommend de-funding and terminating a federal code section or regulation or its associated agency or office. At the conclusion of its deliberations, the CVRS Work Group shall submit the code section, regulation, agency, program or bureau selected for de-funding and termination, to the manager of the CVRS website, for posting.

Within 30 days after said posting, each recommended defunding and termination measure shall be voted on by each and every CVRS Work Group. Each Work Group shall cast one vote, representing the majority vote of that Work Group's members casting a vote on that item.

Section 17. Each Work Group's vote shall be the vote of the U.S. congressman who represents that district. No member of Congress shall influence, counter-mand, veto, or otherwise interfere with final decisions of a CVRS Work Group or Supergroup.

No member of Congress shall recruit, entice, hire, contract, coerce or otherwise obtain the services of any staff member, agent or intermediary to influence or otherwise interfere with a final decision of any CVRS Work Group or Supergroup.

Section 18. De-funding and termination of any federal code section or regulation shall occur within 180 days of a vote having been cast with a simple majority of all votes cast, in favor of de-funding and termination.

Each such vote shall be posted on the dedicated secure CVRS website server for public access within 72 hours after the vote is cast, on the CVRS 'More Constitutional Government' portal.

Section 19. Pursuant to this legislation, the SCDNEP shall provide adequate funding and staffing to maintain a comprehensive database of each and every federal agency, bureau, code and regulation under review including date of commencement of review and effective date for de-funding and termination..

Section 20. No member of Congress or staff of any member of Congress shall interfere with any CVRS Work Group, other than each legislator's staff randomly selecting from voter registration or tax rolls, the citizens to serve on a CVRS Work Group.

Section 21. A CVRS member must serve a minimum of 90 days, and may serve on a Work Group for four consecutive years. No CVRS member shall serve for more than eight years in aggregate, with a minimum of two years intervening between periods of service.

Work Group members shall provide 30 days' notice prior to resigning or retiring from service.

Every CVRS member rendered incapable of service due to death or disability shall be immediately replaced with the next name in the service queue in that district and said replacement shall be summoned to begin service within 10 calendar days.

Section 22. No person shall serve on a CVRS Work Group if (s)he is presently employed by any agency of government or has been so employed within the preceding three years.

Section 23. Any current or former CVRS member receiving a financial benefit of more than $100 by virtue of his/her positive decision to retain a federal code section, regulation, agency, bureau, program or project shall be guilty of a federal felony.

4) The **Clean Bill Act**, stipulating:

Section 1. No omnibus bill shall be permitted. All bills passing out of any committee in Congress shall treat only the subject found in the title of the bill, and shall not exceed 50 pages, single-sided, double-spaced, 12-point type.

Section 2. No committee shall add any amendment, rider, or earmark or authorize any agency, bureau, department, expenditure, office, power, program or regulation that cannot be demonstrated is directly entailed in the subject and title of the bill.

Section 3. All bills when filed shall list the names and contact information of every private-sector individual and entity who initiated and/or proposed or suggested elements of said legislation.

5) The **Secure Borders Act**, stipulating:

Section 1. Each citizen of these United States has an in-alienable right to defend his own life, liberty, and property.

Section 2. Attending that right is the duty stipulated in Article I, Section 8, Clause 15 of the U.S. Constitution, for Citizen Militia to "execute the Laws of the Union, suppress Insurrections, and repel Invasions".

Section 3. Congress hereby acknowledges each border State's legislature's special right and duty stipulated in Article I, Section 8, Clause 16, to appoint the officers and train the Militia of that State.

Section 4. To aid in its duty per Clause 15, Congress shall provide for immediately finish constructing a secure border barrier, with reasonable alternatives employed for riverine sections of the U.S.-Mexico border, and Congress shall waive environmental, regulatory, and bureaucratic requirements such that the border fence project shall avoid the time and cost overruns common to federal government projects.

Section 5. Congress shall provide for an increase in border federal troop strength, airborne assets, and electronic detection as to furnish a demonstrably effective impediment to illegal crossing by any means.

Section 6. Congress shall coordinate this effort with the legislatures and their duly authorized Citizen Militia (where applicable) of the sovereign States of California, Arizona, New Mexico, and Texas, and shall accept all reasonable aid and alliance with said legislatures along their own sovereign borders, to timely construct said wall and/or fence.

Section 7. Congress shall immediately discontinue and de-fund all agencies, bureaus, policies and programs that encourage, facilitate, or support illegal immigration.

Section 8. As the Islamic belief system is well established and self-described as a militant organization and an exclusive, invasive law-code, Congress will assure that any individual shall be barred from immigration into this republic who is reasonably believed to adhere to sharia law, regardless of whether the aspiring immigrant's domicile of origin is an officially Islamic state.

Section 9. As stipulated in Article I, Section 8, Clause 15 of the U.S. Constitution, the several States retain the power to enforce this legislation by appropriate State legislation and duly authorized Citizen Militia enforcement within their respective jurisdictions.

6) **Senate Joint Resolution 6** of the 111th Congress, ending the illegal alien 'anchor baby' practice.

7) The **Congressional Anti-Corruption Act**, stipulating:

Section 1. SEC insider trading rules shall apply to members of Congress. It shall be a federal crime for a member of Congress, directly or through proxies, trusts, or other entities, to purchase or sell stock in any company materially affected by legislation of which the member of Congress may be reasonably expected to have knowledge.

Section 2. No incumbent or former member of Congress may lobby Congress on behalf of any domestic interest for a period of five years after leaving Congress, or on behalf of any foreign interest, for life.

Section 3. For any member of Congress to require any member to raise money as a prerequisite to being considered for or offered a seat or leadership role on any committee of Congress, shall be a federal felony.

Section 4. As stipulated in Article I, Section 8, Clause 15 of the U.S. Constitution, the several States retain the power to enforce this legislation by appropriate State legislation and duly authorized Citizen Militia enforcement within their respective jurisdictions.

8) The **Citizens' Privacy and Liberty Act**, stipulating:

Section 1. The American people's own persons, houses, papers, telephone, email, and other communications, vehicles and effects shall be free from any and all government surveillance, collection, seizure, storage, or detainment unless preceded by issuance of a specific, bona fide judicial warrant issued upon probable cause, as stipulated in the Fourth Amendment to the U.S. Constitution.

Section 2. With the benefit of the doubt accruing to the citizen, any portion of the FISA, RFPA, USA Patriot Act, NDAA, and Intelligence Authorization Act of 2004 or any similar legislation presently in effect that violates the Fourth Amendment, are hereby repealed.

Section 3. Congress shall bear responsibility and accountability to the American People to assure that any operations of the FBI, NSA, CIA, or any other federal intelligence agency, <u>or any major U.S.-based technology provider</u> shall scrupulously refrain from infringing on the privacy, or on the freedom of speech and expression of any American citizen, whether residing in any of the 50 sovereign States or residing temporarily overseas.

Section 4. It shall be a federal felony for any individual, corporation, or federal entity to engage in any optical, electronic, airborne, or satellite surveillance, collection, seizure, storage, detainment, tracing, or tracking of any American citizen, his property, or his communications, whether by means of traditional devices and methods or by 'nanobots', mini-drones, sniffer aircraft, satellite, concealed cameras or sensors, or any other means, unless the citizen has requested such 'service', or until a judicial or Grand Jury warrant is issued upon probable cause, supported by oath or affirmation and particularly describing place, items, or data to be searched and persons or things to be seized.

Section 5. No visa of an American citizen seeking to return to one of the 50 sovereign States, shall be revoked without due process of law.

Section 6. As stipulated in Article I, Section 8, Clause 15 of the U.S. Constitution, the several States retain the power to enforce this legislation by appropriate State legislation and duly authorized Citizen Militia enforcement within their respective jurisdictions.

9) The **Religious Treason Act,** outlawing religious laws or seditious activities in the name of any foreign religion, state, or legal system operating within these United States, stipulating as follows:

Preamble. As explained in hundreds of passages in the Quran itself as well as in precise detail in the book <u>The Quranic Concept of War</u> by Pakistani General S.K. Malik, the belief system established by Mohammed in the 7th century is full theocracy; a system of law and government. Islam demands adherence by all, obedience by all Muslims, and payment of a dhimmi's tax by all non-Muslims.

As Europe reels under a new Muslim invasion, we are prudent to recall the words of U.S. supreme Court Justice Joseph Story, who wrote in his massive work on the Constitution, "The real object of the First Amendment was not to countenance, much less to advance Mohammedanism, or Judaism, or infidelity, by prostrating Christianity, but only to exclude all rivalry among Christian sects and to prevent any national ecclesiastical establishment."

Ending immigration of potential enemies of America and our Constitution is neither the establishment of religion or impeding the free exercise of religion; rather, it is within Congress' responsibility to support the U.S. Constitution and the security of the sovereign States of this republic.

Section 1. Because Islam is <u>a means of warfare against all rivals</u>, and given the common tactic known as taqiyya which instructs Muslims to deceive in the interest of furthering Mohammed's system of law and government, the United States shall not allow immigration of any foreign national who adheres to Islam.

Section 2. For the same reason, adherence or allegiance to Islam shall disqualify any American citizen from taking public office at school district, city, county, state or national level.

Section 3. It shall be a federal offense for any elected or appointed U.S. federal public servant to travel to a foreign country with such travel funded by a foreign government or by a foreign or domestic private foundation or lobbying organization on behalf of any foreign country, people, or religion.

Section 4. Every lobbying group for any foreign country or religious cause — specifically any lobbying organization for Israel or any Islamic state — is required to register within 180 days of passage of this legislation, under the Foreign Agents Registration Act of 1938.

Section 5. Every applicant for U.S. naturalization shall be required to swear under oath his or her full allegiance to these United States of America and their laws. Any reasonably suspected of adherence to Islam or any other faith that calls for or sanctions in its established doctrines forcible conversion, supplanting American Law, or substantive discrimination against other faiths, shall be required to make an unambiguous public, videotaped renunciation of that faith.

Section 6. It shall be a federal offense for any educational or religious institution, public or private, to promote or incite violence, war, or a foreign code of law on the basis of any religious teaching, tradition, law, or on any other basis than the liberty and security of these United States of America.

Section 7. All individuals including American nationals, immigrants, resident aliens, and foreign diplomats, and all institutions within these United States found in violation of this law shall receive a warning and fine for the first infraction. A second offense shall warrant forfeiture of the individual's U.S. visa, indictment for treason or sedition, and seizure of assets held within these United States.

Section 8. Upon the first instance in any of these United States of attempted murder by conventional explosive or mass attack (three or more victims) by any individual or group associated with, or on behalf of, a religious belief or legal system, using any potentially lethal object (firearm, knife or vehicle) there shall issue a nationwide warning of a ban on all gatherings in, or use of, any and all facilities affiliated with said religious belief system within these United States.

Section 9. Upon the second instance described in Section 8, there shall issue a ban throughout these United States on all gatherings in, or use of, any and all facilities affiliated with said religious system within these United States.

Section 10. Upon the third instance described in Section 8, all property and other assets held by or in favor of, said religious system within these United States shall be seized and where applicable destroyed, and willful adherence to said system of belief or law within these United States shall thereafter be classified as sedition and if sufficiently egregious, treason.

Section 11. Upon the first instance of an individual or group associated with a foreign religious or legal system, discharging in any of these United States a nuclear, chemical, or biological device capable of inflicting mass casualties: all U.S.-based land, buildings, training facilities, bank accounts, and other assets of said religious or legal system shall be seized and where applicable, destroyed.

Section 12. As stipulated in Article I, Section 8, Clause 15 of the U.S. Constitution, the several States retain the power to enforce this legislation by

231

appropriate State legislation and duly authorized Citizen Militia enforcement within their respective jurisdictions.

10) The **Internet Liberty Act**, stipulating:

Section 1. It shall be a federal felony for any individual or group within federal government or within any major technology service provider who — unilaterally or with other individuals, groups, organizations, or governments — disables or censors any citizen's access to the Internet so that it becomes inaccessible to the average computer or other Internet device in these sovereign States.

Section 2. As stipulated in Article I, Section 8, Clause 15 of the U.S. Constitution, the several States retain the power to enforce this legislation by appropriate State legislation and duly authorized Citizen Militia enforcement within their respective jurisdictions.

11) The **Constitutional Supremacy Act**, assuring the sovereignty of the American People and States, stipulating:

Section 1. No provision of a treaty or agreement, public or secret, conflicting with this Constitution or not made in pursuance thereof, shall be the supreme Law of the Land or be of general force or effect.

Section 2. No provision of a treaty or other international agreement shall become effective as internal law in the United States until it is enacted through legislation in Congress acting within its constitutionally enumerated powers.

Section 3. No Continuity of Government (COG) order may contravene, suspend or violate the U.S. Constitution in any particular.

Section 4. Per Article III, Section 2, Clause 2 of the U.S. Constitution, Congress hereby stipulates as an Exception that no federal court shall have jurisdiction in any matter arising under this Act.

Section 5. Any vote regarding advice and consent to ratification of a treaty shall be determined by yeas and nays and names of all persons voting for and against shall be entered in the Journal of the Senate.

Section 6. It shall be a federal felony for any individual or group to engage in or to materially support actions that threaten the legal or financial sovereignty of any of the sovereign States of America without the knowledge and consent of the legislature of each and every State whose citizens would be affected, regardless whether such action may formally constitute treason.

Section 7. Within 12 months from passage of this Act, Congress shall cease all foreign aid of a military nature to any government, regime, entity, or individual.

Section 8. Within 24 months from passage of this Act, Congress shall cease all foreign aid of a non-military nature to any government, regime, entity, or individual. Said aid shall be immediately reduced by 33% for the first 12 months and by 66% for the second 12 months.

12) The **American Sovereignty Restoration Act** of 2017 (HR193) of the 115th Congress, and stipulating:

Section 1. This bill repeals the United Nations Participation Act of 1945 and other specified related laws.

Section 2. The President shall terminate U.S. membership in the United Nations (U.N.), including any organ, specialized agency, commission, or other formally affiliated body.

Section 3. The President shall close the U.S. Mission to the United Nations.

Section 4. The following shall hereafter be unlawful: a) Any funds for the U.S. assessed or voluntary contribution to the U.N.; b) Any authorization of funds for any U.S. contribution to any U.N. military or peacekeeping operation; c) Expenditure of funds to support the participation of U.S. Armed Forces as part of any U.N. military or peacekeeping operation; d) U.S. armed forces serving under U.N. com-mand; and d) diplomatic immunity for U.N. officers or employees.

13) The **Lawful Wars Act**, reiterating Congress' duty to declare wars, repealing the War Powers Resolution of 1973 and barring any administration from initiating foreign hostilities or mobilizing U.S. military in foreign lands without a Declaration of War; requiring Congress to assure that such mobilization or hostilities are necessary to defend against a demonstrable threat to these United States.

14) The **Federal Pork Sunset Act,** stipulating:

In Fiscal Year 2019, federal government doled out over $700 billion in illicit funds to the States, counties, and cities across our republic. The long tradition of such 'pork' projects with strings attached has perverted the citizen's view of his place atop the Constitution's hierarchy and allowed Washington D.C. organized crime to assume the role of benevolent master, with the sovereign States and cities as so many piglets at sow-teats. This criminogenic arrangement has rendered our local, county and State public servants willing to do whatever they must, to receive their share of funds (originating from the people themselves) from countless unaccountable, largely invisible federal agencies. This criminal activity must end.

Section 1. For three (3) fiscal years after passage of this Act, all revenues sent by federal government as grants to States and their subdivisions shall be remitted as a single block grant to each State, with no federal conditions attached, i.e., the States having liberty to determine all uses of said funds.

Section 2. Commencing on the first day of the fourth fiscal year after the date of passage of this Act, any federal grant to a State or subdivision thereof shall be a federal felony.

15) The **Minuteman Act**, pursuant to Congress's power to "provide for...arming...the Militia" contained in the U.S. Constitution, stipulating:

Section 1. The National Firearms Act of 1934, Omnibus Crime Control and Safe Streets Act of 1968, the Gun Control Act of 1968, the Firearm Owners Protection Act of 1986, and the Brady Handgun Violation Prevention Act of 1993 are hereby repealed.

Section 2. No statute, regulation, executive order, or other directive with the purported force of law of federal government, present or future, or that of any State or subdivision thereof, shall infringe on or burden the right of any citizen of, or legal resident alien in, any State who is eligible for membership in that State's Militia to purchase, own, possess, transport, or sell, whether interstate or intrastate, any firearm, ammunition, or related accoutrements suitable for service in a Militia as that term is used in the U.S. Constitution.

Section 3. No statute, regulation, executive order, or other directive with the purported force of law of federal government, present or future, shall infringe on or burden, except on the same terms as apply to any other business, the right of any person to engage in the commercial design, manufacture, repair, sale and distribution, or other trade or occupation involving firearms, ammunition, and Militia accoutrements.

Section 4. As stipulated in Article I, Section 8, Clause 15 of the U.S. Constitution, the several States retain the power to enforce this legislation by appropriate State legislation and duly authorized Citizen Militia enforcement within their respective jurisdictions and subdivisions.

16) The **Non-Conscription Act**, stipulating:

Section 1. Neither Congress nor any president or federal court has the power to conscript Americans of any age into involuntary national service or servitude of any kind.

Section 2. As stipulated in Article I, Section 8, Clause 15 of the U.S. Constitution, the several States retain the power to enforce this legislation by appropriate State legislation and duly authorized Citizen Militia enforcement within their respective jurisdictions.

17) The **Return of Sovereign Lands Act**, stipulating:

Section 1. Upon acceptance as a sovereign State of these United States, all lands and resources within said State become the sovereign property of the American People living within said State, and the individual right to private property is no more sacred than the collective right of sovereign property for every sovereign government on earth. The federal government has no lawful authority or claim of sovereignty over — or claim to minerals or other natural resources in, on or under — any land on earth, except as stipulated in Article I, Section 8, Clause 17 of the U.S. Constitution.

Section 2. No sale of any land or resource within any of the sovereign States shall be made by the U.S. government or any entity thereof on behalf of said government, effective immediately, except such surface land as stipulated in Article I, Section 8, Clause 17 of the U.S. Constitution.

Section 3. The United States government shall, within 24 months of the passage of this Act, relinquish all claims to, or jurisdiction in, all sovereign places other than those lands specifically stipulated in Article I, Section 8, Clause 17 of the U.S. Constitution as being within the exclusive legislative domain of Congress.

*Section 4. The federal government has no constitutional authority to **seize** private or State sovereign land, water, timber, oil, gas, minerals, or other natural resources in, on, or under such land in any State, for any reason, under any conditions.*

*Section 5. Other than purchases from the States for military installations, federal government has no constitutional authority to **accept** lands or resources via a State constitution or legislative act.*

Section 6. As to purchases from the sovereign States for military installations, federal government has constitutional authority to purchase lands in a State only with "Consent of the Legislature of the State in which the Same shall be". Said consent of the State Legislature must be accompanied by a majority-vote approval of the People of that State via single-issue referendum or plebiscite.

Section 7. All present federally claimed, held, or controlled lands and any minerals, water, forests and timber, or any other resource within each sovereign State shall revert within 24 months to full control and ownership of the State in which it is located, to be managed and controlled as the People of that State shall determine. The costs of transferring control of formerly federally-claimed lands and natural resources shall be borne by the State in which said lands and resources are located.

Section 8. All federal land-use regulations, national forest and park acts, and like federal controls, restrictions, and prohibitions that deprive private owners of the full use and enjoyment of their private properties pursuant to the laws of the several States, shall be repealed within 12 months of passage of this Act.

Section 9. As reparations for the past federal use and control of sovereign State lands, all federal government improvements, fixtures, facilities, equipment, vehicles and other appurtenances located within each sovereign State (except on military installations) shall become the property of that State, effective immediately. The legal transfer of all said public property located within each State shall be administered by the government of that State, and shall include executive, legislative and judicial branches and Citizen Militia as applicable.

Section 10. Congress shall provide to the sovereign People of the United States, within 12 months of passage of this Act, its detailed plan to relinquish control of all foreign military bases and to cease funding for, and operations of, all foreign land-based military and civil government operations, transferring foreign civil governance to the governments or people of those sovereign lands, within 36 months of the passage of this Act.

Section 11. Irrespective of any local independence movements within sovereign foreign lands outside the 48 contiguous and United States, all noncontiguous, foreign, and/or 'U.S. possession' claims shall revert to the full, un-fettered control of the peoples of those sovereign lands (including Hawaii and Alaska, neither of which People ever applied for statehood but were instead invaded and claimed by Washington D.C.) at their own expense and with no additional expense borne by American citizens after 24 months from passage of this Act.

18) The **Lawful United States Money and Banking Act** which will contain elements of, but be more comprehensive than H.R. 459, 833, 1094, 1095, 1098, 1496 and 2768 and SB 202, stipulating:

Section 1. The American people have delegated the power to 'coin Money' only to Congress, and have delegated to Congress only the power to 'coin' Money.

Section 2. Congress lacks any authority to delegate or to fail, neglect, or refuse to exercise this power.

Section 3. The Legal Tender Act of 1862, the Federal Re-serve Act of 1913, and all subsequent amendments of those acts, have been unconstitutional since their enactment.

Section 4. The special privileges now attaching to Federal Reserve Notes— that such notes shall be redeemed in lawful money by the United States Department of the

Treasury, shall be receivable for all taxes and other public dues, and shall be legal tender for all debts, public and private—have since enactment been in violation of our Supreme Law.

Section 5. As remedies for these violations of the Constitution, Congress shall establish as an alternative to the Federal Reserve System and notes, a system of official money consisting solely of gold and silver, with silver coins valued in 'dollars' at the prevailing exchange rate between silver and gold in the free market.

Section 6. This new, lawful U.S. money shall be produced through immediate free coinage of whatever gold and silver may be brought to the United States Mints; including sale of the existing national gold stocks, replaced by silver stock if the gold-silver ratio suggests silver as preferable for the initial coinage.

Section 7. Said reserves and coinage and/or fully-convertible paper or electronic receipts for physical gold and silver, shall be substituted for Federal Reserve Notes as rapidly as maintenance of stability throughout America's economy will permit, in all financial transactions of the general government.

Section 8. The Federal Reserve Act of 1913 (as amended) shall be further amended such that: a) after the effective date of such legislation, the Federal Reserve System shall have no official relationship to the general government, and b) Federal Reserve regional banks shall obtain new charters from the States consistent with the laws thereof or cease doing business as of the date on which the Secretary of the Treasury shall certify that all financial transactions of federal government are being conducted solely in gold and silver or fully-convertible paper or electronic receipts for physical gold and silver.

Section 9. The States have always enjoyed the right as sovereign governments and a duty pursuant to Article I, Section 10 of the Constitution to employ gold and silver coin or fully-convertible paper or electronic receipts for physical gold and silver, to the exclusion of any other currency as the medium of exchange in their functions. Neither Congress, nor the president, nor any court, nor any international or supra-national body, nor any private parties have any authority to require a State to employ anything other than gold and silver coin or fully-convertible paper or electronic receipts for physical gold and silver, for such purposes.

Section 10. The practice of fractional reserve banking is to be ended within 12 months of passage of this legislation, and all American financial institutions shall be required to maintain in their vaults 100% reserves against loans made. Any financial institution accepting deposits, that is unable to pay on demand all such deposits in gold and/or silver or fully-convertible paper or electronic receipts for physical gold and silver, the directors, officers, shareholders, partners, trustees, or *other owners and managers of said institution shall be personally liable (their own personal assets subject to seizure) to satisfy unpaid deposit balances under the laws of the State in which the demand for payment of such balances is made.*

Section 11. It shall be a federal felony for any person to enact or enforce any tax or financial burden on: a) any exchange of one form of United States money for another form of money thereof, notwithstanding that the nominal value of one form may be different than the nominal value of the other form involved in the transaction; or b) the movement of privately-owned United States money by any private citizen, to or from the United States to or from any other domicile that said private citizen may desire, provided said funds are not being demonstrably used in, or do not demonstrably result from, illegal activity.

Section 12. This legislation shall apply to Federal Reserve Notes, base-metallic and debased silver coinage, and all paper currencies of the United States until the date on which the Secretary of the Treasury shall certify that all federal financial transactions are being conducted solely in gold and silver or fully-convertible paper or electronic receipts for physical gold and silver, and thereafter only as Congress deems necessary.

19) The **Intelligent Republic Act**, a reform law based loosely on the Smart Nation Act, sponsored by Congressman Rob Simmons (R-CT), must provide for orderly dismantling of all secret intelligence operations of federal government as recommended by former CIA officers Kevin Shipp and Robert Steele.

The National Security Act of 1947 created the CIA and the National Security Council, which is accountable only to presidents. *Congress, which represents the People and the States, allowed itself no oversight of the NSC.* That criminal act of legislation never defined or limited what the CIA can do or cannot do, but also clearly cannot and must not authorize, allow, or fund covert operations closed to congressional oversight.

Even if the House Permanent Select Committee on Intelligence and the Senate Select Committee on Intelligence attempted to de-fund the most egregious crimes of this criminal agency, the CIA makes this impossible. First, it makes all of its budget line items and appropriations classified, keeping its operations secret from Congress thus making it impossible to de-fund the agency in part.

Second, the CIA maintains blackmail dossiers on all members of Congress so that no legislator would dare reduce that criminal organization's programs or funding. Thus, this criminal operation as well as the deeply corrupt FBI, must be dismantled, outlawed, and defunded _in full_.

With illicit funding generated by foreign drug operations, these criminal agencies give themselves vast, unconstitutional powers over the American People and even over American elections and those of foreign countries.

Secret agencies unaccountable to the American people are unconstitutional and have increasingly destructive impact on American security, liberty, and public morale. It is clearly unconstitutional for federal government to create foreign operating agencies, fund private offshore contractors, or create alliances with foreign countries, whether for intelligence or supposed 'defense'. Such corrupt traditions violate the Constitution by usurping the authority of Congress and the Militia.

The Constitution stipulates that the Citizen Militia shall _"execute the Laws of the Union, suppress Insurrections, and repel Invasions"_. Thus, all networks, cells, and offices for intelligence in the American republic _must_ operate under the local aegis of the Citizen Militia and are ultimately the duty and authority of the American People themselves. Each unit of Citizen Militia, according to the Constitution, is to follow _"the discipline prescribed by Congress"_, with officers appointed by and training, equipment, logistics supplied by its State legislature.

~ ~ ~

We The People reserve the right to revise and extend the list of federal government arrogations, violations, and usurpations brought to our attention for remediation by AmericaAgain! members via our State courts and through reform legislation.

Notwithstanding the long tradition of congressional corruption and arrogation warned against by James Madison, the numerous retained powers of We the People includes power to allow _no implication beyond the powers specifically enumerated_ to our federal servant; for our benefit, not theirs. As members of AmericaAgain! and its TACTICAL CIVICS™ chapter network, we resolve to enforce the Law of the Land under Amendment X; the People and States retain all powers not specifically enumerated to federal government.

For many generations, Washington D.C. has arrogated to itself powers nowhere granted to federal government by the sovereign People or States. We The People shall now put the shoe on the other foot, exercising our almost limitless retained powers as clearly stipulated in Amendment X, but only to enforce the U.S. Constitution and its limitations on our federal servants. We intend to thus tighten the chains of the Constitution via our Indictment Engine™ and the Grand Juries of our States to criminally indict members of Congress and State legislatures whose violation of the supreme law and our liberty are found to coincide with felonies in their State criminal statutes.

We shall bring our members of Congress home from doing the bidding of powerful individuals in party machines behind the scenes – to now work beside us and under our watchful eyes in their own home districts which shall now be smaller and more difficult for powerful interests to corrupt.

Violations of State criminal statutes are exclusive original and appellate jurisdiction of the courts of the State in which the parties reside. No State being a party to these actions, nothing in the Constitution or federal law can be construed to allow federal courts to steal jurisdiction and exonerate such perpetrators.

AmericaAgain!, through its TACTICAL CIVICS™ chapter network, seeks to rekindle the lawful, pre-constitutional Grand Juries and Militias in each County, for we share the founders' concerns about government – now including many State governments – seeking to disarm the People, their sovereign and violating the U.S. Constitution and their state constitutions with impunity. It is the duty of all citizens, as codified in the Fourth, Fifth, and Sixth Amendments to the U.S. Constitution, to serve in their county Grand Jury to check and superintend their servants in county and municipal government, and any other servant, whether in state or federal office who lives and works in the county, to investigate any credible complaint or presentment of potential criminal behavior by said officers.

And it is also the duty of all citizens who are physically and mentally fit for the duty, to be armed and trained to fulfill the Citizen Militia functions in Article I, Section 8, Clause 15 of the Constitution. Per Clause 16, it is the duty of the States to provide officers and training for Citizen Militias, yet no State legislature has yet fully performed such duty. Until the State legislatures do so, it is the People's express and retained power as well as our God-given right, to have our County governments fill the void, or even to defend ourselves.

We seek to be better stewards of the natural resources that God has entrusted to us – rather than allowing our government in our name, to help corporations plunder resources of foreign countries.

This organization is explicitly, unashamedly Christian. It will *perpetually* hold to, support, and defend the Christian doctrine of the Apostle's Creed, and will require of all national leadership and regional trustees, an oath or affirmation of that statement of faith. Although this be a perpetual trust, should it ever fail to glorify Jesus Christ and defend the faith and norms attached thereto, *it shall be dissolved.*

In our membership and operations we seek no theocracy; but the American civilization was founded as a Christian – not Atheist, Jewish, Muslim, Hindu, Buddhist, Catholic or Mormon – commonwealth. None of those beliefs, or any other, has produced equally efficacious or humane law, economics, or social practices. Although some Founding Fathers were not orthodox Christians, the vast majority were. A survey of America's original colonial documents of government, law, economics, and social life demonstrates that America is founded on Christianity and no other belief system. A survey of the history of atheism, 1947 political Judaism, Islam, Hinduism, Buddhism, Catholicism, and Mormonism have no such historical record of accomplishments. Yet we only exclude Muslims because that is a system of government and law at war with ours; it is not merely a 'religion'.

In building, reinforcing, promoting, refining and organizing our TACTICAL CIVICS™ chapter network, we refuse to operate in any unlawful, seditious, riotous, rebellious, paranoid, or terroristic manner. We also refuse to allow this tactical mission of We the People to be co-opted, overseen, or infested by politicians, lobbyists, or operatives from any government or political party, foreign or domestic. We will organize and operate locally as free citizens in the privacy of our homes, businesses, and churches – or in public parks and any venue that suits us as owners and residents of such places – expecting to have no government infiltration, or coercion as is common to tyrant regimes.

Should our member of congress, state legislator, or governor refuse to cease violating the law; should he prevaricate and bloviate as politicians do, or conspire anew with like-minded scoundrels and oligarchs who purchased his first allegiance – we will seek his criminal conviction in State Court; the longest possible State Penitentiary term; and as actual and punitive damages for massive fraud and conspiracy, we will seek to have our State Court seize all assets held under any structure, in any jurisdiction, inuring to his benefit or that of his family or descendants.

To any state or county prosecutor, district attorney, judge, constable, sheriff or other public servant who refuses to oversee justice as your oath of office demands, We The People will see that your complicity in potential high crimes is included in a separate felony presentment to your Grand Jury, jointly deployed with our community or county Militia.

No defendant in Congress can plead ignorance of the U.S. Constitution or ignorance of federal laws over which he is responsible – even those for which he voted without reading. Ignorance of the law is no defense for public servants who swear an oath to support the U.S. Constitution, only to violate it daily, as was done in the 'COVID-19' scheme of 2020.

We the People will offer immunity from indictment to a member of Congress only if that defendant, in writing with notarized witnesses from among our membership, agrees to withdraw support for or cease acquiescence in the crime(s) for which we seek his indictment; sponsor or co-sponsor legislation outlined above, drafted by citizens; and refrain from supporting any amendment thereto.

AmericaAgain! and its TACTICAL CIVICS™ chapter network is an effort conceived by free, productive citizens of these sovereign States of America who believe that by God's grace, a diligent minority can restore liberty, property, rule of law, honest elections, and the collective sovereignty of We the People that we guaranteed ourselves in the U.S. Constitution.

Each public servant leaves a public record in history. Their response to their sovereigns now enforcing the Constitution will demonstrate either their repentant fidelity or their ignominious corruption.

We give thanks to God in the name of Jesus Christ His Son, and ask His blessing on this formerly godly republic, that we may be AmericaAgain!

We The People of the fifty United States of America

National Day of Thanksgiving

Original, November 22, 2012   (Rev 112- Nov 22, 2021)

APPENDIX I

Tactical Civics™ Declaration

The charter members of Tactical Civics™ are, for the first time in mankind's history, forging a responsible, repentant Remnant into an educated, organized, lawful force of Popular Constitutionalism, and helping our Congress become history's first distributed legislature. *That is no small feat.*

What Obama and the Dragon Brought

Hatched in the Lincoln administration, we began witnessing the kicking, screaming, clawing, biting death of 150-year-old American Communism when Hussein Obama removed Communism's mask and the Chinese dragon took 'Resident' Biden's invitation and removed its mask as well. Now, the CCP is helping to transform Washington DC into a brazen, arrogant, clinically insane Communist stronghold. *The Russiagate, Shampeachment, BLAntifa riots, Plandemic masking and jabbing operation, and Election Steal 2020 are the attempted overthrow of America.*

At least 100 million normal, productive Americans in the heartland will never stand for this. As the criminal, ruthless 10-by-10-mile city state on the Potomac has finally shown the world its true colors in 2015-2022, it's awakening America's Heartland. Until Tactical Civics™, We The People did not know what to do about it. *Most still don't.*

What America's Going to Do About It

But now, we in the repentant remnant *do* know what to do...

First, we are turning off Washington DC; watching and listening to organized crime as it sinks into its final pathetic years as a world power. We're increasingly tuning it out. For us normal folks, watching this idiocy in the federal, state, county, local, and school district palaces is like sitting in an insane asylum. We're outta there, and taking our money, too (more on that, below).

Second, We The People are walking away from Google, Facebook, Twitter, all mainstream media, Hollywood, and any tech company that decides to de-platform or ban us. Fantastic; you're dead to us, too. We'll find alternatives. *You won't.*

Third, We The People will pay no more attention to the sociopath political machines of Atlanta, Baltimore, Chicago, Dallas, Detroit, Houston, Los Angeles, Phoenix, Minneapolis, New York City, Philadelphia, and a couple of dozen other feral hellholes. In America's 31,000 small towns and all the rural homesteads in between, we intend to take control back, and *not* by the rigged game called politics. We're going to live our lives as normal, God-fearing, God-glorifying Americans. We refuse to give another minute to the sick values of God-hating, collapsing urban sewers. Hey, big cities: that's why your real estate values and tax bases are plummeting. Get a clue.

Fourth, We The People are restoring our Grand Jury and constitutional Militia in every one of the 3,141 counties, boroughs, and parishes in these sovereign States.

Fifth, We The People working on the app development team at Tactical Civics™ plan to develop, refine, and launch the Indictment Engine™ mobile app to scan every proposed state or federal bill before it becomes legislation, and if it violates the Constitution, generate felony presentments to be sent to the Grand Jury of the counties of every sponsor and co-sponsor (conspirator and co-conspirator of the attempted felony) in each perpetrator's State Judicial District.

Sixth, We The People intend to force 27 more State legislatures to ratify the original First Right in the Bill of Rights, requiring that no US congressional district exceed 50,000 persons; the only subject on which George Washington felt strongly enough about to address during the four-month constitutional convention in 1787. America's 31,000 small towns and millions of rural Americans will have representation in the U.S. House and Electoral College for the first time in a century.

Seventh, We The People intend to then bring Congress home to work under *our* watchful eye, as they obviously have not 'checked and balanced' one another in generations. In Article I, Section 8, Clause 17, we grant that Congress shall have 'exclusive legislative jurisdiction' in that 10-by-10-mile plot of land on the Potomac. So once we bring them home and have normal American statesmen filling those seats, we will take control of the agencies and bureaucracies that fill that ruthless, criminal city-state that plunders and threatens the whole earth,

244

beginning with its own sovereigns, enriching the few thousand wealthiest and most ruthless humans on earth.

Eighth, through 6600+ Citizens Volunteer Research Service (CVRS) teams created by our Non-Enumerated Powers Sunset Act (NEPSA), We The People will review, red-line, de-fund, and outlaw ('sunset') every agency, bureau, department, office, program, and regulation that We The People did not *specifically* authorize in our Constitution and have no need for. This review will be *at the People's sole discretion,* with each member of the U.S. House *required* to sign off to his/her CVRS team's decisions. When a majority of CVRS teams has red-lined an agency, program, or regulatory line item, it is de-funded, shut down, and outlawed. *Period.*

We The People are serious about organized crime. Any congressman found to have interfered with or attempted to change any CVRS team's decision will have committed a felony, as will be stipulated in NEPSA and similar State statutes.

Ninth, We The People intend to immediately de-fund the US Department of Education (Indoctrination) and assure that no public, private, or religious school shall have any nexus with federal government, except as stipulated in our proposed *Religious Treason Act,* outlawing religious laws or seditious activities in the name of any foreign religion, state, or legal system operating within these United States, stipulating,

"As explained in hundreds of passages in the Quran itself as well as in precise detail in the book The Quranic Concept of War by Pakistani General S.K. Malik, the belief system established by Mohammed in the 7th century is theocracy; a system of law and government. Islam demands adherence by all, obedience by all Muslims, and payment of a dhimmi's tax by all non-Muslims".

Any such 'school' is seditious and destructive to America's rule of law. We The People are shutting down jihad.

Tenth, We The People intend to start keeping what we earn. As explained in the book, *A Tax Honesty Primer,* without a dollar of individual income taxes needed, the combination of corporate tax revenues, federal excises, imposts, and import duties are *more* than sufficient to fund what We The People authorize government to do.

Note on Parental Choice in Child-Rearing

We will support other efforts that are not included in our formal mission's trust deed; especially every state reform law providing parental school choice vouchers, beginning with tax credits and equal to 100% of state per-pupil expenditure, no strings attached, for each student who is homeschooled or enrolled in a private school. Liberating American minds from the propaganda and counter-factual American history programmed into us for the past century is vitally important.

Note on Private Property in this Republic

The same is true of ending *ad valorem* property taxes in this Republic. The rapacious state legislatures in their palaces, in the name of bureaucrats have *outlawed* private property in America, in favor of wasteful, bloated pork programs and bureaucratic empires over which the owners of homes, farms, and shops have no control or voice, yet by which predators, parasites, and their sheriffs and collections lawyers hold us hostage for life, as the people of every Communist country. This practice of a monarch holding the People hostage for life to the crown began with William the Conqueror in 1066 A.D. and was exported to the American colonies by King James, along with chattel and indentured slavery.

It is time for this cruel, despotic practice of feudalism to end in this Republic! When an American has paid in full for a piece of property, that property should be the free, clear property of its owner, with no level of government having its hooks (and its collections lawyers' and sheriffs' hooks) in that private property. It's always been a fundamental tenet of American self-government that the People be truly self-governing; that a grasping, communistic majority cannot seize the property of the minority against the minority's will or hold that minority in lifelong servitude to cover ever-growing expenses of fat, lawless bureaucrats.

But the huge state has led to an increasing number of Americans opting for careers in the cancerous, lawless, limitless 'public sector', which at this point is closer to Karl Marx's system than to that of our Founding Fathers.

Preparing For Your Chapter

We The People are now rising up and reporting for duty in our own counties from coast to coast, to create and maintain a 3,141-county *permanent* law enforcement against organized crime and corrupt arrogations from our federal, state, county, city, and school district palaces. *Enough is enough!*

There are 19 sweeping reform laws in the AmericaAgain! Declaration that Tactical Civics™ chapters will be pushing in decades to come. But no population has ever done anything like this before. Yes, it's just what's in our Constitution. Yes, the Internet and social media makes it a no-brainer. But by God's grace and the counsel of the Holy Spirit over more than a decade in the lives of 44 volunteers, Tactical Civics™ is the first organization to finally put all the pieces together.

The 'Great Reset' seems to be destroying America; but today, every corrupt careerist in government is thinking like *the cantina scene in A Bug's Life* when Hopper tells the other grasshoppers that their lives of leisure are over. The sleeping giant is waking up, and our mission is the point of the spear: lawful, peaceful, full-spectrum, and long-term.

So far, we are like infants in a crib, just figuring out our shapes, colors, and letters. So until you know the materials, don't hold your first formal meeting. But as soon as you do the Chapter Builder Boot Camp, you can gather with one or two or a handful of new acquaintances to show them the new way of life that lies ahead for the responsible remnant.

We cannot adequately stress that your first task is: join your County Chapter, follow the step-by-step instructions, and *learn the mission.*

Your First Chapter Meeting

Each Chapter Leader must watch our 28-minute Tactical Civics™, then play it for all new members at introductory county chapter meetings and discuss it. If you have time, show the PowerPoint presentation.

All approved chapter leaders will need our three field handbooks:

Chapter Leader's Field Handbook Volume 1 walks you through every step: holding your first meeting (press release, blogger resources to announce it); when, where, and how to run regular meetings; how to prepare your county for your annual Tactical Civics™ gala event; how to recruit responsible, concerned citizens; how to spot and quickly eject moles, *agents provocateurs*, and showboats; how to help launch a true constitutional Militia unit in your county; how to recruit Tactical Civics™ Affiliates in local small businesses; how to work with area churches; how to train/brief county residents in their Grand Jury duty and authority, and much more.

Field Handbook Volume 2 introduces you to the Grand Jury; things you never knew will inspire and liberate you as political parties were never able to do. It presents our model County Grand Jury Ordinance and teaches you how to get it enacted in your county, and how to get a Grand Jury page added to your county government's website where citizens can volunteer for Grand Jury and submit confidential presentments (reports of potential felony activity in the county).

Field Handbook Volume 3 is the constitutional Militia operating manual: what it is, how to restore it, and how to operate your local or county unit. It presents our model County Militia Ordinance and teaches you how to get it enacted in your county. While our members may join their true Militia unit, Tactical Civics™ is not Militia; we only support and aid local constitutional Militia. Before reading this book, you must read our book, *Time to Start Over, America: Introducing American Militia 2.0™, Restoring Our Founding Fathers' Law Enforcement, Riot & Border Control, and Social Glue*

More on 'militia' vs. Militia

America's 50-year-old 'militia movement' *is not constitutional Militia.* While a minority of the movement is comprised of honorable men, the majority are not serious and many are downright dangerous. This is why that movement has stigmatized the very word 'militia', thus killing the desire in able-bodied American men to serve in constitutional Militia. That is why our organization does not carry water for the 'militia movement', infiltrated by Antifa and FBI *agents provocateurs.*

Of course we are working with sincere leaders in that movement, who want exactly what we want. But if you deal with 'the movement', you will meet Alpha Male private militant group leaders who think their group belongs to them. In truth, it does; every existing armed group using the label 'militia' today is a private club, not the public function that the Founding Fathers stipulate in the Constitution.

Like anything done by well-meaning Americans claiming they're a legitimate civil function: *show it to me in the Constitution.* We do not mean to antagonize, but we also will not be intimidated by men who are essentially working for FBI, Antifa, and others who seek to keep Militia from ever being restored in our land. That may not be their intention, but the Constitution is the only sure test. Any group leader who is sincere, will work with his corresponding county chapter of Tactical Civics™. He will work to get our Militia Ordinance passed in your county government's public meeting, at the same meeting just after we get our Grand Jury Ordinance passed.

If he refuses or conveniently 'forgets' or drags his feet week after week in that one good faith action step, you will know that the well is poisoned. Move on. That leader has no interest in properly executed, constitutional Militia and will eventually destroy the unit or at least waste a great deal of time and your chapter morale before you get it.

We recommend to any potential Militia leader: if you can start with a clean sheet, do it. Recruit men who are tough, smart men of their word, who will show up for training and muster; who are godly, rational, and respectful. We call our program American Militia 2.0™ because too many 'militia' groups are like false flag Antifa cells hidden among America's frustrated, honorable men who want to do their duty but can never seem to find a group with a real plan.

Regarding Pastors

'Men of God' need to start acting the part. We have several pastors in our number; all the same kind of man. They don't march to the tune of a franchise and they don't lead a flock for a salary, house, and benefits.

America's careerist pastors are even more stiff-necked than 'threeper' Alpha Males. That's why George Barna reported over a decade ago in his book *Revolution,* that 25 million Christians had walked away from church buildings and back to Jesus. The number is surely much larger now. On both sides of the Atlantic, pastors have a great deal to repent.

The local church can be every bit as vital as the local gun dealer, shooting range, or Militia unit. Repairing these ruins without pastors makes no sense. Our 7-week Crash course is a book called *Mission to America,* and is perfect for church small groups, and *Tactical Civics™ For Church Leaders* was written for American pastors to stop avoiding our civic duties while making the excuse, "we don't do politics". *Our Romans 13 duty over the Constitution and rule of law is not politics!*

What a Massive Job Ahead!

Well, yes; that's true. And what a zoo all around us, predators and parasites threatening to outnumber the honest and productive if we, like Europeans, continue to avoid our duties.

Tactical Civics™ is full-spectrum and long-term, and it looks extremely difficult. But those who go through our Training Center step by step will learn that this mission is designed for the newbie; we break this new way of life down into simple steps and individual study units and action projects. It will be much easier for the next generation, and even easier for the one after that.

But for now, we repeat the old aphorism...

People who say that it cannot be done should not interrupt those who are doing it.

About the Author

David M. Zuniga is a graduate of the University of Texas (BS, Architectural Engineering) and was for 28 years a professional engineer designing schools, churches, industrial, and commercial buildings and their structural, plumbing, HVAC, electrical, and site civil systems. He has also been a cattleman, custom homebuilder, commercial contractor, SCUBA instructor, cross-culture church planter, missionary pilot, land surveyor, and subdivision designer/developer.

Having founded four classical Christian K-12 schools in three states, he designed a curriculum with Latin, Logic, Rhetoric, and the Great Books of Western Civilization.

Shocked at the government fraud of 9/11, beginning in 2006 he spent 14 months in monastic seclusion, prayer and study of 110 key books. He wrote the first draft of the *AmericaAgain! Declaration* and refined the document with help of many fine Americans including constitutional radio show host Mike Church and constitutional scholar and author Edwin Vieira Jr.

Establishing AmericaAgain! Trust with his brother in 2009, David wrote his first book *This Bloodless Liberty* in 2010 to convey his vision. In 2015 he published *Fear The People,* introducing a full-spectrum action plan to restore popular sovereignty and rule of law. In 2018, he began writing the 5-volume Tactical Civics™ series and several other standalone books to break this new way of life into brief books for action. With his co-founders, in January 2021 David helped launch the Tactical Civics™ Training Center. By October, Americans had launched over 200 county chapters.

David has been a guest on Infowars Nightly News and is a recurring guest on radio shows across the republic. His published articles have appeared on many blogs, forums, and alternative media.

David has two children and six grandchildren. They live in the Hill Country of Texas where they serve no king but King Jesus.

Made in the USA
Monee, IL
04 June 2023

35251105R00144